Maghrebian Literature in French

Twayne's World Authors Series

David O'Connell, Editor
University of Illinois, Chicago

TWAS 727

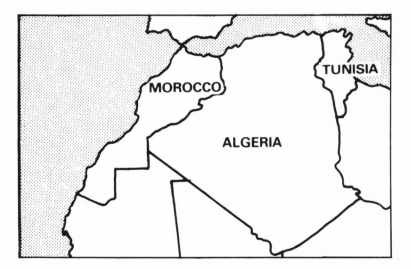

THE MAGHREB
Photograph courtesy of Maps on File,
Martin Greenwald Associates, Inc.

Maghrebian Literature in French

By Joan Phyllis Monego

Twayne Publishers • Boston

Maghrebian Literature in French

Joan Phyllis Monego

Copyright © 1984 by G. K. Hall & Company
All Rights Reserved
Published by Twayne Publishers
A Division of G. K. Hall & Company
70 Lincoln Street
Boston, Massachusetts 02111

Library of Congress Cataloging in Publication Data

Monego, Joan Phyllis.
    Maghrebian literature in French.

    Bibliography: p.
    Includes index.
    1. North African literature (French)—History and
criticism.   2. Africa, North, in literature.   I. Title.
PQ3980.M6   1984   840'.9'961   84-4573
ISBN 0-8057-6574-3

Contents

About the Author

Joan Monego is Director of Adult and Continuing Education for Triton College at its Oak Park extension center. In 1975 she completed her Ph.D. in Romance languages and literatures at Case Western Reserve University where she was an N.D.E.A. scholarship recipient and a university fellow. Her doctoral research focused on selected works of the Algerian writer Mohammed Dib. In 1978 she traveled in Morocco. She has taught French in Japan, for Triton College, and at Oak Park and River Forest High School, Illinois. Her work has appeared in the <u>French Review</u> and <u>Lutheran Education.</u>

Preface

This volume is intended as an introduction to Maghrebian
literature in French for a nonspecialist English-speaking
audience. Natives of Algeria, Morocco, and Tunisia began
producing quality literary works in the French language
in the 1950s. Yet it was only in the 1960s that the significance of this production came to be recognized and a
few researchers in France and Africa attempted to synthe-
size into a unified history the writings and those events
which gave birth to them. One of the persons to distinguish himself in this area is the eminent scholar, teacher, and literary critic, Jean Déjeux, who has devoted
himself tirelessly to recording the development of
Maghrebian francophone literature. His magnum opus,
Littérature maghrébine de langue française, the
single most complete volume on this literature, and his
Bibliographie méthodique et critique de la littérature
algérienne de langue française: 1945-1977, are indispensable to the study and appreciation of the topic, and
we are indebted to him. Other writers too have helped
clarify the sociological-historical-political settings
which gave impetus to Maghrebian francophone literature,
among the most important Albert Memmi, Abdelkébir
Khatibi, and Isaac Yetiv. The studies of all these
researchers are written in French, however. Coverage of
the field in English has been limited principally to
literary criticism of specific books, or has dealt only
briefly with small segments of this production. With
today's current interest in Third World countries and
their culture, we feel the time has come to open this
area to a broader public and, hopefully, to thereby
create a greater awareness and sensitivity to the peoples
of the Maghreb and to their unique contribution to belles
lettres. Our purpose here then is to sketch the sociohistorical background of Maghrebian francophone literature,
and to briefly present some of its leading exponents and
their works. In no way do we mean to imply that the list
of representative authors selected for this study is com-

plete. Our choice has been limited by space; many fine writers had to be omitted.

Special thanks are due to David O'Connell, without whose support, encouragement, and assistance this volume would not have been possible, to Mette Shayne, in the Africana library at Northwestern University, and to Beatrice Soroka for her careful proofreading of the manuscript.

Joan Phyllis Monego

Chronology

7th C.   Beginning of the Islamization of North African Berber tribes by invading Arabs.

1518-1830   Ottoman Regency in the Maghreb.

1830   France occupies Algiers. Beginning of French colonization of North Africa.

1881   Bardo treaty imposes French protectorate on Tunisia.

1912   Treaty of Fès establishes French protectorate over Morocco.

1920   Randau's Algerianist manifesto calls for an autonomous Algerian literature distinct from that of France. The Society of Writers of North Africa is founded in Tunisia. The Association of Algerian Writers results from a split in this group.

1919-1935   The Algerianist period, marked by the production of a genuine North African literature, inferior from a literary standpoint, but proper to the Maghreb and independent from that of France.

1935-1955   Period of the "Ecole d'Alger" and "Ecole nord-africaine des lettres"—regionalist currents led by Gabriel Audisio and Albert Camus, characterized by Mediterranean sensitivity which ignored the Berber-Arab ethnic heritage.

1940-1945   French literary activity, stifled in France by the German occupation, moves to Algeria. Period of increased rapport between French and Algerian writers.

1946   Jean Amrouche's essay, "Eternal Jugurtha" crys-
        tallizes the identity crisis of the North
        African, colonized by succeeding generations
        of invaders.

1952-1956   The "generation of 1952," led by Mouloud
            Mammeri, Mohammed Dib, Mouloud Feraoun, Albert
            Memmi and Driss Chraibi, produce the first
            wave of high quality creative works in French
            revealing the interior and exterior world of
            the colonized.

1952   Mammeri's La Colline oubliée and Dib's La
        Grande Maison published.

1953   Memmi's La Statue de sel and Feraoun's La
        Terre et le sang published.

1954   Chraibi's Le Passé simple and Dib's L'In-
        cendie published. 1 November, Algerian war
        of national liberation begins.

1955   Publication of Mammeri's Le Sommeil du juste,
        Memmi's Agar, and Chraibi's Les Boucs.

1956   Chraibi's L'Ane published. Kateb's
        Nedjma marks a departure from traditional
        documentary vein. France recognizes the
        independence of Tunisia and Morocco.

1957   Memmi's essay Portrait du colonisé, précé-
        dé du portrait du colonisateur published.

1962   July, France recognizes the independence of
        Algeria.

1962-1967   Proliferation of creative works celebrating
            the Algerian war effort; experimentation with
            new literary techniques, and renewal of
            themes.

1962   Djebar's Les Enfants du nouveau monde pub-
        lished. Dib's Qui se souvient de la mer
        marks new direction in his production.

1963   Founding of the Union of Algerian Writers

(U.E.A.). Resentment toward Maghrebian writers residing permanently in France.

1964   Dib's Cours sur la rive sauvage published.

1965   Mammeri's L'Opium et le bâton published.

1966   Kateb's Le Polygone étoilé published. Disintegration of the U.E.A. due to polarization of members into Arab-language versus French-language groups.

1967   Chraibi's Un ami viendra vous voir shocks by its departure from North African concerns.

1968   National Cultural Colloquium in Algiers. Failed effort to get writers and artists to reorganize cultural disciplines along socialist lines.

1974   Convocation of Algerian Authors. Misgivings between writers of the "old guard" and the new.

1974-   Ongoing debate about the future of French-language literature in the Maghreb nations, which claim Arabic as the official language.

Chapter One

Retrospective Panorama

Birth of a Literature

Between the two world wars, a new francophone literature
was born in North Africa. It was not the product of
French European writers, nor of their descendants, but of
Arabs, Berbers, and Jews. Imitative and mediocre for the
most part, it caused no great stir. But around 1950 it
reappeared, this time original in its content, polished
in its style, and bearing a significant message. It had
some representatives from the French protectorates of
Tunisia and Morocco, where French influence had exerted
itself since 1881 and 1912 respectively, but its most
fruitful source was the French colony of Algeria which
was then in the throes of radical discontent resulting
from intensive European colonization that had continued
unabated since 1830. Clearly this literature was distinct from any that had preceded it.

To many it came as a surprise that North Africans of
the Maghreb (1), that is, indigenous people of modern day
Algeria, Morocco, and Tunisia should, after centuries of
living down a reputation as a barbarous, inferior, and
backward lot of irrelevant humanity, suddenly be producing creative works of high quality, and gleaning
French literary awards. The new current provoked strong
reactions on both sides of the Mediterranean. Most
French, imbued with the long-standing prejudice that
nothing good could come from the natives, dismissed the
new works as conventional and unimportant. Some, however, rejoiced at what they considered the ultimate success
of their efforts at colonization: the assimilation of
French culture, thanks to which the colonized peoples
were able to express themselves as well as those from the
mainland (les Métropolitains as they were called), and
to make their own contribution to French belles lettres.
Algerian critics too took note. Some, conditioned by the
colonizer to see themselves as inferior, judged the new
literature as second-rate. Others believed, for various
reasons, that the works did not truly represent North

1

African society: they were written in French instead of
the native Arabic; they were published in France and destined for a French-European reading audience; they received foreign literary prizes; they were not committed
to the cause of national liberation but had as their purpose the entertainment of a foreign public. As more
works appeared, a lively polemic developed, bringing even
greater attention to authors unknown at that time. As
the movement for national liberation gradually took
shape, some North African critics were particularly
severe in their judgment, asserting that only works which
directly served the cause for liberation were valid and
acceptable.

This literature was certainly not the first to
describe the society and culture of North Africa, yet it
was recognized as unique, distinct from that which had
preceded it, and in a totally different vein from that of
the well-known "Algerian" writers, Albert Camus, Gabriel
Audisio, or Jules Roy (2). With the passage of time,
critics identified it as a new school or movement. What
separated these latest creative endeavors from those that
issued from the pen of other writers who shared a common
geography was the point of departure. Before 1950, the
celebrated North African writers whose works circulated
among a French reading public were of European descent.
In a world which divided its populations into two groups,
colonizers and colonized, they belonged to the camp of
the conquerors. And it was from this position of
strength, this vantage point, that they voiced their
feelings and concerns. While they claimed the Maghreb as
their homeland, while they aptly used it as a backdrop
for their works, in fact their mentality remained European.

During the 1950s a new strain of native North African
writer emerged. Unlike his timid and technically deficient predecessors who for three decades had been weaving
tales and verses full of local color sure to appeal to
their foreign readers, these newcomers, who had been
thoroughly molded in the process of acculturation, were
proficient in their craft. And, most important, they
were determined to describe their position of the colonized vis-à-vis the powerful colonizer. For the most
part they came from Algeria, the country upon which colonization had the greatest impact. Their works represented
a totally different point of view as, candidly, they lay
bare their soul and explained the effects of colonialism

on their race. As autochthones writing in the language
of the colonizer works that were theoretically destined
for consumption by the colonized, their position was
inherently ambiguous. They were simultaneously the
object of paternalistic praise for enlarging the scope of
art and the target of condemnation for playing into the
hands of the enemy. Extremists at either end missed the
point. An original literature had been born and it was
necessary to come to terms with it. The Algerians soon
realized what a powerful arm it was and skillfully made
use of it to press the cause for independence.

For years to come one would hear reference made to the
spontaneous birth of this new movement, a reference that
was not entirely without truth. The 1950s saw the beginnings of a new current which was to continue unabated to
our own day. But no phenomenon springs forth from a
void. We must look to the interaction of historical
events, geography, sociological factors, and a psychological climate to explain the genesis of this movement.
The flow that gathered force in the Maghreb, and in
Algeria in particular, can only be fully comprehended
from these perspectives. The complaints voiced in the
literature, the shortcomings, abuses, and metaphysical
torment exposed therein are integrally bound with centuries of religious, cultural, and political influence
and conditioning. For that reason we diverge briefly
from our literary history to present a quick sketch of
the sociohistorical context from which Maghrebian francophone literature sprang.

The Maghreb: Sociohistorical Panorama

The historical sketches that follow are necessarily
brief. Many specific details and names of important
personages have been deliberately omitted. The purpose
of this terse historical review is to highlight those
elements—anthropological, religious, cultural, historical, and political—which shaped the evolution of the
North African people, because those elements are an
integral part of their literature.

EARLY PERIOD (3). The lands which comprise the
region that we today call French North Africa entered
recorded history just before the end of the second millen-
nium B.C. Phoenicians, Carthaginians, and Romans came to
her shores to exploit her and to do business with her.

Her native inhabitants, the Berbers, were described by classical writers as a fierce race. The name "Berber" derives from the Greek barbaros, which the Greeks and the Romans used to call peoples who spoke neither Greek nor Latin. The origins of the Berbers remain a mystery. Scholarly investigation has produced many hypotheses but no definitive solution. They are a composite Caucasian race formed of dissimilar ethnological elements. They have their own language, Berber. While it is possible that a common Berber tongue existed in ancient times, by the close of the classical period it is known that the Berber language was already broken into several mutually incomprehensible dialects. They did have an alphabet, which is still used today by the Tuaregs of the Algerian sahara, but it is inconvenient to write and read and did not favor the development of a common literature or common linguistic bond. Instead, the Berbers adopted the language of their various conquerors, for literary, religious, economic, and administrative purposes. From earliest times the social organization of the Berbers had been along tribal lines. Whether nomadic or sedentary, from rural or from urban areas, they lived in small autonomous groups to which members owed their final allegiance. Their laws, government, and religion were highly personalized and therefore most effective at the lowest levels of their application. A Berber national consciousness never existed, a fact that was to have far-reaching consequences.

In the seventh century, after the death of the Prophet Muhammed, Arab armies swept across North Africa from Arabia to carry the message of Islam. It was the Arabs who used the appellation Maghreb (the land of sunset) to designate the lands west of Egypt. They were met with protracted resistance by the strong Berber tribes. It took almost a century of effort for the Arabs to complete their push across North Africa and into Spain. As they went, they converted many to the new religion. The historian Jamil M. Abun-Nasr says that "the Islamization of the Berbers went further than their Arabization, and in many ways the latter process was the product of the former" (4). Because Islam was as much a system of legal administration as a religious code, because its authority extended to the temporal as well as to the religious spheres, its adoption, even in its heretical forms, had lasting significant implications. The Arabs had as their goal a politically and religiously unified land under a central head to which all tribal interests would be subordinated. Arab rule was a severe form of tyranny, mitigated only by its inefficiency. North Africa remained for centuries an aggregate of free Berber states on the fringe of the Arab caliphate.

In the eleventh century first the Almoravids, a religious brotherhood, then the Almohads swept across the continent into Spain. The Almohads, the greatest North African dynasty in history, gave the Berber people a measure of collective identity and political unity. They created the idea of an "imperial Maghreb" under Berber aegis that survived from dynasty to dynasty.

Unlike their predecessors, the dynasties which emerged in later centuries did not have religious reform as their chief mission. Gradually, in rural areas, the ulama, Muslim religious scholars responsible for interpreting and elaborating on the codes of Islamic law, were supplanted by spiritual guides called marabouts, divinely favored wandering holy men endowed with special qualities of grace and blessedness (baraka). The traditions perpetuated by these mystics, seers, and miracle workers antedated Islam in the Maghreb. Not only did the people look to these men for spiritual guidance, but, as official government authority waned, they turned to the marabouts for political leadership as well. Small autonomous republics sprang up all over the Maghreb as a common form of government. At the same time religious brotherhoods multiplied. In essence each of these represented a miniature corporation for the support of folk religion. The Maghreb's brand of Islam was a blend of the intellectualism and orthodoxy of the ulama and of the superstitious emotionalism of the masses, and so it would remain into the twentieth century. Mouloud Mammeri would be heard to decry its more backward practices in his novels, and Mohammed Dib would use it as a central topic in one of his.

As Muslim power declined in Spain, the Christian kingdoms landed troops on the North African Mediterranean coast. Fearful of an eventual full-fledged European invasion, tribes in these vicinities negotiated truces with Spain and agreed to pay tribute. They also called on the pirates to help them repel the Christians, allowing them, in 1510, to use Algiers as their base of attack. The Barbarossa pirates then seized the city, but their position was tenuous. Menaced by Spain on the one hand and a nervous citizenry on the other, their leader

recognized the suzerainty of the Ottoman sultan over the
territory in his control, and was appointed regent there.
Thus was Algeria reduced to a vassal state of the Ottoman Turkish Empire. Turkish was proclaimed the official
language. Neither Arabs nor Berbers were admitted to
government posts. The territory under Turkish control
was governed, theoretically, by a dey, and was subdivided
into cantons that were under the direction of caids,
usually chosen from the heads of tribes. The caids continued to play a part in administration right up to
independence. In practice the three provinces that the
Turks carved out of the Maghreb were never unified under
a central government. Tribalism continued as the main
form of social organization.

In the three centuries of Ottoman control, right up to
the time of the French takeover in 1830, piracy flourished. It was common practice to seize and hold hostages
for ransom. The economy of Algiers depended on slave
trade and slave labor. Thus the Maghreb gained a reputation as a decadent uncivilized place. The Turks' main
interest in controlling the land was the extraction of
wealth through piracy and tax collections. The period of
Ottoman regency was one of stagnation.

FRENCH COLONIAL ALGERIA. A dispute between the
French consul and the dey of Algiers led to a French
attack on the city in 1830 (5). The French expedition
was successful. The dey resigned, and by convention
France was awarded sovereignty over the whole Ottoman
territory of Algeria. In the name of suppressing piracy
and slavery and of liberating a backward society oppressed by tribal anarchy, the French army steadily
expanded its influence in the coastal cities. In the
rural regions, however, it met with opposition. For
fifteen years the Algerian resistance leader, Abdel
Kader, struggled to gather tribes in waging a war against
the Christian invaders who employed brutal means to crush
their opponents. He realized the importance of presenting a united front. Though he pursued his mission relentlessly, the superior strength of French arms forced
Kader's surrender in 1847. A century later Algerians
would recognize and venerate him as the first hero of
Algerian independence.

In governing their vast colony, France allowed the
native population only a limited measure of control at
the local level. In her zealous effort to organize
affairs, she imposed designs which tore at existing

social structures, imposing artificial divisions of tribal land, for example. Her application of the French
legal system galled. She recognized the indigenes as
French nationalists (by virtue of the fact that Algeria
had been annexed to France in 1834), but not as French
citizens. They were protected by French law, while
allowed to remain under the jurisdiction of Islamic law
in litigation regarding personal matters. In order to
become a French citizen, however, they were required to
reject Islamic law and accept the full authority of the
French legal code. Inherent in this act was the renunciation of their religion, an act of apostasy which relatively few made.

The immigrants who came to settle in Algeria were from
many different countries. Apart from the French were
large numbers of Italians, Spaniards, Maltese, and
Alsatians. These were the colons, or pieds noirs
("black feet"), as they came to be called (6). They were
largely peasant farmers and working class in origin, and
they were hungry for land. French law, which initially
was aimed at the protection of native property, was easily circumvented. Some colons managed to acquire vast
tracts of land or to establish big economic concerns.
These were the grands colons. There was very little
inbreeding of colon with native. The colon was suspicious of the Muslim, did not want to establish a rapport
with him, and wanted to go about his life as though the
native were not there. Distanciation, depersonalization,
and alienation were forms of oppression which greatly
afflicted the indigene while passing unnoticed by the
outside world.

After so many centuries of being the prize of diverse
conquerors, it is easy to understand the Algerians'
anguish over the question of identity. The novelists of
the 1950s and 1960s devoted much of their effort to the
examination of this burning issue.

Of course the French did make some positive contributions as part of their mission civilisatrice. In the
area of education, French schools accepted small numbers
of Muslim students who studied with Europeans. The cur-
riculum was entirely in French and totally excluded
Arabic studies, which were deliberately downgraded. Within a generation a class of well-educated gallicized
Muslims, the évolués (literally "evolved ones") was
thus created. It was in this privileged group of
Muslims, strongly influenced by French culture and politi-

cal attitudes, that a new Algerian self-consciousness developed.

SEEDS OF UNREST--ALGERIAN NATIONALISM. Strains of Algerian nationalism developed after World War I. Algerians had served with the French army on the Continent. The higher standard of living that they observed in France and the democratic political concepts which were a way of life there but which were denied the Muslim majority back home deepened their resentment. A small number of activists began calling for reforms of the legislative process where disproportionate representation gave the foreign minority majority rule. Both sides spoke of assimilation and integration, but the colons, fearful of being plunged into a Muslim sea, staunchly resisted any measures which would lead to the diminution of their power. Many French back home disagreed with their country's colonialist policies. World War II reinforced earlier sentiments. More and more the Algerian became aware that he was living on the margin of society. As petitions for reform were denied, there developed in the Algerian a growing conviction that his only recourse was to violence. On 1 November 1954 the Front de Libération Nationale, or F.L.N., called on all Muslim Algerians to unite in a national struggle. The bitter war, which would be fought at the price of many lives and much destruction, was not won until the summer of 1962. But the aftermath of the war was particularly devastating. It saw the exodus of the professional European community. Since its members represented, for the most part, all occupations from which the Muslim population had been excluded by colonial policy, the country was temporarily paralyzed and in chaos.

THE TUNISIAN PROTECTORATE. Early Tunisian history can be profitably studied as part of the history of the Maghreb as a whole, with some important differences. While even today Algeria has a substantial ethnically identifiable minority group in the Berbers, this is not the case in Tunisia, where Berber tribes were thoroughly Arabized at a very early date. Tunisia too was forced to submit to an Ottoman Regency, but although she was nominally part of the Ottoman Empire, in fact she was governed by a powerful bey who founded a hereditary dynasty that was to last until 1957. Tunisians were superior in their politics and culture to the Algerians and given to commerce rather than piracy. Above all, Tunisia wanted to avoid an excuse for foreign intervention. In the nine-

teenth century, however, a dishonest treasurer led the
country into bankruptcy and opened the door for French
economic and political penetration. A Tunisian elite
sought reforms and modernization to keep their country
independent, but modernization implied European participation in Tunisian economic affairs. The Tunisian urban
elite was forward-thinking. Under their persuasion, in
1861 the bey promulgated a constitution that was the
first written constitution in the Islamic world. He also
created a secular Supreme Court, empowered to review
decisions of the religious courts. The provincial
notables and tribal chiefs saw the constitutional government as an attack on local tribalism and autonomy. Popular resentment and tribal rebellion led to the suspension
of the treaty in 1864. The experiment had failed, but in
the twentieth century the restoration of the Constitution
of 1861 would become the premise of the demand for independence by the nationalist movement.

Under the pretext of pursuing rebel tribesmen, who had
raided across the Algerian border, in 1881 France moved
in with her army. Then, arguing that Tunisia was a backward and impoverished country, the French representative
urged the bey to sign the Bardo Treaty that put Tunisia
under France's "protection." France left the beylicate
intact and through its facade issued all her instructions
for running the country. The urban elite readily assimilated French values as the French proceeded to bring
about the reforms and modernization that they had failed
to instigate earlier. Most important, Tunisian development was brought about by corporate development of the
land rather than by European settlement. As always,
however, the contributions made by France were directed
primarily to benefit France and French investments. By
1892 more than one fifth of Tunisia's arable land was
French-owned, but 90 percent of that was in the hands of
only sixteen landowners and companies (7).

Traditional education in Tunisia was highly developed.
Unlike the Algerian model, the bilingual, bicultural
school system that was offered to a mixed student body
under the French protectorate worked successfully throughout the entire country, achieving a synthesis of Arabic
and French culture. This undoubtedly contributed to the
breakdown of tribal organization and the gradual transformation of Tunisians into a cosmopolitan society. The
tribal system, as a significant element in the Tunisian
social complex, thus died out. Many students went on to

France for higher studies. These well-educated gallicized Tunisians became the core of a highly motivated
nationalist movement which began to call for emancipation
in 1907 and in every decade thereafter. Their actions
provoked repressions by the authorities. When in 1955
France promised total independence for Morocco, she could
not refuse to grant Tunisia the same. The country became
independent in 1956. Unlike the example of Algeria and
Morocco, French colons did not flee the country and a
strong staff of professionals remained. Tunisia had a
relatively smooth transition despite the tensions caused
by the war raging across her border.

THE MOROCCAN PROTECTORATE. Like Algeria and Tunisia, in early times Morocco's population too was made
up of jealous autonomous tribes who knew no authority
above the tribal level. In Morocco, the decaying Berber
dynasties were followed by sharifian Arab dynasties (from
the word shurfa which designates families claiming
direct descent from the Prophet). They introduced the
makhzen or central government, a concept alien to Berber
traditions, and vested religious and secular authority in
one head, the sultan. While in theory the sultan had
absolute rights, in practice he had not sufficient means
to enforce them. While the sultanate was not hereditary,
the fact that one ruler and one government were thus
recognized implied an intent for unity. The Arab tribes
intermarried between the Berbers, except in the remote
mountain areas which remained pure Berber. Orthodox
Islam and Berber folk religion with its very active
marabouts coexisted. The marabouts stressed community
solidarity and mutual self-assistance, thus lending
psychological support to the masses in a way that the
official institutions—mosques and courts—could not.

Unlike Algeria and Tunisia, Morocco succeeded in
resisting the Turks, thus preserving her separate identity. The European nations coveted Morocco. Due to an
archaic system of financial administration, corruption,
and tribal rivalries, she became increasingly dependent
on foreign powers whose domination she wanted to avoid.
European countries, and France in particular, made loans
to her, which she was unable to pay back. Instability
within the country provided them with an excuse to intervene in order to protect their investments. Because of
Morocco's strategic position on the African continent, in
the late nineteenth and early twentieth century European
powers engaged in much diplomatic maneuvering with her,

more with a view to obviating conflict among themselves
rather than for the purpose of restoring internal stability in Morocco. In 1906 the conference of Algeciras
granted that every nation have equal access to Morocco,
but made it clear that French influence would predomi-
nate. In 1911 the irresponsible and weak sultan Hafid
was besieged by his own subjects for having yielded to
the European infidels, and called on the French for military assistance. Germany saw the military occupation as
a threat to her. Differences were settled by the Treaty
of Fès in 1912, which established a French protectorate
over Morocco.

Spain was given a similar though lesser position in
the north. The treaty called for "a new regime com-
prising the administrative, judicial, educational,
economic, financial, and military reforms which the
French government may see fit to introduce" (8). The
sultan retained his status as reigning head of state,
theoretically, but most of the internal jurisdiction was
transferred to France. It took France twenty-two years
to subdue the dissident tribes and bring all of Morocco
under her control. For all practical purposes, Morocco
was reduced to the status of a colony, the real power
being wielded by the French resident general. He was
assisted by the caids, who functioned as executive
assistants of the French regional administrators. In all
areas, French assistance to Morocco was geared to further-
ing the economic growth of France.

As in Algeria, the influx of French colons led to the
expropriation of vast tracts of the most fertile land.
French quickly became the official language. A small
Muslim elite was admitted to the French education system.
By the 1920s these students would be organizing secret
societies to fight for Morocco's political independence.
Nationalist activities multiplied in the 1930s as the
result of the French-inspired Berber Dahir promulgation.
This was supposed to help the protectorate through the
recognition of Berber customary law in those areas where
it existed, but it had the effect of splitting the country into Arab versus Berber, with the former arguing that
the authority of the sultan was thus infringed upon.
Ordinary Moroccans joined the intellectuals in rallying
against the French.

World War II saw the Moroccans fighting side by side
with French armies in Europe. The nationalist hope that
the Allies would help them achieve an independent Morocco

was disappointed. Their activities were suppressed, but
parties multiplied. Finally, in 1955 the French National
Assembly accepted a policy of "independence with interde-
pendence." The sultan, Mohammed V, promised to institute
reforms to change Morocco into a democratic state under a
constitutional monarchy, personally assuming the title of
king in 1957. A new administrative structure, headed by
Moroccans, was set up to replace the old. With the sign-
ing of the French-Moroccan Agreement on 2 March 1956,
Morocco achieved complete independence. She was unified
in name, if not in substance. She passed through a difficult transition period, but in no way could her experience be compared with that of Algeria.

Literary History of the Maghreb: Beginnings

For more than a century there existed a French-
language literature said to be of the Maghreb. In fact,
however, it was actually the product of French people who
had come to visit or live in North Africa, or who had
been born there. With the emergence of writers of indigenous stock who used French as their medium of expression, it became necessary, for the sake of accuracy, to
make a distinction in terms. Strictly speaking then, the
rubric "North-African literature of the French" (littérature nord-africaine des Français) or "French
literature of the Maghreb" (littérature française du
Maghreb) applies to the first group of writers, Europeans, or their descendants. Creative works of the
second group, the true natives, whose mother tongue was
usually not French, fall under the heading "Maghrebian
francophone literature" (littérature maghrébine de
langue française). In order to understand how and why
the latter, which is the principal object of our study,
distinguishes itself radically from the former, we need
to examine the characteristics of both.
NORTH-AFRICAN LITERATURE OF THE FRENCH. Long
before the French occupation of Algeria in 1830, visitors
from European countries gave written accounts of the
mysterious uncivilized North African people who practiced
bizarre customs. Christian missionaries, government
envoys, geographers, historians, and writers confirmed
stereotype images of the Muslim world that had prevailed
since the days of the Crusades. The trend was to continue into the twentieth century. First, from the pens

of French soldiers came diaries and memoirs that spoke of adventure. Then, French writers, tired of the petit-bourgeois atmosphere of their homeland and in search of fresh sensations, followed. These were the écrivains touristes ("tourist writers"), as Memmi called them (9), for whom Algeria held the lure of the Orient, exotic, mysterious, exuding intrigue. Théophile Gautier, the Goncourt brothers, Feydeau, Fromentin, Flaubert, Maupassant, Gide, all came in pursuit of literary inspiration. For them North Africa was "an accidental enrichment of their palette" or "a land of evasion" (10). The preconceived notions and the cliché-ridden mythic vision that they brought with them were satisfactorily confirmed during their brief sojourns. In North Africa they were able to satisfy their thirst for the picturesque and steep themselves in the ambiance of a carefree sensual life-style. From 1830 until the turn of the century a picture-postcard literature perpetuated the stereotype. The colorful tableaux presented in these works exalted the natural beauty of the land while ignoring its inhabitants, except as part of the decor. The image which prevailed in the mind of the French reader was therefore inaccurate because it was grossly incomplete. For decades writers continued to write on Algeria. But as the French and other European immigrants—Spanish, Italian, Maltese—implanted themselves in growing numbers, a new generation of settlers who qualified themselves as Algerians was born. Unlike their forebears, outsiders who made only short visits, this race of Algerians was rooted in Africa. As insiders they held a different viewpoint. They saw Algeria as a land to conquer, a frontier to settle and reshape. They saw themselves as budding pioneers who would bring forth a new society. They sought a heritage and a national identity. They were the new generation, the écrivains français d'Afrique du Nord ("French writers of North Africa"). As Algeria became politically and financially emancipated from the Motherland, new themes reflecting the sociohistoric change emerged in literature. Two very different orientations developed.

In 1891 a French school teacher, Louis Bertrand, left France—which he found too soft and petty—to become an instructor in Algiers. For half a century he would promulgate through his novels his pet theory of latini-té, according to which contemporary French North Africa was seen as a continuation of Roman Africa, which had

never ceased to live. Speaking of French colonialism
Bertrand wrote, "we have done no more than recover a
province lost from Latin civilization" (11). French
colonialism to him marked the beginning of an African
renaissance: "We are the true Africa, we the Latins, we
the civilized" (12). Conveniently ignoring the centuries
of Arab and Turkish influence, Bertrand sought to find
the roots that he had severed by leaving France. Eager
to flee the stagnating society in France, Bertrand was in
search of an unaffected, energetic, robust Mediterranean
race that fully embraced life. He viewed Africa as much
more than "a store of decors or a voluptuous alcove"
(13). Precise observations and realistic descriptions
fill his pages. But he was suspicious of the indigenous
people, seeing in them an enemy. Islam had destroyed the
civilizing efforts of the Latins and had transformed the
natives into a barbarous backward race.

While Bertrand's views were simplistic and racist,
while they failed entirely to place the native in his
Arab-Muslim cultural dimensions, they did bear significant influence on the generation of French Algerian intellectuals that was to come, and lead ultimately to the
Algerianist movement.

The next important name in the evolution of French
Algerian literature was that of the Algerian-born writer
Robert Arnaud, who signed himself Robert Randau (14). It
was he who coined the word "Algerianism." Algerianism
was not a school but a movement, a philosophy which conceived the notion of Algerians united in a single
Algeria. Randau sought to develop an emancipated "original" literature of Franco-Berber inspiration. His
preface to a collection of poetry published in 1920
constitutes a veritable manifesto of Algerianism. In it
he called for an autonomous aesthetic and the most current representation of the Berberesque soul (15). Randau
declared that "there must be a North-African literature
because a people which has its own life must also possess
its own language and literature" (16). Firmly rooted in
his native African soil, Randau fostered the growth of a
vibrant literature which stood apart as distinct from
that of France. He placed equal value on the European
and the indigene as regards their humanity, but while he
saw the natives as a group that would be integrated into
the new Franco-Berber race, his perspective was that of a
paternalistic colonialist. He viewed them as an inferior
and decadent people who must be converted to the European

way of thinking. It was the task of the colonialists to carry out this mission. Yet even as he wrote, Randau must have been aware of the basic misunderstanding that existed here. Muslims and Christians regarded each other with suspicion and continued to lead separate lives.

In Tunisia, meanwhile, Arthur Pellegrin was investigating North African literature and produced a critical study in 1920 (17). He perceived no conflict in the use of the French language to express the reality of North Africa and believed in the existence of a distinct North African school. That same year, a Society of Writers of North Africa was founded in Tunisia. It had as its organ the publication Nord Africains (1919-29), which was succeeded by La Kahena. A split in the Tunisian society led to the birth of a new group, the Association of Algerian Writers, which in 1924 began publishing a literary magazine, Afrique, and instituted a grand prize for Algerian literature.

A substantial number of creative works appeared over the years 1919-35, dubbed the Algerianist period. These described assorted milieux, recorded past history, related observations on Muslim customs, but failed in one major area. They treated Algeria as though it were France, and as if the assimilation of the two cultures and two races were an accomplished fact.

The Algerianist movement was important not for the works that came out of it, but for the principle that was its guiding force: the production of a genuine North African literature, proper to that land, and independent from that of the mother country.

By 1935 the Algerianist movement was on the decline and the focus of attention turned to a new theme, that of a Mediterranean Algeria, a land of sun and sea. It concentrated its regard on the cities of the littoral rather than the interior. Gabriel Audisio used the term "Ecole d'Alger" for the generation of writers whose works were bent along those lines, while Camus called it the "Ecole nord-africaine des lettres." Jean Déjeux, one of the most eminent scholars in the area of North African literature, comments that it was not so much a school as a way of feeling (une sensibilité) (18). Some of the best-known francophone authors were attached to this current, of which Audisio and Camus were the leading proponents: Emmanuel Roblès, Jules Roy, Jean Pélégri, to name a few. Like the Algerianists, the adherents of the new fashion favored the development of a regionalist

literature. They too ignored the immediate past and the
Arab-Muslim heritage. Mediterranean sensitivity, however, proved an insufficient basis for the creation of a
country and a national identity.

Albert Memmi, the noted Tunisian expert on the literary history of North Africa, detects a certain ambiguity
in the stance assumed by the Algerianists. For all their
claims to create a new national literature, he suggests,
their natural ambition was "to be French writers among
the others—or among the best" (19). Their literature
not only failed to take into account the native, other
than as an element of decor, it also seemed to be founded
on the idea of separation from the original motherland,
France. These writers, Memmi proposes, were strangers in
the land of their birth. Camus's works may easily be
interpreted along these lines. Certainly their titles
would seem to support that view: L'Etranger (The
Stranger), Le Malentendu (The Misunderstanding),
L'Exil et le Royaume (The Exile and the Kingdom), La
Chute (The Fall), L'Homme Révolté (The Rebel),
Les Justes (The Just Ones).

Regardless of the school or current to which the North
African descendants of the Europeans belonged, they remained tied to Paris. When the Algerian war for independence heated up and when the creation of an independent
Algerian state became imminent, many returned to Paris
rather than retain citizenship in an Arab-Muslim country.

MAGHREBIAN FRANCOPHONE LITERATURE (20). Gradually
under the pressure of colonialism, Algeria began to be
remolded. By the turn of the century the more intellectual members of the native population began to perceive the
advantages of mastering the French language. Those who
believed that the country was destined to remain part of
France saw it as a means of assimilation. Still others
sought it as a tool through which they might defend their
rights and protect their liberty.

The first publications in French by native writers
took the form of essays and treatises on political and
social questions: World War I, the integration of the
native population with the French colonialists, the integration of Algeria with France. From 1880 to 1945 the
issues of "Algerian malaise," the "Algerian problem," and
the "dilemma of the native population" were reiterated.
By 1920 the problem of identity, of how to be Algerian
and French at the same time, had already been posed and
would continue to be an issue. Also at this time, short

stories and novels by autochthone writers began to make
their appearance. The following names and titles are
associated with this period: in Tunisia, Tahar Essafi
and Mahmoud Aslan; in Algeria, Caïd Ben Cherif (Ahmed,
Ben Mostapha, goumier, 1920), Abdelkader Hadj Hamou
(Zohra, la femme du mineur [Zohra, the miner's wife,
1925]), Slimane Ben Ibrahim (Khadra, danseuse des Ouled
Nail, 1926]), in joint authorship, Chukri Khodja (El
Eudj, captif des Barbaresques [El Eudj, captive of the
Barbaresques, 1929]), Mohammed Ould Cheikh (Myriam dans
les palmes [Myriam in the palms, 1936]), Ali Belhadj
(Souvenirs d'enfance d'un blédard [Childhood memories
of an inhabitant of the Bled, 1941]), which won the
Algerian grand prize for literature that year, Aïssa
Zehar (Hind à l'âme pure ou l'histoire d'une mère
[Pure-hearted Hind or the story of a mother, 1942]), and
the Zenati brothers (Bou el Nouar, le jeune Algérien
[Bou el Nouar, the young Algerian, 1945]). From the
point of view of style, these works were mediocre. They
imitated the academic models studied in the classroom.
Their authors were restricted by the demands of writing
correctly in a foreign language and were preoccupied with
syntax and spelling. This is not really surprising, con-
sidering the difficult process of assimilation that they
were undergoing. Not only had they to master a foreign
tongue sufficiently well to function in the arena of
everyday affairs, they also had to develop an aesthetic
sense for a literary genre, the novel, which was foreign
to Muslim letters. In their concern for mechanics they
overlooked many subtleties of the imported art form and
ignored the finer points of structure and form. Even the
Western way of thinking was alien to them. In content
too the works of the native writers were restricted.
Aimed at a French-reading public, they had certain characteristics in common. They emphasized the ethnographic
and folkloric aspects of North Africa, thereby appealing
to the Frenchman's yearning for the exotic. While on
occasion they pointed out the negative effects of colonialism on their culture, they did not omit the perfunctory
homage to France for all the good she had done for them.
They were superficial, failing to sound the depths of the
native soul or to inquire into the essence of his being.
They envisaged their society with the look of the colonizer.

   While many were happy that for once the native was
thus depicted by his own kind, in fact, so concerned were
these writers with attracting French readers that the

image they projected was one that tried to remain faithful to the European's view. The deeper problem of identity, of what it meant to be oneself when one wanted to be
African and French at the same time, lay untouched.

In the domain of poetry, only one name stands out
during this early period, that of the Algerian Catholic
Jean Amrouche, whose two collections of poems, Cendres
(Ashes, 1934) and Etoile secrète (Secret star, 1937),
are of the highest literary quality, in the line of
Patrice de La Tour du Pin, Milosz, and Ungaretti, according to Déjeux. "That entire production is an obsession-
al quest of paradise lost, of the living sources of
childhood, of the ancestor, or prenatal purity" (21),
themes cherished and more fully developed by writers
after the turn of the century. These original works were
followed by a translation of Berber songs of Kabylia,
Chants berbères de Kabylie (1939), and an essay,
"l'Eternel Jugurtha" (1946) (22), which explores the
depths of the Maghrebian essence. Amrouche, who referred
to himself as a "cultural hybrid," tried to bridge the
gap between two cultures. "No one more than he had the
taste for beautiful speech, for draping the phrase, for
eloquence worthy of the ancient rhetoricians" (23),
writes Jean Déjeux of him.

A literature of native North Africans about North
Africans had been in existence for four decades before
the beginning of the war for independence in 1954.
Creative works by autochthone writers were included in
anthologies and literary magazines, but they were invari-
ably lost among the contributions of French writers,
which far exceeded them in number. And, as we have
noted, with few exceptions, neither their content nor
their style was exceptional. Clearly Maghrebian writers
were as far from literary emancipation as they were from
political self-sufficiency.

World War II and its aftermath marked a turning point
in the development of this literature. In 1940, as
France was stifled by the German occupation, attention
turned to Algeria, where literary production flourished.
Algiers became the capital of free France and the birth-
place of many new and quality periodicals (24), including
L'Arche (1944), under the direction of Jean Amrouche,
La Nef (1944), a competitor, directed by Robert Aron,
and Forge (1946), under the editorship of Emmanuel
Roblès and El Boudali Safir, to name three of the most
important. While La Nef and L'Arche moved to Paris

after the Liberation along with many writers who had come
temporarily to Algeria, during their tenure in Africa the
directors of these publications expressed a desire to
promote French-Arab relations by printing the finest
literary contributions of Arab-Berber writers. Intellectual French Algerians chose to break the barriers of
prejudice and to meet on equal terms with educated
natives. Dring this period literary circles, clubs, and
associations were very popular: French-Muslim friendship
circles, Friends of As-Salam, the Association of Muslim
Students of North Africa, the Association of Algerian
Writers, to name just a few. Conferences with guest
speakers were regular functions; aspiring authors of Arab
and Berber origin mixed freely with African-born French-
men and visiting writers from France took an active role
within the most productive intellectual literary assem-
blies. A bond of cultural and literary humanism developed providing a climate of confidence. Within this
supportive framework and reassuring atmosphere Arab and
Berber writers were encouraged to give expression to
their true feelings. Most important, they abandoned
their former habit of seeing themselves through the prism
of the colonizer and replaced it with a bold and candid
depiction of their circumstances, thus putting an end to
the conventional popular images imposed by the colonizer.
This radical shift in viewpoint owed largely to the
unsettling effects of the war, which Mouloud Mammeri so
aptly describes in one of his novels: "this war has
thrown everything into confusion. No one knows any
longer where the way is" (25). Like Europe, North Africa
was in ferment, the people were aroused and anxious for
change. Intellectuals and militants began to draw
together with a view to altering their unhappy lot.

Two historic incidents, intended by the French to
crush Algerian nationalism, served only to polarize the
Muslim and colon communities. The first was the 8 May
1945 uprising and consequent retaliation at Sétif, near
Constantine, which resulted in the death of some one
hundred Europeans and anywhere from one to six thousand
Muslims, depending on whose statistics one uses. The
second was the failure of the 1947 Statute of Algeria,
which according to the Algerians fell far short of their
demands, but which according to the colons accorded too
much control to the native population. These events and
the general unrest left in their wake were soon to be
reflected in the literature of the Maghrebian writers.

Jean Amrouche's 1946 essay, "L'Eternel Jugurtha," is perhaps the finest expression of the predicament of the colonized. After years of miming the language and culture of others, Jugurtha finds only emptiness when he turns to examine his own soul. Realizing that his identity has been suppressed, he decides to come to grips with reality. In the early 1950s, the Algerian people seemed to share Jugurtha's experience as they gradually became cognizant of their situation. At the same time, Algerian intellectuals, responding to an inner urge to reflect their country's plight, began to set down their thoughts in novels and poems. Acting independently of each other, they produced a composite picture of their culture and their history.

Contemporary Maghrebian Francophone Literature

THE "GENERATION OF 1952." By 1950 North African writers had passed through their initial phase of development, the difficult period of acculturation which was marked by inadequate command of the tools of their craft and a superficial point of view, and they began to embark on a new course. The most important of North Africa's novelists emerged during this period, producing well-written, thought-provoking works of fiction: Mouloud Feraoun, Le Fils du pauvre (Son of the poor man, 1950) and La Terre et le Sang (Earth and blood, 1953); Mouloud Mammeri, La Colline oubliée (The forgotten hill, 1952); Mohammed Dib, La Grande Maison (The big house, 1952); from Tunisia, Albert Memmi, La Statue du sel (Pillar of Salt, 1953); from Morocco, Driss Chraibi, Le Passe simple (The simple past, 1954). The significance of these novels has been aptly noted by Albert Memmi in his introduction to the Anthologie des écrivains maghrébins d'expression française:

> For the first time, North Africa can be seen to take itself on. Accepted, assumed, or discussed, she ceases to be a simple decor or a geographic accident. These new authors are at grips with their country as with the essential of themselves. . . . It was necessary to dare at last to grasp at one's own life, at that of one's fellow citizens, at the relations with the colonizer. It was necessary, in sum, to discover and affront one's veritable domain, one's specific

object. And that isn't to be taken for granted when
one has lost the habit of disposing of one's own destiny. (26)

The first generation of accomplished Maghrebian writers, dubbed the "generation of 1952," opened the initial
chapter in the history of Maghrebian literature, for
which the years 1910-50 served only as a preface. Its
rapid evolution was closely allied with the North African
countries' efforts to achieve political independence and
to make the transition to self-sufficient statehood.
Independence and transition were only steps in a long
process involving individual and collective awareness and
historical events, which, in turn, were set against a
background of sociopolitical conditioning. For the purpose of facilitating our understanding of the development
of this literature, we propose a multidimensional approach which reviews the phases of its growth, its characteristics, and its principal themes.

The initial stage of modern Maghrebian francophone
literature covers the years 1950-56. This was a period
of rumbling discontent that began mildly with a literature that may be characterized as ethnographic or documentary because of the large place given to descriptions
of locale, daily activities, costumes, and folklore.
Prudently, at first, it disclosed the suffering endured
by the people, their qualities of forebearance, and their
love of the land. These writings were aimed at touching
the heart of the European reader. As actual historical
events grew more violent, however, the writers became
bolder, devoting less time to description and more to an
interrogation as to the nature and origins of their
difficulties. There was much soul-searching in the works
of this period, accompanied by many conjectures as to the
exact source of their ills. Discontent with the foreign
presence, the conflict of generations, dissatisfaction
with outdated customs, and a calling into question of
traditional values were often-heard topics. Ethnographic
literature gradually gave way to a literature of refusal
and contestation in which authors bore witness to abuses
from both internal and external sources, and openly lay
blame. These works were aimed at drawing the attention
of the European reader to the seriousness of the North
African's plight as they protested the indignities and
injustices that had been unduly brought down upon an
entire people. At this time writers became aware of

their social role, and their writings were an expression
of their commitment to effect a change in their stagnant
situation. Because they spoke of internal evils and
exposed to the colonizer weaknesses inherent in their
native tradition as well, they were accused of playing
into his hands.

The first half of this decade was a time of gestation
during which the hero was seen struggling for a personal
form of liberation. Rejection of one's own heritage,
flight, and assimilation with the Other would be a route
elected by many. At this stage the hero had merely begun
his anxious quest.

During this period poetry had not yet reached its
full development. While the proliferation of journals
encouraged literary expression, Maghrebian poets tended
to copy, even plagiarize, the popular French laureates,
from Musset to Aragon to Eluard, or to yield to pompous
grandiloquence, boorishness, or facile repetition of
worn-out themes.

THE ALGERIAN WAR OF LIBERATION: 1956-64. The
period 1956-64 was marked by works which described the
struggle of the French national war of liberation. They
were of two types, first a literature of combat, which
might be in a pathetic or in a revolutionary vein, but
which was consistently patriotic. In it bitterness com-
mingled with the burning hope of bringing forth a free
nation. Second, there appeared a littérature de témoignage, or literature of testimony, in the form of
memoirs, chronicles, and narrative accounts based on
historic events. Collectively they formed a document of
the recent past. In some cases their literary quality
left much to be desired; in others, rules of syntax and
form were deliberately broken to render more forcefully
the ferocity and vitality of the prise de conscience
which was sweeping across the Maghreb. These works were
indicative of the general need to take a stand and affirm
one's commitment as a member of the single-minded whole
as it asserted its unique and proper identity, and for
this reason they are referred to as a littérature de
l'affirmation de soi ("literature of self-affirmation").
This was a period of anger and bitterness, which counted
the sacrifices and the victims of war, and yet it was
also one of exaltation that reveled in the victory of
liberation and of a newly discovered national identity.

Among the important writers of this period we may cite
Kateb Yacine, for his novel Nedjma (1956), a work that

makes use of a disconcerting form and style to explore ancestral myths, and Mohammed Dib, especially for his work of fiction Qui se souvient de la mer (Who remembers the sea, 1962), a further experimental attempt to render reality in a strikingly unconventional way. A host of others are also worthy of mention: the Kabylian writers Malek Ouary, Le Grain dans la meule (The grain in the millstone), and Mouloud Mammeri, Le Sommeil du juste (The sleep of the just), both in 1956, Malek Haddad, La Dernière impression (The last impression, 1958), Je t'offrirai une gazelle (I will give you a gazelle, 1959), l'Elève et la leçon (The student and the lesson, 1960), Le Quai aux Fleurs ne répond plus (The flower quay no longer answers, 1961), Hachemi Baccouche, Ma foi demeure (My faith remains, 1958), Henri Kréa, Djamal (1961); from Morocco, Driss Chraibi, l'Ane (The donkey, 1956), La Foule (The crowd, 1961), Succession ouverte (Heirs to the Past, 1962).

In the domain of poetry, there were scores of contributors, but few major works of quality among the reams of mediocre panegyrics, fastidious pastiches, and moralizing prose poems cranked out "for the occasion." A number of collections of high quality are worthy of mention. Le Malheur en danger (Misfortune in danger, 1956), from the pen of Malek Haddad, centered on the fatherland and those who gave their lives for it. Jean Sénac's Le Soleil sous les armes (The sun under arms), subtitled Eléments d'une poésie de la résistance algérienne (27), constituted a veritable manifesto of the resistance and caused quite a stir when it appeared in 1957. This thin yet explosive volume called the people to action and instilled in them the hope of a certain future. It was in this volume that Sénac submitted the definition of the Algerian writer as "any writer having definitively opted for the Algerian nation" (28). The strong commitment of Algeria's literary artists is evident from such titles as La Révolution et la poésie sont une seule et même chose (Revolution and poetry are one and the same thing, 1957) by Henri Kréa, and Le Toujours de la patrie (The foreverness of the fatherland, 1962) by Nordine Tidafi.

There was a scarcity of works for the theater, with less than a dozen available in printed form. Among the more noteworthy examples we may cite Henri Kréa's Théâtre algérien (1962), Hocine Bouzaher's Des Voix dans

la Casbah (Voices in the Casbah, 1960), and in particular Kateb Yacine's Le Cercle des représailles (The
circle of reprisals, 1959), which explores the mythical-
historical foundations of the fatherland.

Among the essayists, special mention must be made of
Frantz Fanon (1925-61) for his sociohistorical studies,
l'An V de la révolution algérienne (1959), published
in English as A Dying Colonialism, and Les Damnés de
la terre (The Wretched of the Earth, 1961). Though
Fanon was a black man born in Martinique, he played a
role as a leading spokesman of the Algerian revolution.
His works served as handbooks of revolutionary practice
and social reorganization. For his efforts Fanon was
awarded, posthumously in 1964, the National Prize for
Letters. Mostefa Lacheraf, the Algerian sociologist and
historian, published a collection of studies, L'Algérie, nation et société (1965) on the history of Algerian social structures. Other men, better known for their
political contributions than for their books, are also
worthy of note: Ferhat Abbas, La Nuit Coloniale (The
colonial night, 1962), Amar Ouzegane, Hocine Aït Ahmed,
and Mohammed Boudiaf.

The period 1956-64 (29) was intensely fruitful from a
literary standpoint. Spurred on by the objective of
Algerian national independence, writers boldly and passionately gave vent to the feelings and aspirations which
they had for so long held in reserve. The political plat-
form of the Soummam Congress in August 1956 acknowledged
the contributions of literary artists whose novels,
poems, and plays exalted the nationalist cause. The
Congress only reiterated what Mohammed Dib had perceived
six years earlier, that "all the forces of creation put
in the service of their oppressed brothers will make of
culture and of the works which they will produce so many
arms of combat. Arms which will serve to conquer liberty" (30).

1964-75. The period 1964-75 was once again a time of
self-interrogation as the free nations, and Algeria in
particular, meditated on their future. Déjeux refers to
the works of this period as a littérature de contestation et de dévoilement ("literature of contestation and
disclosure"). This was a period of anguish, at the heart
of which lay the burning issue of whether to advance
along Eastern or Western lines, to follow one's heritage,
imbued as it was with Islamic tradition, or to opt for a
pagan, capitalist-oriented technological society. With

Algerian independence came the exodus of thousands of
pieds noirs on whose expertise had depended the administrative and economic future of the country. Algeria had
to admit that she needed French know-how, though what
role the former conqueror would exercise was an open question. The victory of 1962 left Algeria with a multitude
of grave problems. For eight years emphasis had been
placed on winning the revolution; little if any attention
had been given to developing a feasible concrete plan for
forging a new society. The years which followed independence were tumultuous and fraught with knotty issues.
Among other things, social injustices and inequalities,
and a resurgence of the ills inherent in the peasant
class, pointed to the shortcomings of the revolution and
the need to come to grips with reality. Writers did not
ignore their social role during this time of crisis.
"The writer is the expression of the worries of society,
of its doubts, and even of its struggle against itself,
of its negative side" (31), aptly noted Albert Memmi.
This was a time of metaphysical turbulence, when once
again the question of what it meant to be an Algerian
called for an answer. The unity of purpose which had
predominated during the war dissolved afterwards to give
place to factional differences. The task of bringing the
masses into the twentieth century was equally perplexing
and directly related to the question. Elementary and
secondary education was seen as an essential key, but
what should be the language of instruction, French or
Arabic? (The lack of qualified Arabic instructors
resulted in the choice of French, at least temporarily.)

   The literary works of the postwar years tended in two
directions. On the negative side, there was a conformist
clinging to outmoded forms and themes, the repetition of
uninspired conventional formulas and a tendency to glori-
fy the past in monotonous unrevolutionary ways. Hundreds
of poems and short stories in newspapers and periodicals
were in this vein. They relived the war—names, places,
dates, and bloody details—and thus limited themselves to
only one brief chapter in the history of the nation. On
the positive side, writers of talent and imagination
plunged into the distant past as into the cradle of civilization in search of the roots of their identity. They
were audacious in their quest of the new responsible free
citizen. They posited an optimistic yet inquisitive
hero, one who was anxious for social change, who denounced hypocrisy, indolence, superstition, a false sense

of values, and a fixed mentality. Accusations and blame
were no longer to be conveniently inveighed against the
departed colonizer. The source of failure and shortcomings lay within each person and had to be sought there,
not without. The moment of self-examination, that of the
spirit, was in order. The North African needed to create
an identity for himself, to re-create himself. Responding to the need for individual self-discovery, writers
had recourse to experimental techniques quite unlike
anything seen before in their works: surrealistic
dreams, fantastic voyages through man's psyche, a fusion
of myth and symbolism, the elimination of all temporal
restraints, and, in the most extreme cases, passage into
delirium, albeit at the risk of abstruseness. By unbur-
dening themselves of exterior trappings, writers were
able to penetrate the truth within. One dreams and one
dreams oneself (32), is Déjeux's way of describing this
experience. Mohammed Dib with Cours sur la rive sauvage (Run on the untamed shore, 1964), La Danse du roi
(The dance of the king, 1968), Dieu en Barbarie (God in
Barbary, 1970), Le Maître de Chasse (The master of the
hunt, 1973), Habel (1977), and Kateb Yacine, Le Polygone étoilé (The starred polygon, 1966) were the leading proponents of this inquiry into man's essence.
Writers such as these, already familiar to the French-
reading public, responded to reality by finding new
directions. Meanwhile a fresh generation of writers
emerged. Among the novelists, Mourad Bourboune for Le
Muezzin (1968), Rachid Boudjedra for La Répudiation
(1969) and L'Insolation (1972); in Morocco, Khair-
Eddine for Agadir (1967) and Corps négatif (Negative
body, 1968), Abdelkébir Khatibi for La Mémoire ta-
touée (The tattooed memory, 1971); in Tunisia, Albert
Memmi for Le Scorpion (1969) and Le Désert: ou la
vie et les aventures de Jubaï Ouali El-Mammi (The
desert: or the life and adventures of Jubaï Ouali
El-Mammi, 1977).

Among the poets, the postwar period in Algeria saw two
major trends. To the first belonged those who, trauma-
tized by the war and frozen in the past, could only
reiterate the worn out "patriotic" themes of combat, suffering, and metaphysical anguish. Their so-called "revolutionary" verse was no more than a mediocre and
repetitive logorrhea. Lamenting the stagnant course that
this genre had taken, Jean Sénac encouraged a new generation of nonconformist poets through national radio and

television broadcasts in 1968 and 1969. In 1969 he spon-
sored a poetry conference and recital at the Algiers
French Cultural Center. As a result a new generation of
voices was heard alongside the already established poets:
the violent iconoclast Rachid Boudjedra, Hamou
Belhalfaoui and Mourad Bourboune, in search of a new man,
the sensitive Mostefa Lacheraf, and many more—Malek
Alloula, Ahmed Khachaii, Youcef Sebti, Rachid Bey, Abdel
Hamid Laghouati, Hocine Tandjaoui, Anna Gréki, Djamal
Imaziten, Boualem Abdoun, Guy Touati. Not all of these
poets have published collections of their works. In many
cases, their poems have appeared scattered in newspapers
and periodicals. And even among those who have published
one or two collections, the matter of quality and authenticity remained an open question. Still the memory of
the revolution persisted, together with an inner need to
voice past suffering and future hopes. Among the majority could be found a commitment to a social cause, that of
renewal of the individual, allied with the firm determination to effect positive change in the country as a whole.

In Tunisia the trend went toward a literature of Arab
expression, with few exceptional poets of French expression. Among the important names to be retained: Salah
Ettri, Mustapha Kourda, Ahmed Chergui, Badreddine
El-Abbassi (died 1966), Salah Garmadi, Ahmed Hamouda,
Abdelmajid Tlatli, Mohammed Aziza, Moncef-Tayeb Brahim,
Azz-Eddine Derradji. The war was not a topic of interest
to Tunisian writers, and the vituperative hatred common
to Algerian poets was largely absent from their works.
Tunisians were given to a lyrical expression of their
innermost feelings and were more inclined to write in a
serene vein on such topics as love, the fatherland,
primordial innocence, and the sea. A more assertive
tenor was to be heard in the 1970s, however, with the
publication of a new cultural review, Alif (33), that
called for writers to be mindful of cruel realities, to
denounce injustice, and to unite with all the underde-
veloped countries in the struggle to restore man to a
place of dignity within society.

In Morocco a more impetuous direction was established
by Abdellatif Laâbi (34) and his collaborators through
the cultural review Souffles (1966-71). This bimonthly
periodical, conceived originally as "une revue essentiellement poétique et littéraire," took on a new tone in
short time to become "une revue culturelle et idéolo-
gique" (35), in the words of its director. Embracing not

only the cause of the Arab Maghreb but of all oppressed
peoples, Laâbi consistently called for new revolutions,
political, social, and literary. Vehemently he demanded
action, a shaking up of the old order, and the restitu-
tion of justice. The writer was called upon not to shut
himself up in a kind of mystical sect whose special jar-
gon cut him off from society. Instead he was to be a
combatant who should take his place beside those of other
professions in a broad campaign against neo-colonialism,
imperialism, and bourgeois and technocratic ideologies,
in sum, against the exploitation of the masses. Laâbi
denounced "marginal and inauthentic currents" (36) which
ran through Maghrebian literature—folkloric, intimate,
doleful, ethnographic. He deplored the inaction of those
writers who shed crocodile tears over human misery yet
never applied themselves to advancing the cause of the repressed. In his view, liberation was a goal yet to be
achieved. Laâbi's militant cries did not produce a corps
of "vigilante" poets, but the new generation did concern
itself with the formation of a "new man." Among those
who pursued the theme of rebirth we may cite Mahjoubi
Aherdane, Mohammed-Aziz Lahbabi, Zaghloul Morsy, El-
Mostefa Nissaboury, Tahar Ben Jelloun, Tahar Zary, Nordin
Sail, Hamid El-Houadri, Mounir Chahdi, Abdelkader Lagtaa,
Ahmed Janati, Abdel Majid Mansouri, Mohammed Loakira, and
Ali Khamar. Like so many of their Algerian counterparts,
they sought to establish an identity, to create a new man
of substance with roots in the ancestral past.
      The name of Abdelkébir Khatibi must not be omitted
from our enumeration. While better known as a novelist,
essayist, and sociologist, the Moroccan Khatibi is also a
poet. With the combined wisdom of his various disciplines, he discerned the development of a peculiar trend
among the poets of French expression. In an article for
Le Monde (37) he explained that the originality of
Moroccan poets lay in their effort to break the very arm
of the colonialists, which they had appropriated and now
used to serve their own ends: the French language. By
ordering French grammar along the lines of Arab syntax
and by including neologisms drawn from Arab dialects,
they succeeded in alienating the French language from
itself, a sort of reverse procedure of the spiritual and
psychological alienation that they had undergone at the
hands of the colonialists. This device was most successful as the poet lapsed into trancelike Rimbaldien states
that enabled him to escape temporal entrapment. Khatibi

himself had a penchant for the oneiric, bordering on delirium. To "break" the language of the oppressor, to make it foreign to the Frenchman, even at the risk of unintelligibility, was a way of freeing oneself from the grip of the detested colonizer.

In the face of these new political, sociological, and linguistic problems, literary production continues to grow. Another generation of writers has emerged. In Africa and in France stories and poems appear regularly in newspapers and periodicals; new novels and anthologies make their way to the bookstores on a frequent basis. The young in particular, determined to make their voices heard, avail themselves of all possible outlets—press, television, and cinema, as well as the more traditional routes. As Déjeux has pointed out, "the crisis is not a crisis of production, but a crisis of thematics and of the quality of writing" (38).

Themes in Maghrebian Francophone Literature

From the early fifties to the eighties, themes common to Maghrebian literature express the view that the native had of himself as a result of French intervention in his life and country as well as of internal pressures exerted by the ancestral codes of his heritage. They further reveal his emergence from an Other-dominated existence to an emancipated one. Not that he necessarily found answers to all his metaphysical inquiries, or that he even felt the final goal had been attained, but a forthright and open formulation of issues directly touching on his being have helped to liberate his spirit.

The themes particular to this literature may be summed up in key words which in themselves form a system of references. The indigene saw himself as a "bastard son," neither Maghrebian nor French, "castrated," "alienated," "dispossessed," an "outcast," an "exile" in his own land. His relationship with his own heritage proved equally disturbing, as seen in his revolt against the ancestors and the repudiation of his heritage. He saw the colonizer as l'Autre (the Other"), as mistress France—often represented symbolically as la Ville ("the City")—whom he wanted to possess. Angry, dissatisfied with himself and his status, he disclaimed traditional values, family, and homeland, turned toward France, and submerged his identity in order to make himself into the image of the

Other, by whom he hoped to be accepted. From here flowed
the themes of "hatred of the father," "repudiation of the
homeland," and "flight," followed by attempted "assimilation" and "integration" with the foreigner, the quest for
l'altérité ("Otherness"). But with mistress France's
rejection of him, his only option was to return to the
sanctuary of family and ancestral values, whence sprang
the themes of the "mother," "paradise regained," la
terre ("the native soil"), "blood," and "the brotherhood
of the people." The colonized often depicted himself as
being in la grotte ("the Cavern"), a sort of primordial
womb, a place of innocence. The problem was how to come
out of the "dark night" of the Cavern and confront the
oppressor in the bright light of the sun, or of how to
find the way out of the labyrinth. From 1954 to 1962 it
seemed that the war of independence would resolve all
these anxieties, hence a literature of combat glorifying
the Algerians' struggles to attain a noble end predominated. In fact, however, the 1962 victory in Algeria was
a springboard for further interrogation and self-examination. Tunisians and Moroccans too shared in these
concerns: a reexamination of fundamental questions,
repudiation of petrified ancestral values, demythifica-
tion, the liberation of women, emigration, revolt against
bourgeois society and technocratic ideology, a search for
the new man, the quest for authenticity, a return to
pagan times in the hope of finding the foundation of
one's race in the primitive purity of the pre-Arab-
Islamic era.

The Dilemma of the Maghrebian Writer

For two decades, from 1950 to 1970, North African
writers, and Algerians in particular, probed the drama of
a people in the throes of crisis. Their literature mir-
rored the collective experience of a whole people as it
rethought its entire existence, progressing from dependence to self-affirmation. Writers both supported and
helped to crystallize the national stocktaking (39).
They gave an account of the process of colonization and
the means by which it might be crushed. They delved into
the psychological trials which plagued the masses as well
as the elite. They sounded the depths of man's being as
he tried to answer the question, "Who am I, among my fellowmen and in relationship to others?" Déjeux notes

that this literature was "that of a conflict of civilizations" (40), with reproaches levied against the native
civilization as well as the foreign one.

If the literature before 1970 expressed collective
realities, that which followed tended to voice individual
inclinations or the interests of small groups. Some writers became preoccupied with social issues, others with
destroying the "cult of the past," still others pursued
their personal obsessions. The deep crisis of identity
remained a major preoccupation among writers who realized
the indigene's craving to recover "his own interior
Maghrebian permanence" (41). Hence the theme of the
absent father led to that of a return to pagan times
where the North African might find the vital source of
his existence: delight in the natural joys of the earth,
spontaneity, freedom from outside restraints and criticism. But the problem proved, and remains, insoluble, as
seen in the fact that the North African was and is a
hybrid of East and West, unable to escape this double
formation.

The future of the modern North African states is
fraught with difficulties, as revealed through the pens
of their writers. These problems continue to cry out for
discussion and resolution. The very fact that this situation exists may be a source of hope for the future of
Maghrebian francophone literature which, far from being
only a monument to the past and destined to dry up short-
ly has, in Jean Déjeux's thinking, just gotten its
second breath. In a later chapter we shall examine this
view and weigh it in the light of other considerations
that will bear on the future course of this literature.

Chapter Two
Mouloud Mammeri

From Liberty to Liberation

"To confront [the] reader with the deepest and sometimes
most desperate truth about himself" (1) is the goal which
Mouloud Mammeri endeavors to accomplish. It is the mission that he set out to fulfill, even when it meant opening himself to the reproach of his fellow countrymen.
Gradually and subtly, he pulls away the mask of Algerian
and colonialist alike, forcing his readers on both sides
of the Mediterranean to search their souls. The experience is painful, but necessary if man is to achieve inner
peace and give meaning to his existence. For the colonized, whose identity had been stripped during the long
years of foreign domination, who had been buffeted by the
machinations of alien and native forces alike, the ordeal
leads to reconciliation. The conflict of Eastern and
Western cultures subsides as he comes to realize that
each has an intrinsic value that contributes to the
enrichment of his life. Piercing the barrier of prejudice, he frees himself from spiritual bondage and finds a
measure of serenity in this quite imperfect world. This
is the path which Mammeri has trod, the path which,
through his fiction, he bids his reader follow. The journey is long, taking him from the Forgotten Hill, against
which he had turned his back, to an awakening from his
Sleep of the Just, and culminates in a firm commitment to
his people and his nation as he refuses Opium and the
Rod. Enlightenment, true liberty, and a sense of fulfillment, these are the rewards that come from a sincere
search for truth. Finally, in the 1970s Mammeri comes to
realize that the experience that his nation passed
through is not unique. Drawing a comparison with the
Spanish colonizers of old, in his most recent work he
weighs the issue of purportedly superior civilizations
overtaking inferior ones, a dilemma with which his own
country had to come to grips and which others today still
face.

Biographical Notes

Mouloud Mammeri was born on 28 December 1917 at
Taourirt-Mimoun in Grand Kabylia, the mountainous area in
the north of Algeria which lies between Algiers and
Bougie and which is bordered on the south by the Djur-
djura Mountains. As a Kabylian he is a member of the
distinct Berber ethnic group, which makes up one quarter
of Algeria's population. Despite their early conversion
to Islam, the Berbers persevere in the practice and safe-
guarding of their own customs. They are fiercely jealous
of their independence and are characterized by a strong
spirit of clan (2), a feature which stands out in the
author's novels.

Mammeri enjoyed the comforts of the educated middle-
class family from which he issued. His father held the
respected position of amin or village mayor. Mammeri's
mother tongue is Kabyle, a language distinct from Arabic.
His study of French began at an early age when he
entered the village elementary school. His father, who
held a certificate of French studies, strongly encouraged
his education, sending him off at the age of eleven to
live with an uncle in Rabat, Morocco, where he attended
the Lycée Gouraud. This move was a cultural shock for
the youngster, who came in contact with Western culture
for the first time. In the city he had access to French
language publications, through which he came to learn
about a world whose existence he had not suspected. This
led the adolescent to reexamine and question the traditional beliefs that he had always held sacred. The
startling impact of this cultural jolt was to remain with
him for many years. This period in his life is reflected
in his second novel, Le Sommeil du Juste.

After four years in Morocco, Mammeri returned to
Algeria, where he prepared two baccalauréats at the
Lycée Bugeaud. From there he went to the prestigious
Lycée Louis-le-Grand in Paris, with the intention of
later pursuing higher studies. He spent two years studying in the French capital. In 1939, while on vacation in
Algeria, the war broke out and as a member of the Ecole
d'Aspirants de Cherchell, he was mobilized with the Ninth
Algerian Artillery Regiment. Released from duty in October 1940, he enrolled in the Faculté d'Alger. This
same year Mammeri began keeping a personal journal in
which he recorded his experiences and those of his

Kabylian friends. He was again mobilized after the
American landing in North Africa in 1942 and, like his
fictional hero of his second novel, over the following
years he participated in campaigns in Italy, France, and
Germany. Following the war, Mammeri stayed in Paris
where he earned his license in literature. In 1947 he
returned to Algeria and taught French literature as well
as the Greek and Roman classics in Medea and at Ben
Aknoun.

Mammeri's private journal was growing all the while,
and about this time the idea of transforming these pages
into a novel occurred to him. In an interview (3) published in 1967, after his career as a writer had been
established, Mammeri explains that after he had made the
decision to work toward this goal, he wrote more for himself than for his readers. This propulsion to set his
life down on paper fulfilled two inner needs. First, it
allowed him to recapture his youth: "It was for me a way
of reliving it and of getting rid of it" (4). Writing
was thus a means of self-analysis, an opportunity to clarify the forces that had molded him, and a device through
which he crystallized the meaning of existence. Furthermore, it provided him with a means of venting his inner
frustrations by projecting himself into the center of a
marvelous adventure from which he felt he had been excluded: "The values for which it seemed to me one could
live had been elaborated by other men for a society different from mine in a context in which none of my people
played any part, except accidentally. I had hopes of
filling the void" (5).

When Mammeri realized that his work might well be
published, he had to eliminate two thirds of it. Many
portions were too personal, others too critical of the
colonialist power. If the book were to have a French
reading audience, circumstances of that period prevented
the inclusion of explicit censure of the French regime.
Uncertain of what response he would receive, Mammeri sent
the unsolicited manuscript to the Paris publisher Plon.
Six months later he received their affirmative reply.
La Colline oubliée (The forgotten hill) appeared in
1952, and was followed by a second work of fiction, Le
Sommeil du juste (The sleep of the just), in 1955, also
published by Plon.

In 1957, while the bloody battle of Algiers was
raging, Mammeri was drafting a play, "Le Foehn" (the
word, of Swiss-German origin, means a violent wind), but

had to destroy his manuscript and flee to Morocco, where he stayed until Algeria's independence in 1962.

Mammeri is presently a professor at the University of Algiers and director of the Bardo Center for Anthropological, Prehistoric, and Ethnographic Studies. In 1965 a third novel, L'Opium et le Bâton (Opium and the rod), was published by Plon. In addition to the novels, in 1967 Mammeri's film scenario, Le Village incendié (The burned village), was printed in the periodical Révolution Africaine (6), and his play "Le Foehn" was staged at the Théâtre National Algérien in Algiers. Still attached to his Kabylian roots, Mammeri translated into French the work of the Kabylian poet Si Mohand and wrote an introduction for the book, entitled Les Isefra, poèmes de Si Mohand ou Mhand. The bilingual text was published by Maspero in 1969. In 1970 L'Opium et le Bâton was freely adapted for the screen by Ahmed Rachedi and appeared under the title "Thala." In 1973 the Librairie Académique Perrin in Paris published in one volume Mammeri's most recent contribution, La Mort absurde des Aztèques, an essay, followed by Le Banquet, a play about the Spanish conquest of the Aztec Empire and the imposition of a superior culture on a barbarous race.

While Mammeri's mother tongue is Kabyle, he chose the French language as the vehicle of his literary expression. Having done all his studies in French, he has an excellent command of the language and, unlike Malek Haddad, an Algerian compatriot for whom the use of French was a form of exile, he suffers no inner conflict in using the idiom of the dominating colonialists. He saw the adoption of French in Algeria not as an ignominious mark of enslavement imposed by a superpower, but as an instrument that would enrich and would bring modernity and advancement to his country.

The Novels

The three novels which comprise the first phase of Mouloud Mammeri's oeuvre represent three stages in a painful journey of the soul as it is torn between two cultures. In each the hero undergoes an interior crisis which brings him one step further along the difficult path to enlightenment. Feelings of bitterness, disenchantment, and alienation mark this metaphysical quest for self-fulfillment until the hero finally comes to

correctly identify the only goal which can lend meaning
to life: the collective cooperative struggle for Algerian independence.   La Colline oubliée represents the
first stage of the hero's itinerary: repudiation of the
ancestral heritage.

Set in a small Kabylian village, this novel, which
opens in the spring of 1939, focuses on a group of ambi-
tious reform-seeking young men.   Led by the main protagonist Mokrane, they enumerate the objects of their
contempt: a crippling spirit of resignation, the perpetu-
ation of age-old religious traditions replete with magic
and superstition, unquestioning adherence to the dictates
of one's elders and to fossilized social custom, and
poverty and misery brought on by the colonial regime.
Anxious to give meaning to their existence and create a
better future, the young men join the military service,
but contrary to their expectations, they are not given
the opportunity to serve in areas where they may distinguish themselves.   The youth lose faith in their
diplomas and return home disillusioned.   In their village
they are trapped by the very restrictions and evils from
which they had hoped to escape.   An illustration of this
is provided in the example of Mokrane and his wife Aazi,
whom he dearly loves.   When Aazi fails to conceive, she
is taunted by the villagers and her husband is urged to
repudiate her.   Their union, like that of all couples in
Mammeri's fiction, is doomed to failure.   Mokrane dies in
a snowstorm when he attempts to reach Aazi who has
written him the joyous news of her pregnancy.   The young
peoples' aspirations are dashed.   For Menach, another
member of the disillusioned group, only one solution
remains—flight, self-exile.

The publication of La Colline oubliée in September
1952 produced diverse reactions (7).   The French press in
Algeria labeled it in familiar stereotyped terms as a
"splendid Kabylian novel" (8) and a "novel of the Berber
soul" (9).   Given the uncomplimentary picture which it
gives of the indigenes, the French could easily exploit
it to serve their own ends.   The powerful European colonialists who controlled the press saw this book as an oppor-
tune political instrument which might stir up ethnic
antagonism and regionalist separation, and thus destroy
autochthon efforts to build a nationalist front.

Understandably, the Algerian critics' response was
scathing.   Mohammed Cherif Sahli, in an article entitled
"The Hill of Abjuration" (10), criticized the novel for

its lack of engagement. Disregarding the book's literary merit, he censured it for its failure to conform to
the only criterion which he, along with many others,
judged to be admissible during that period: the promo-
tion of the movement for national liberation. A work was
valid only insofar as it served this cause and advanced
the downfall of French colonialism. Mohammed Dib's
Grande Maison, released by Seuil scarcely a few days
after La Colline, conformed to this standard and so did
not draw the same volume or kind of attention. Sahli was
surprised that the first book of an unknown author should
be published in Paris and regarded with suspicion the
laudatory remarks that appeared in the French press.

Mammeri defended himself by stating that any book that
depicted realities in Algeria served the Algerian cause.
Another Muslim writer, Mostefa Lacheraf, continued the
polemic. In an article entitled "The Forgotten Hill or
the Anachronistic Conscience" (11), he accused the author
of regionalism and of unjustly presenting an isolated community as representative of an entire country. He also
urged that through omission and commission, Mammeri had
deformed the truth and he had deliberately evaded the
political issue. Even a friend of the author, Mahfoud
Kaddache, while praising the work for its artistic qualities, expressed disappointment and chagrin over the off-
handed manner in which social traditions and religious
beliefs were mocked (12). The reader who understands the
historic context of the Algeria of 1952-53 can appreciate
Kaddache's view. At a time when traditional values
seemed the only refuge against colonial alienation and
depersonalization, the proposal to reform the deeply
ingrained social and religious codes to which the people
clung seemed like a dangerous threat. Algeria needed a
unifying factor to draw her people together against the
common enemy, not an internal debate that would further
splinter her already extended factions.

In La Colline oubliée Mammeri lays bare the ills of
his people. He expresses bitterness over the poverty and
misery which mark his country, over lack of employment
which forces men to leave their families and go abroad in
search of work. But clearly he places the largest burden
of guilt on his own people, giving only minor attention
to the abuses brought on by colonialism. Furthermore, he
does not propose any viable solution to his nation's problems. He challenges the existing traditional hierarchy,
and he poses the reform of the social and religious codes

as a necessary but unattainable end. In sum, he depicts
the maladies of his countrymen as inborn and inescapable.
His message to the nation is confusing and disappointing. He leaves the reader with an overall negative feeling about the future of Algeria.

Like other works of fiction produced by what was coming to be called the "generation of 1952," La Colline
oubliée is an ethnographic document of lucid realism
and penetrating insight in which local customs, religious
ceremonies, and provincial mentality are vividly described. It testifies to the critical situation of the
moment, the growing malaise of a colonized society that
was stirring from passive acceptance to open contestation. While it ignores the theme of a national struggle
for liberation, it poses a number of burning questions
that attracted the attention of the younger generation of
educated Algerian readers. The book aroused their curi-
osity, if not their sympathy, and brought about an open
debate of delicate issues. Insofar as it contributed to
a climate of critical self-evaluation, it promoted the
cause of the nation.

From a literary standpoint, La Colline oubliée was
one of the few works of quality to be written by a native
Algerian about Algerians. The novel's literary merit is
attested to by the fact that in January 1953 it was
awarded the prestigious Prix des Quatre Jurys (13).

It remained for the more mature and politically bolder
Mammeri to clear up the ambiguities and doubts he had
planted, a task that he attempted in his second novel,
Le Sommeil du juste. The three-year interval between
the publication of the first novel in 1952 and that of
the second in 1955 saw increased strain in French-
Algerian relations, which finally culminated in the open
declaration of war on 1 November 1954. Perhaps the
developments of this period persuaded Mammeri to speak
out unequivocally against the French. Without totally
relinquishing a negative view of his people and country,
and while continuing to point out his peoples' weaknesses, he blames the French for destroying the very fabric
of their being.

Le Sommeil du juste marks the second phase in the
hero's path to metaphysical enlightenment: an awakening
to the hypocrisy of Western doctrine and philosophy. The
action is set in the year 1940. The main protagonist,
Arezki, having repudiated traditional values which he
sees as dead and outmoded, seeks a new philosophy and a

new existence to fill the void. He goes through a
painful initiation process during which he attempts to
integrate himself with the power block, the French who
hold control, "the others." To this end he applies himself to the assiduous study of their language, philosophy, and behavior, hoping thus to be assimilated into the
ranks of what he had been led to believe was a superior
humanity. Although he mimics their ways, he fails to
gain their acceptance. In a symbolic gesture of rejection, the most emphatic in the novel, Arezki burns all
his books. "I piss on ideas" (14), he cries out, as the
noble theories of two centuries of revered sages go up in
smoke.

Arezki goes to Europe, where he hopes to shed his
"difference," but here too his efforts meet with failure.
Finally, his illusions shattered, Arezki returns to his
homeland, to the "forgotten hill." There, caught up in
the intrigues of a 300-year-old tribal feud, the innocent
Arezki is mistakenly accused of the murder of a clan
enemy, and, in what amounts to a mockery of justice, is
sentenced by a French judge to twenty years in prison.
It is from this incident that the book derives its title.
The judge, and by implication the French who sit in
judgment upon the whole country, sleep "the sleep of the
just," confident that they are performing their duty and
defending society. It is an accident of birth which has
brought Arezki so low and has set the judge so high, the
young man reflects: "He doesn't know that it is by
chance that he is on the right side of the bar and I on
the other. He doesn't see how fragile is the line which
separates the fault from the judge. If for one instant
he ceased to be lulled by the false security of the code
. . . he would recoil scared stiff to discover that the
society which he defends could owe its pardon only to my
docility" (15).

Like La Colline oubliée, Le Sommeil du juste does
not propose any solutions to Algeria's dilemma, but it is
unmistakably committed to the struggle against colonialism. It warns against the false promises of liberty and
equality, of pledges made but not honored. It admonishes
the colonized who would too eagerly place their trust in
Western civilization, whose assurances are not to be
counted on and whose interests are suspect. It demonstrates that the colonizer's avowals of friendship and
guarantees of progress are false. In sum, it prepares
the way for rebellion.

In Le Sommeil du juste Mammeri reaches his peak. He
pulls together content and form, technique and artistry,
in a skilled blend that both serves the cause of his
people and responds to the reader's demand for quality
fiction (16).

The final stage in the journey of the dark night of
the soul is reached in L'Opium et le Bâton (1965), set
in the year 1957 while the Algerian war is raging. The
hero, Bachir Lazrak, a medical doctor with a successful
career, learns that he cannot run away from his problems
or avoid them by clothing himself in the guise of "the
others." Most important, he discovers that he cannot
succeed by merely acting as an individual. He must join
the collective cause. Persuaded to relinquish his com-
fortable existence in Algiers that he has attained as a
result of French schooling (the opium which seduced him,
paralyzed his will, and made him oblivious to the truth),
he awakens from his "sleep of the just" and goes to the
maquis to assist his people who suffer the oppression of
the rod wielded mercilessly by the French. Refusing both
opium and the rod, he commits himself to his fellow
Algerians in their combat for national independence.
This is the culmination of the hero's quest. Authentic
liberty is found neither in freedom from responsibility,
nor in isolated pursuits, but in commitment to the service of others and the nation. Only when the hero relin-
quishes his individual quest for liberty and dedicates
himself to the broader cause of liberation does he give
meaning to his life.

L'Opium et le Bâton responds totally to the demand
for engagement required of the Algerian writer. With
great realism it depicts the cruelty of the French and
the physical and spiritual damage inflicted by them.
From this point of view the novel is a complete success.
Furthermore, it delicately probes the thoughts and
motives of the protagonists, leading the noted Algerian
writer and critic Abdelkébir Khatibi to praise Mammeri
for introducing the psychological novel into Maghrebian
literature of French expression. Regretfully, as the
didactic factor gains importance, the lyric elements seen
in Mammeri's earlier works, especially his first novel,
diminish. The realistic concrete depictions of the evils
wrought by war are somewhat repetitive. L'Opium et le
Bâton may be cited as a well-written example of the
littérature de combat that flooded the literary scene
in the years immediately following independence.

New Directions: An Essay and a Play

Eight years elapsed before another major work emerged
from the pen of Mammeri, this time in the form of a
twelve-page essay, <u>La Mort absurde des Aztèques</u>, and a
three-act play, <u>Le Banquet</u>, published in one volume in
1973. Like so many Maghrebian writers, Mammeri came to
see his country's experience in broad terms. He understood that the destruction of social groups by the
onslaught of "civilization," specifically or "progress"
imposed by the white man, is a phenomenon that recurs
periodically over the centuries. These foreigners, who
secretly covet the riches of the lands they invade while
outwardly proclaiming their mission to deliver the backward peoples of the earth from their barbarity, destroy
civilizations in the name of progress. To illustrate his
point, Mammeri focuses on the collapse of the Aztec
Empire in 1519. Within a twenty-month period, a great
race of people disappeared, owing to the Indians' superstition and the white man's cleverness and cruelty.

The parallel which Mammeri chooses is an excellent
one. As explained in the play, which is based on historical fact, the Aztecs expected and feared the arrival of a
white god, Quetzalcoatl, who was soon due to return.
When Cortes and the Spaniards came to Mexico, the Indians
took him to be the incarnation of this great god. By a
curious mechanism, the powerful Aztec Empire, which had
been centuries in the making, was wiped out in less than
two years. This is attributed in large part to the
Indians' psychological attitude, which led them to accept
the superiority of the white man and to bow down before
it. Here was "a world which accepts itself as condemned
in the face of another which believes itself invested by
God . . ." (17). For Mammeri the situation was "a real
laboratory experiment" (18), a case which echoes what his
own people had suffered and what scores of other underde-
veloped societies face in the twentieth century: "They
undergo as an unbearable shock this regular, implacable
advance of the event, the unfolding of an absurd mechanism. It is not a war, it is a funeral march" (19).

Mammeri inveighs against ethnocide carried out in the
name of progress. Specifically he faults Western civilization for the domination of the world by one overriding
ideal set inexorably in motion to sweep away any group
that will not be transformed by it: "Now it is clear
that as the years pass, more and more vast portions of

humanity bury themselves in the royal paths of technical,
material, efficacious, and programmed Western civilization" (20).   The advanced nations of the world hold out
to the less developed ones the hope of material well-
being, half threatening them to believe that this is the
only possible course.   Whole nations flock to join this
mainstream only to discover that the prestigious image
that they breathlessly pursue conceals a host of weaknesses.   Mammeri is severe in his judgment: "Western
thought is essentially unifying and reducing.   It has
invented the unique and devastating God, the jealous God.
There is no place in [Western thought] except for a sole
truth.   For it the other's crime is his 'otherness':   the
other is always intolerable.   He is the crack which
threatens to break the stupidly round closing of our
being" (21).

Without overtly proclaiming the theory of the noble
savage, Mammeri indicts Western civilization for succeeding in everything except in making men happy: "Work
itself, which is the basis of his riches, hinders him
from enjoying them.   Leisure is weighed out to him by the
ounce, he is programmed and jailed in the hooked paren-
theses of two weeks a year; they sell it to him in pack-
ages, tied, pasteurized, weighed" (22).   In what amounts
to a totally subjective view of life, Mammeri calls work
a damnation, saying that man was made for Eden, there to
enjoy the warmth of other human beings.   The author concludes on a note of black optimism, convinced that civilized man is gradually becoming disgusted and angry at
himself, and already dreams are beginning to encroach
upon hard reality.   These perceptions correspond indeed
with views now being expressed by workers who complain of
burn-out and stress.

Mammeri is a talented writer deeply sensitive to the
responsibility of his vocation.   His works give testimony
to his position as an engagé writer, of one who fur-
thers man's hopes by bringing him to a clearer understanding of himself and his society.   As with his compatriots,
Mammeri's concern goes beyond the narrow confines of his
own particular case.   Like Memmi he is able to grasp the
universal dimensions of the process of colonization and
its aftermath.   If the truth that Mammeri sees arouses
anguish, sadness, and even anger, it is because this is
not a perfect world, wherever one lives.

Unlike Dib and Chraïbi, who choose France as their domicile, Mammeri opts to remain in Algeria near his people. There, as a respected man of letters, he guides and instructs them in helping them acquire a balanced and lucid perspective of history, past and present. He is a writer and a citizen of whom they may well be proud.

Chapter Three
Mohammed Dib

An Inquiry into the Depths

Certainly the best known, most prolific, and most versatile of the North African writers to use the French language is Mohammed Dib. Poet, novelist, <u>conteur</u>, playwright, and journalist, Dib's steady literary output, from 1952 to the present, and the merit of his oeuvre have earned him a major position in the literary history of his country. Déjeux rightly calls him one of the most constructive, profound, and lucid Algerian writers. Not content with a facile superficial review of men and events, Dib has never relinquished his goal of pursuing to more profound depths and in a singular manner the hidden side of reality. His work "presents itself as a more and more penetrating investigation of the human person (what is the human being, the couple, liberty, destiny) as much in reference to the Algerian terror (yesterday's colonized and today's Algerian advancing toward a greater demand for liberation) as in relationship to man wherever he is. This work is the search for a reconciled humanity" (1). Through Dib's writings come renewed insights into the dilemmas of the Algerian people and human beings the world over.

Biographical Notes

Mohammed Dib was born on 21 July 1920 in Tlemcen, into a bourgeois family that had known better times. His father worked as a master carpenter. While his family was not economically well-off, as a youth Dib did not experience the unhappy existence described by him in his first novel. He led a normal childhood, attending school first in Tlemcen and later at Oujda in Morocco. Although he did not attend a religious school to study the Koran, he was brought up in an atmosphere permeated by Muslim beliefs and practices. Through formal education and family and social contacts he acquired both Arabic and French as native languages. His family knew or was

44

related to many inhabitants living in different sectors
of the city. Through them he got to know a variety of
social conditions and milieux.

When Dib was eleven years old, his father died. Only
then did he begin to confront some of the difficulties
which gradually transformed his life. As a teenager he
wrote mainly poetry but also some prose, and dabbled in
painting. In the twelve-year period from 1939 to 1951 he
worked in a variety of occupations. From 1939 to 1940
Dib was employed as a school teacher in a remote Algerian
village near the Moroccan border. His students, for the
most part, were the sons of nomads. From 1940 to 1941 he
worked in Oujda as an accountant for the army. In 1942
he was with the army engineering corps, then the Algerian
Railroad. From 1943 to 1944 he was a bilingual French-
English interpreter for the Allied armies in Algiers.

In 1945 he returned to Tlemcen, where for three years
he drew designs and supervised the fabrication of one-of-
a-kind carpets. In 1948, by invitation of the Service
for the Movements of Youth and Popular Education, Dib
spent three weeks at a meeting in Sidi Madani near Blida.
The conference was also attended by Jean Cayrol, Jean
Sénac, and Albert Camus. That brief sojourn changed the
course of Dib's life. Hitherto his writings had been composed instinctively, on impulse. The reunion at Sidi
Madani led him to see writing as a serious endeavor. His
vocation as a novelist began to take form as he seriously
pursued work on what was to later become the trilogy Algérie. That same year Dib made his first trip to
France. During the period 1948-51 Dib joined the Communist party and the militant agricultural union, actively helping to organize the fellahs into syndicates in the
region of Oran. Simultaneously he worked as a journalist
for the progressive newspaper Alger Républicain (at
the same time as Kateb Yacine). He wrote news reports,
politically committed columns, poems, and reviews of Arab
theater for that publication as well as for Liberté,
the official organ of the Algerian Communist party. Dib
claims that he does not have happy memories of those
days.

Finally he gave up his position with Alger Républicain in order to be able to devote full time to his
novel. In 1951 he married a French woman, Colette
Bellissant, by whom he has four children. A year later
he again traveled to France. He sent the manuscript for
the first book of his trilogy to the publishing house of
Seuil in Paris. That novel, La Grande Maison, was pub-

lished in 1952. The first printing was sold out after one
month and the book was reprinted. Thereafter its popularity was so great that it had to be reprinted almost on an
annual basis. The second part of the trilogy, L'Incendie,
followed in 1954, and the final book, LeMétier à tisser,
was published in 1957, again by Seuil.In between Dib sent a
collection of short stories to Gallimard, which published it
under the title Au Café in 1955.

While Dib was making progress in his literary career,
the situation in Algeria was disintegrating. In 1955,
less than a year after the outbreak of the Algerian war
for independence, Dib was one of two hundred persons,
Algerian and French, to sign the manifesto "Algerian
Fraternity," which sought to draw together the two peoples. During the period 1956-59, while the war was heat-
ing up, Dib worked as an accountant and commercial
correspondent to supplement his income. In 1959 two new
works were published: Baba Fekrane, a short story for
children, by the firm of La Farandole in Paris, and a
fourth novel, Un Eté africain, by Seuil. That same
year Dib was expelled from Algeria for his outspoken
political stance. He moved to Mougins, in the department
of the Maritime Alps, where he lived with his wife's
parents. That event marked a turning point in his
career. Forced to abandon his personal belongings and
his homeland, Dib had to make a new beginning, rethink
his entire existence, his beliefs, his career. He
traveled in Eastern Europe and in 1960 returned to Morocco to work on a film scenario of La Grande Maison.
That project was never completed. In 1961 Gallimard
published Ombre gardienne, a collection of poems, which
was followed by Qui se souvient de la mer, an apocalyp-
tic novel on the war of liberation, issued by Seuil in
1962. This work, which greatly departs from the author's
initial writing style, introduces Dib's second literary
phase. It was followed in 1964 by Cours sur la rive
sauvage, again at Seuil, in which the theme of the Algerian cause is temporarily set aside in favor of an
unwonted metaphysical exploration of the human psyche.
In 1964 Dib moved to the suburbs of Paris, settling finally in La Celle Saint-Cloud, not far from Versailles. His
literary output continues to flow steadily. In 1966
Seuil published Le Talisman, a collection of short stories, followed by two novels, La Danse du roi (1968)
and Dieu en Barbarie (1970), and Formulaires (1970),
a book of poems.

During the mid-seventies, Dib's first three novels

were serialized on Algerian television, proving quite successful. However, the later novels depicting the political and technocratic regime of independent Algeria are
not distributed in that country. In 1974, the year his
folktale L'Histoire du chat qui boude was published by
La Farandole, Dib accepted a post as visiting Regents
Professor at the University of California in Los Angeles.
By the time of his return to France, Seuil had published
yet another collection of poems, Omneros, which was
followed by the novel Habel in 1977. A fourth volume
of poetry, Feu beau feu, appeared in 1979, and Dib's
first drama, Mille hourras pour une gueuse, a transposi-
tion of La Danse du roi, was printed in 1980. All of
these were from the Paris firm of Seuil.

In addition to his major writings listed above, other
creative works, as well as literary and social criticism,
have appeared in diverse publications. Moreover, Dib has
participated in literary colloquiums; for instance, in
the spring of 1976 he served as a member of a literary
jury in Oklahoma. Dib's talent has been recognized and
acclaimed; he has been the recipient of numerous literary
awards, including the prestigious prix Fenéon for La
Grande Maison, the prix René Laporte in 1961 for Ombre
gardienne, the prix de l'unanimité in 1963, the prix du
Collège du Menton in 1964, that of the Union of Algerian
writers in 1966, and of the Academy of Poetry for the
ensemble of his works in 1971.

Mohammed Dib remains a popular and much-read author.
The success of his works is attested to by the fact that
many of his books have been translated into various languages. La Grande Maison, for example, is available in
no fewer than eleven translations, including Chinese and
Eastern European languages. With man and freedom as his
subject matter, Dib easily appeals to readers of many lands.
While admitting that he writes above all for the Algerians
and the French, so that they may better understand themselves and each other, Dib has stated that his ambition
is to attract all readers: "The essential is the fundamental humanity which is common to all of us; the things
which differentiate us will always remain secondary" (2).

The Novels

THE FIRST MANNER: AN ALGERIAN BALZAC. In the
late forties Dib conceived the idea of writing an immense
novel on Algerian life, similar to what Balzac had done

on French life. Inspired by the Comédie Humaine, Dib
envisaged a large-scale work composed of many novels
describing the occupations, life-style, and social mores
of members of all classes. This vast oeuvre, as Dib perceived it, was to be a magnificent fresco of the Algerian
society of the times. The books that make up the trilogy
Algérie are the products of this initial conception.
In them the reader glimpses various milieux of society,
but mainly he sees in all of them the dynamism of the
ordinary people on the brink of awakening to a new
future. The three novels echo the major problems which
assailed Algeria during the years 1939-56: famine and
misery, a lethargic populace paralyzed by strict attach-
ment to the Islamic principle of resignation, and a tyran-
nically ruled society. These themes run throughout the
novels, yet the reader must not allow himself to be so
overwhelmed by these specifics as to miss the ultimate
dominating thrust of these works: an effort to alert the
reader to an awakening national consciousness while at
the same time drawing his attention to the injustices
that were being perpetrated on a subjugated people. Dib
sought to warn his French readers about the unrest that
was stirring in his homeland as a result of the severe
want and oppression brought on by the colonialist regime
and, simultaneously, to point to the ultimate consequences of such conditions. Algérie is a document that
bears witness to the truth that many were disinclined to
believe.
     Dib's sweeping tableau of Algerian life begins with
La Grande Maison (The big house, 1952), set in the
city of Tlemcen during the years 1938-39. The central
hub of activity is Dar Sbitar (3), the Moorish-style
apartment complex built around a central courtyard, with
its scores of indigent residents squeezed into cramped
cell-like quarters. The building, from which the book
derives its title, is representative of the living conditions of the masses of urban poor.
     Among the occupants of Dar Sbitar are the stalwart
widow Aïni, her ten-year-old son Omar, and two younger
daughters. Like all of Dib's female characters, Aïni is
strong and determined. Through her example the reader
learns how individuals of little means manage to survive
on a day to day basis. But it is Omar, a mere lad, no
longer a child yet still not a man, who is the central
figure of this novel. The three books that make up
Algérie trace his apprenticeship into life and through

him explore the major concerns and issues of the period:
the question of national identity, the cruelty of the
French overseers, the injustice of colonial law, the
fatalistic resignation of the native populace, the meaning of liberty, the idea of revolt. In his youthful innocence, Omar lends a unique view to life's occurrences as
he questions and ponders his role in the activities of
which he is a part. He is both the lens through which we
see the world and a mirror in which the world is reflected. So well does Dib succeed in weaving conversations
between Omar and the dozens of people he encounters that
we almost forget that the novel is in fact narrated by an
omniscient third person. From the opening pages, Omar
functions as the medium through which questions are posed
and problems laid bare. He is both a tool through which
the author proposes key issues for his readers' consideration and a synthesis of the Algerian people. Like the
latter, he has yet to grow and mature mentally, to formu-
late a position and stand by it. Like them, he pursues
his shortsighted course, gaining occasional insights of
an altered future. Like the restless individuals with
visions of freedom, Omar rejects self-limiting perceptions and tenaciously refuses to "accept existence as it
offered itself to him. He expected something other than
this life, this dissimulation, this catastrophe which he
surmised" (4).

    There is a clear parallel between Omar's relationship
to his family and Algeria's relationship to France. Omar
is baffled and confused by the conflicting codes that
govern his existence. On the one hand, as a dutiful
child he must obediently and uncomplainingly do as he is
told; on the other, as the male head of household, he
must assume the responsibility of finding a means for all
to survive. Similarly the masses of people may be
likened to children who must obey the orders of "mother"
France, which has jurisdiction over them. But, while
they must submit to this authority, they are at the same
time expected to assume responsibility for their own well-
being. Torn between this dual role of child and adult,
Omar, and the nation, experience great anguish. Just as
the child looks forward to freeing himself from the
constraints that bind him, so too must the nation.

    Despite the misery portrayed on every page of this
novel, its overall outlook and conclusion are optimistic.
At the story's end, Omar encounters a silent crowd assembled in the street. He feels the strength and energy of

the group, "sure of itself, of what it carried within
itself, still unaccustomed but strong and ferocious.
They had always been helped not to think; presently their
own adventure surged up before them, full of obscure
threats, strong-willed; and all these men and all these
women stood naked before their inner selves. They had
left their heart disengaged, at rest. But misfortune hit
them with its fist and they were waking up" (5). Solidarity will overcome tyranny, suggests Dib. Standing in the
crowd, Omar no longer feels like a child; he senses that
he is part of a great whole, a member of the brotherhood
of man as it awakens to its collective destiny. The end
of the novel portends a new beginning.

La Grande Maison appeared only a few days after
Mammeri's Colline oubliée (September 1952). Jean
Brune, comparing the two works in the Algiers Dépêche
Quotidienne, hailed Mammeri's novel as "a work fit to
enter the prestigious Olympus of Art," while labeling La
Grande Maison as a pamphlet which "stirs up malice with
arguments borrowed from propaganda" (6). Both novels
offer a view of the Algeria of 1939, yet the two are
totally different in nature. Dib's novel is boldly
accusing, strongly engagé, strategically aimed, shot
through with invitations to rise up and revolt. In this
respect, Brune was not completely inaccurate in his judgment. The Algerian writer Jean Sénac acknowledges the
revolutionary content of the novel, but views this as a
desirable quality (7).

Some critics of the early fifties, Algerian and
French, entirely missed the point of the novel. Because
of the numerous pages devoted to descriptions of hunger
and deprivation, they never saw beyond the most superficial level of interpretation. They criticized the novel
for showing Algerians to a disadvantage, for wallowing in
misery, and for presenting too negative an outlook. In
fact, this novel portrays Algeria and Algerians in a
realistic light up to that time unknown in the history of
the country's literature. Dib was dismayed by the
critics' reactions. The May 1953 issue of Progrès, a
Communist party organ, took the author to task, arguing
that he ought rather to exalt man and praise the en-
lightened rising lower classes. This position was in
keeping with the Stalinist socialist ideology of the
times, but it did not correspond to fact. The famous
French Communist writer Louis Aragon defended Dib against
these attacks by the Algerian Communist party, referring

to the author as an "Algerian Jean-Christophe who has not yet emerged from childhood" (8).

The scope of Dib's exposé on Algerian society is enlarged in L'Incendie (The conflagration, 1954), which transports the reader out of the narrow confines of the city to the open space of a rugged countryside village in the summer of 1939. Here the novel focuses on the fellahs, the simple people who compose a significant portion of Algeria's population. Despite their archaic existence, the fellahs are a force to be reckoned with, for almost "all that makes up Algeria is in them" (9). As the novel illustrates, the destiny of the entire country rests with this seemingly insignificant heap of wretched humanity. L'Incendie offers numerous examples of colonial tyranny and traces the slow unraveling of the thought processes that finally bring the peasants to believe that their actions can effect a change in their circumstances. Deciding that the time has come to create a new soul, the fellahs stage a strike and witness the extent of their power.

The unity of the endeavor is expressly underscored as workers' unions in the city lend moral and financial support to the fellahs' cause. This display of solidarity is a key point, showing that urban and rural worker share a common goal. Dib encourages them to eradicate the distinctions which set them apart. The strike is effective, but not without incident. An Algerian traitor collaborates with the French by deliberately setting a fire that brings the police in in full force and leads to the arrest of the strike leaders. The title of the novel derives from this incident, whose symbolism is clearly stated: "A fire had been lit and never again would it go out. It would continue to creep blindly, secretly, underground; its bloody flames would never cease until they had cast their sinister brilliance over all the land" (10). The will to revolt has been born and is purified in the crucible of fire. It stands ready to shake the entire colonialist system.

Le Métier à tisser (The weaver's trade, 1957), the concluding part of Dib's trilogy, transports the reader back to a dreary Tlemcen, crowded with beggars who have drifted in from the countryside in search of work. In this winter of 1942 Aïni manages to have her son Omar apprenticed to a weaver. Thereafter he is doomed to spend his days toiling in the dark malodorous cellar of an exploitive Algerian boss. In these cramped darkened

quarters, which he shares with a dozen other workers,
Omar encounters yet another segment of society, the
artisans and hand laborers. They are of all ages and
political inclinations. Amid the clack of the flying
shuttlecocks, Omar is witness to the ideas and emotions
that they unrestrainedly voice. Their condition and
their concerns are the focal point of the narration. The
kindling of man's will to act and to finally seize his
liberty is the central issue: "People who have arrived
at the point where they are nothing, where they are zero,
people like that could do only one thing. . . . Demand
everything" (11). An extreme remedy is needed to cure an
extreme ill, cries one worker: "We have sunk too low.
We could not become men by ordinary means" (12).

In the semidarkness of the pitlike atelier, itself
symbolic of men's souls and the state of the nation,
bristling conflicts ensue. Finally a fight between Omar
and another worker leads to the former's dismissal. The
novel concludes open-endedly with the landing of American
troops in November 1942.

The Algérie novels, chronicles of prerevolutionary
Algeria, give testimony to the circumstances and urgent
concerns of the beginning stages of unrest in that country. Characterized by the careful recording of details
and precise representation of reality, from the point of
view of style and structure they belong to Dib's first
period. They were followed by Un Eté africain (An
African summer, 1959), which, due to its treatment of the
characters' psychological motivations, is already considered a transition piece, one that hints at the direction that is to follow. In this novel Dib continues to
strive to remain faithful to his design of creating a
panoramic view of Algerian society. He juxtaposes members of various socioeconomic stratas, rich and poor,
urban dweller and country peasant, depicting them as they
go about their daily activities. The novel is composed
of a number of independent stories that interrupt each
other. Its major concern is not so much to indicate the
educational, economic, and social differences that exist
in Algeria, but to consider the position that each
individual takes as regards the meaning of existence and
his role in society. On this basis, three postures may
be identified, each represented by a group of characters.
To the first belong those who maintain that the status
quo must be upheld, that man's function is to comply with
the code of tradition. This attitude is seen in the

wealthy Rai family that, against their daughter's will,
seeks to fulfill their obligation through an arranged
marriage. (This thread of the narration provides insight
into the women's problem in Muslim society.) Among the
second are those who decline responsibility, those victims of spiritual degeneration for whom life is devoid of
meaning, as seen in the self-deprecating Djamal Terraz.
Last are those who give meaning to their life through
action with the goal of bettering the condition of their
fellowmen, as illustrated by the village peasants who
derive strength from the network of optimistic cooperative support they have built. The novel introduces
individuals of contrasting backgrounds in order to show
that inner peace, both personal and collective, depends
not on education or wealth, but on the certainty that one
is taking his own future in hand and molding it to
achieve freedom for all.

   THE SECOND MANNER: SYMBOLIC METAPHORS. Dib's
early novels are characterized by a documentary style and
concrete representations of reality. Material needs and
spiritual hunger are graphically depicted in familiar
terms. While the strong ethnographic element of these
novels attracts the reader's interest, Dib himself
realized that the marked repetition of this technique
would only finish by dulling the senses and making the
reader impervious to the nation's anguish. When he began
composing Qui se souvient de la mer (Who remembers the
sea, 1962), hostilities were already at their height.
Dib wanted to describe the material and spiritual devasta-
tion wrought by the bloody conflict and evoke its hellish-
ness as vividly as possible. But he realized that in
comparison with the atrocities of Auschwitz and the shock
of Hiroshima, the Algerian conflict was only another war.
If he were to continue in the same realistic mode of his
early fiction, he could only succeed in enumerating
events, in uttering a numbing litany of horrors, with the
result that, after a short time, the reader would be
rendered insensitive to even the most monstrous and vile
acts of war. Clearly an historic reconstitution of
actual events was not the route to take. To evoke the
unimaginable terror of the revolution, a new framework
had to be found. And as Dib explains in the postscript
of his novel, the inspiration for this new framework came
not from literature, but from art, in the form of Picasso's painting Guernica. There one finds no cadavers,
no blood, no gaping wounds, and yet the viewer is struck

by the dread expressed in this picture. Picasso captured
on canvas the nightmares that haunt the victims of war.
He gave them a form that everyone could recognize. He
evoked the specter of horror. He lent substance to the
unexpressed notion of the terror of war that lurks in
each person's unconscious and in so doing succeeded in
bringing men's fears to the conscious level. This is
what Dib sought to achieve in his novel.

With Qui se souvient de la mer Dib begins a new
phase in his works of fiction, one in which reality is
transformed into a series of oneiric visions and nightmarish hallucinations. The novel's interest lies not in
the hideous acts of war per se, but in the way the mind
perceives the daily onslaught of cataclysmic events. All
experiences are filtered through the mind of the first-
person narrator who perceives and translates reality on
two different registers. In the first mode, the events
of daily life are reconstituted, both as they occur and
as they are remembered, in the traditional manner. In
the second mode, however, spatiotemporal relationships
are distorted and the physical laws that govern matter
are deliberately transgressed. On these occasions the
narrator, though completely awake, perceives his surroundings in surrealistic nightmarish visions. During
hostilities the natural order of things was overthrown in
actual life. The novel seeks to convey this phenomenon
through the evocative power of words. To this end Dib
combines symbolism, surrealism, elements of psychoanalysis, science fiction, the theme of the labyrinth, and the
new novelists' preoccupation with time and space. All of
these are skillfully blended to yield a narrative that
continually stimulates the imagination and challenges the
mind of the reader.

Set in the midst of the war for independence, Qui se
souvient de la mer is, on a literal level, the story of
a man, his wife, and a city torn by war; symbolically and
metaphorically it is the story of the Algerian people and
their struggle to emerge from the bonds of colonialism.
The novel is difficult to decipher. Characters, events,
and places throb with signification. Manifold implications only gradually make themselves understood.

The action takes place in a bi-level city. On the
ground level is the Ville étrangère or foreign city,
the domain of the colonialist regime. Below it is a dark
winding underground whose inhabitants have fallen under
the demonic spell of the forces above. A mole burrows

through the labyrinthian galleries, emerging every once
in a while for a breath of air and causing the structures
above to collapse. Secret underground liberation forces
at work? Yes, but more profoundly, the hidden and forgotten remembrance of the free Algeria of yore. The walls
of the <u>Ville étrangère</u> are in constant flux, moving
closer, dissolving, or reappearing unexpectedly. New
structures are constantly being erected, only to explode.
The foreign city is patrolled by Minotaures (French
soldiers?), harassed by <u>iriaces</u>, predatory birds, or
<u>oiseaux guerriers</u>, "war birds" (spies?, <u>pieds noirs</u>?),
and attacked by <u>spyrovirs</u> (explosives?). Nothing is
constant or predictable, much like life itself. Space is
deformed, objects undergo perpetual metamorphosis. The
city is a stunning metaphor with multiple reverberations.
Its structure suggests two distinct societies, one suffo-
cating the other, while each simultaneously carries on
its daily activities. The subterranean network implies
the secret forces of the resistance at work. It also
corresponds to the dark hidden recesses of man's psyche,
guardian storehouse of the past, living repository of the
country's heritage. Palpitating with life, the underground is the only true city in which the nation's patrimony is preserved.

Amid the turmoil of revolution an element of constancy
asserts itself: the forgotten sea. The sea, principal
symbol of the novel, is a source of wisdom and energy, a
protective, nourishing refuge, the guardian of the collective consciousness of the Algerian people. The sea is
the womb from which new life will issue forth to invade
and topple the foreign city. Over the centuries the sea
withdrew to a cave where it remained forgotten. But its
waves gently lap against the shore; its voice murmurs
softly but persistently. For "qui se souvient de la mer"
("who remembers the sea"), all hope is permitted.

In this novel the sea is personified in the narrator's
wife, Nafissa, whose name in Arabic means breath, soul,
source of life. As perceived by her husband, Nafissa is
no ordinary being. In his mind she is the very idealiza-
tion of woman, envisaged as a <u>guide protectrice</u> and
ministering spirit, source of hope and refuge. The link
between <u>mer</u>/<u>mère</u> ("sea"/"mother") is undeniable.
The sea, as symbol of Algerian identity, preserves the
common heritage, just as woman nurtures and perpetuates
this heritage through the children she carries in her
womb. <u>Mer</u>/<u>mère</u> share a common role. "Without the

sea, without women, we would remain orphans definitively"
(13). Just as woman in her role as mother helps her
children acquire a sense of identity upon which they
build a solid future, the sea, as symbol of the living
past, will enable the people to attain fullness of existence.

In Qui se souvient de la mer Dib exploits the explosive power of metaphor to render dynamically man's reactions to the war of liberation. Dib's unique poetic
vision lends a distinctive quality to his prose. There
is richness of meaning because objects are endowed with
multiple signification. Concepts have depth and color.
Unwonted interrelationships twine the parts into an
intuited comprehensible whole. Nothing "is"; everything
is becoming, in a state of flux, like the cosmos itself.
The reader is not allowed to rest comfortably with one
idea or event since these dissolve or take on new shades
of meaning in an ongoing metamorphosis. Abstract and
complex, yet precise and coherent, Qui se souvient de la
mer describes the structure, destruction, and restruc-
turation of a universe in crisis and explores the spiritual adventure of renewal. Time (past, present, and
future) and space are suspended on different levels
through which the narrator freely passes. Relationships
are deformed, equilibrium is upset, everything is viewed
from an unexpected angle as we move through the subconscious mind of the main protagonist. The composition of
the novel, with its unexpected shifts, dislocations, and
dissolutions, reflects the dynamism of the human psyche
and of history.

The novel was received with surprise on the part of
readers who had become attached to the author's realistic
vein. A quarrel between the realists and the antireal-
ists ensued. In France Pierre-Henri Simon simultaneously
applauded and criticized Dib: "Vertigo is too strong in
Dib. His book reveals a great talent, a writer's vigor
which is at times admirable; but one would have to enter
into a trance to read him well" (14). This kind of judgment refuses to acknowledge the author's intent. In his
postscript Dib provides the key to understanding the
novel, explicitly spelling out the approach that the
reader must take. (One can only wish that it had prefaced
the narration.) Hassan El Nouty rightly refers to the
postscript as a "capital text which responds to a triple
design: it is at the same time an aesthetic commentary,
a defense, and a manifesto" (15). Only a revolutionary

manner of expression could convey some idea of the apoca-
lyptic horror of revolution. In this Dib admirably
succeeds.

If to some Qui se souvient de la mer was shocking
and perplexing in its conception, Cours sur la rive
sauvage (Run on the untamed bank, 1964), the novel that
follows, proved doubly disconcerting, in its content as
well as in its form. In this work Dib sought to break
completely with the depiction of familiar surroundings
peopled by traditional characters. Thus Algeria and her
problems are totally absent as the author turns to the
free pursuit of literature as a creative art form. When
criticized for this blatant lack of political commitment,
Dib responded in an interview: "my concern at the time
of my first novels was to melt my voice in the collective
voice. That voice today is silenced. . . . I have taken
up my attitude of a writer who is interested in problems
of a psychological, fiction-related, and stylistic order.
. . . The time for engagement is over. I was African
when I had to be" (16).

In its subject matter the novel pursues the theme of
woman, a topic that continued to preoccupy Dib. Here she
is no longer envisaged as the strong-willed mother, nor
is she seen as the passive spouse of Muslim tradition,
but rather, she is treated as a being yet to be discovered. Cours sur la rive sauvage is an inquiry into
her role and position vis-à-vis her male counterpart.
To carry out this exploration Dib chose the realm of the
fantastic. Fawzia Mostefa-Kara in her penetrating study
of the novel (17) attempts to explain why. "Under its
envelope of the fantastic, Cours sur la rive sauvage is
an investigation, an inquiry into the destiny of man,
into his immortality, into the role of love that man
bears to woman, into the Beatrician woman who shows the
path to man. The fantastic seems to be the best route to
accede to a profound truth, to explore the invisible,
interior space, the other side of things, the dark second
half of man, 'the other side of the horizon,' to use an
expression of Marcel Proust" (18).

In fact, there is a further reason, intimately linked
with religious and cultural tradition, for revealing the
innermost self only through a veil. Dib himself explains: "Algerians raised in a Muslim milieu consider
introspection a little unhealthy. Of a man plunged in
reflections which seem profane the proverb says, 'It is
someone who leads the cows of Iblis to pasture'" (19),

that is, who invites the devil. Furthermore any discussion of the psychology of love is considered taboo in Muslim society. Dib felt that the novelist needed to overcome this sort of inhibition, but admitted that "psychoanalysis is unthinkable in Algeria for the moment" (20).

Cours sur la rive sauvage, which describes a young man's long voyage of initiation as he goes in pursuit of his beloved, is no simple love story but a complex drama clothed in myth, allegory, and symbolism and inviting multiple interpretations. The novel opens on the wedding day of a young couple, Radia and Iven Zohar. On the way to the ceremony, Iven realizes that he does not really know the woman who is his wife to be. At the wedding reception, Iven assumes a passive role, Radia an active one as before the assembled guests she advances and pierces Iven's breast five times with a needle of light. Iven bleeds and loses his strength. The celebration abruptly takes on the air of a funeral as Iven is borne like a corpse through the crowd. His seeming death, however, marks the beginning of a painful process of regeneration and rebirth. Iven's wedding is a rite of interior renewal. Iven pronounces the name "Hellé" and is catapulted into a shadowy universe, a world whose brutal chaos reflects the psychic transformation which he is to undergo.

We have observed that in Qui se souvient de la mer man's liberation (and by extension that of his homeland) is made possible by a return to woman as mother. She is a symbol of the ancestral heritage, and it is through her that man recovers his identity. But his salvation would remain incomplete if it did not also advance to a more mature dimension, in which woman as spouse is the instrument of his self-realization. In Cours sur la rive sauvage the hero can be reborn only after dying to self. His final goal is the discovery and appreciation of that other half of his own being. To explore and explain the paradoxical relationship of two beings who are at the same time equal, distinct, yet one together, Dib has recourse to Jungian philosophy, which teaches that every human being has within him a male and a female principle, called by Jung the Animus and the Anima respectively. These contrary aspects are in conflict and struggle to be in harmony. As Iven travels through the strange surroundings of an underworld that is his own subconscious, Radia dissolves, only to be replaced by Hellé, who looks

just like his beloved. This phenomenon is a manifesta-
tion of bi-polarity. Like light and darkness, day and
night, Radia/Hellé are the positive and negative aspects
of the same person (21). The woman whom Iven encounters
during his psychic excursion appears sometimes as a
benevolent guide, sometimes in the guise of a destructive
avenging fury who forces him to cross the circles of
hell. Radia/Hellé represent the ambivalent and opposing
feelings that exist within a person, attaction and repul-
sion. Iven's journey teaches him that he will not
realize the fullness of his own being until he comes to
accept his beloved wholly, as a living person whose being
manifests itself in new ways that are ever changing and
still unknown to him.

Iven's journey is long and assumes many forms. Classical analogies are easily discerned. Like Orpheus, Iven
must descend into hell in order to find his beloved.
Like Dante, whose path through the dark wood was illumi-
nated by Beatrice, Iven is guided through the labyrinth
by Radia/Hellé. Like Hercules, who was required to
perform amazing tasks to purify himself, Iven must pass a
series of tests in order to prove his willingness to
advance toward interior renewal. Like Osiris, the
Egyptian god who was killed and dismembered by his
brother, Iven is restored to wholeness thanks to the
healing powers of his wife. These myths are accompanied
by symbols (circle, diamond, golden tulip, quaternity,
voyage by boat, the other bank of the river, old wise
man), and tests of initiation (trap of the Vorasques,
statues, divisions of Radia, struggles with the Takas).
We recognize too the familiar struggle between the old
city and the new one. The former explodes and gives way
to the ville-nova, a new world that is undergoing perpetual transformation.

Iven's progress is slow and ambiguous. Through the
multiple trials he experiences, he comes to learn that
even after accepting his bride as his equal, she shall
always remain "a stranger who would constantly be in the
process of becoming . . ." (22). Love, like life, is in
flux, ever changing, ever challenging, ever exposing yet
another of its limitless facets. But though life allows
no rest, one can, like Iven, advance through it with
security if one has faith in love. Love entails painful
self-examination and death to the self, but from it flows
the reward of fully being.

This interpretation of Cours sur la rive sauvage is

plausible and flows logically from the idea set forth in
Dib's preceding novel. But, as we have noted, the work
is polyphonic, charged with veiled references that rever-
berate with signification. The reader is urged to be
open and not limit his judgment. This work is controversial both in content and in form, and has prompted a
variety of interpretations (23). Its very richness
invites further study.

Dib's literary merit, already clearly established, was
again signaled by this work of fiction. As the noted
French critic Pierre Henri Simon points out, Cours sur
la rive sauvage illustrates that Dib had exquisitely
mastered the tools of the adopted culture. The novel is
"a river taken far from its point of origin, and which
appears rich in particular from the tributaries of culture it has received. [Its author is] an African who has
conquered his right to the city in French belles lettres"
(24).

The probing of man's innermost self continued to occupy the writer, but again renewed and cast in a fresh
mold. From the fluid world of the fantastic of Cours
sur la rive sauvage, we move to the ruminations of
voices that re-create the anguish of wartime and postwar
Algeria.

In La Danse du roi (The dance of the king, 1968), a
man and a woman, both revolutionaries returning from the
maquis, recall the sacrifices they made and the hopes
they had nourished during the fighting. But their hopes
have not been fulfilled; instead, only ingratitude, petty
selfishness, absence, and death welcome their return.
The issue of the victorious revolution is deformed. For
Rodwan and Arfia (25), the principal characters, and for
those whom they represent, the present is empty and pur-
poseless. In a series of récits the past is relived.
Through Rodwan we hear the voice of guilt and the words
of his father which regret the peoples' failure to give
meaning to life. They have let it slip through their
fingers, and as a result were reduced to nothing.
Through Arfia we hear the anguished voices of her com-
panion maquisards, Slim, Bassel, Nemiche, and Babanang as
they sought to flee enemy attack. Rodwan and Arfia are
not the "flesh and blood" characters of Dib's first manner. They are vaguely circumscribed spaces where the
bitter past is brought to life as on a stage (26).

By means of a jeu scénique, an allegorical play
within the novel, the door of the future opens to reveal

a macabre scene. Man's inheritance is no more than a garbage heap over which hovers Azrail, the Angel of Death.
Rodwan, Arfia, and Babanang, at first spectators at this
nocturnal drama, become the main players. It is Rodwan's
own story that he sees enacted before a great rusty gate.
When the latter gives way to reveal piles of filth, Rodwan advances, falling on the garbage. He crowns himself
with a tin can before falling over dead. This is the
"royalty" that he has won after such a bitter struggle.
Death is the victor. In this defeat, however, lies perhaps the seed of new hope, the necessary sad conclusion,
the requisite for a fresh beginning divined by Slim:
"There is perhaps an Algeria to kill. To kill so that
another one, more clean, can come into the world" (27).

La Danse du roi reiterates Dib's concern over the
pernicious internal weaknesses of his country, but adds a
new dimension. The adoption of Western technology by the
now independent Algeria (a subject that will be central
to the two novels that follow). To embrace the West's
ideal of progress—is that not a new invasion, rape, and
dispossession of individual dignity and of the kingdom
that is the inheritance of all Algerians? Dib invites
his reader to weigh carefully present and future directions in the light of past history.

In 1980 Dib rewrote the whole of Arfia's experience
for the stage under the title Mille hourras pour une
gueuse (A thousand hurrahs for a tramp), totally
excluding that portion of the novel that deals with
Rodwan. The action closely parallels that of the novel,
but the language is more vulgar, and there is greater use
of ellipsis. The motley crew of characters, with their
tattered clothes, crude speech, and buffoonery, is reminiscent of Samuel Beckett's tramps in Waiting for
Godot. They are imbued with the same hopeless waiting.

THE THIRD MANNER: A DISCRETE REALISM. The inquiry
into Algeria's future is pursued at greater length in
Dieu en Barbarie (God in Barbary, 1970). To the extent
that it bears witness to key problems facing the newly
created nation, the novel is reminiscent of Dib's first
manner. But the resemblance is superficial. The discrete realism of Dieu en Barbarie is transfused with
implied meanings, extended metaphors, hallucinatory
visions, and whisperings of the subconscious. Once again
the familiar problems are addressed by the main protagonists: the crisis of identity, bâtardise, man's need
to come to terms with himself. The issue under debate

centers on the principles which should form the foundation of the new state. Two opposing courses of action
are proposed, one having its foundation in tradition,
imbued with the tenets of Islam, the other based on
Western ways. Tradition dictates one way of thought and
action, the imported non-Muslim culture expounds a different set of values. Each position is defended by a leading protagonist. The confident self-ordained social
worker Hakim Madjar favors a return to Islamic tradition.
Together with his French wife Marthe he initiates a
group called the mendiants de Dieu ("God's beggars"),
whose members tend to the material and spiritual needs of
the indigent fellahs. They have remained untainted by
the disease of materialistic greed and have, more than
any other segment of society, safeguarded their heritage.
At the opposite pole is Kamal Waëd (28), a government
official who would rebuild Algeria along Western lines.
He would eradicate the Muslim way of life with its inherent weaknesses, and discard the past in favor of the
adoption of foreign ways that would permit Algeria to
take her place alongside the other great world powers.
He is galled by the knowledge that an unknown benefactor
has paid for the education that enabled him to achieve
his high status in society. Unwittingly he has been the
recipient of la part de Dieu, an act of charity that is
one of the fundamental duties of the Muslim faith.

   A third character, the skeptic and cynic Dr. Berchig,
who in the end reveals himself as the secret patron, acts
as a mediator between Madjar and Waëd. A product of
both Oriental and Western thought, he judiciously proposes a middle way.

   In his fiction Dib shatters the fallacy that Eastern
civilizations are barbarians in need of the brilliant
thought of the West. Through Madjar he observes that
"Westerners are themselves torn to shreds and devoured by
their own creation" (29). The West, for all its technology, cannot satisfy man's spiritual longing. In this
light the multiple meanings of the book's title, God in
Barbary, suggest themselves. The materialistic techno-
crats who have renounced their soul in favor of worldly
gain have brought about a modern-day Barbary on their own
continents. But the false god they have erected does not
respond to the individual's deepest needs; an inherent
craving for the true God persists among many and is destined to crack the veneer of self-righteousness.

   The confrontation between Kamal Waëd and Hakim Madjar

reaches a climax in <u>Le Maître de chasse</u> (The master of
the hunt, 1973). Each man proclaims that his way leads
to Truth, but in Waëd's view, when a rival truth imper-
ils his plan for the advancement of civilization and
threatens to plunge the country into its former backward-
ness, that menace must be eliminated. There is no room
for two Truths. Waëd, motivated by jealousy, sends an
armed force against the <u>mendiants de Dieu</u>. Deliberately or accidentally, the fact is never determined, the
hunted Madjar is shot and killed. Like Pilate, Waëd
washes his hands of all blame, attributing the death to
Madjar's foolish notions of truth. Far from eliminating
his influence, however, the murder serves to heighten the
importance of Madjar's message. The fellahs revere
Madjar as a martyr and saint, and vow to preserve and
perpetuate his memory and doctrine. Waëd realizes the
consequences of what has resulted. Madjar's death opens
"a crack, a way," through which the power of the simple
folk may emerge. Madjar is more powerful in death than
in life. With this sacrifice the peasant is restored to
his former dignity as man the king (<u>l'homme-roi</u>).
Death purifies and elevates, bringing resurrection in its
wake. The peasant no longer feels that he lives on the
margin of society but becomes conscious of the vivifying
force that is his. He is the <u>vraie pâte humaine</u>
("true human stuff"), clay destined for a noble Creation.
Together with his fellowmen he is part of an underground
river that will flow through the desert causing new life
to spring up.

With <u>Le Maître de chasse</u> Dib gives full vent to his
mystic vision. He draws on New Testament scriptures,
specifically the passion, death, and resurrection of
Christ, with which he knew his French reading public
would be familiar. The novel develops into a spiritual
prose poem celebrating Life, Truth, Fellowship, and Human
Dignity. It invites man to rise above self-limiting perceptions and to believe in his worth as, in unison with
others, he works to restore wholeness to a suffering
universe. In <u>Le Maître de chasse</u> the ordinary and the
concrete dissolve in an inebriating ecstasy.

While <u>Le Maître de chasse</u> (30) reverently invites
the reader to bathe his weary spirit in hope and faith,
Dib's next novel, <u>Habel</u> (1977), plunges him into the
abyss of loneliness and despair: "Cain today would not
kill his brother. He would push him on the road of emigration" (31). Removed from the sanctifying power of <u>la</u>

Terre/Mère Algeria, the dispossessed hero is crushed by
a foreign land that has no regard for him. Banishment
and its consequences. This is the new framework in which
Dib couches man's metaphysical quest for the meaning of
existence, his craving for the Absolute.

Habel's older brother has driven him out of his homeland for fear that his own power might be diminished.
Dib's fiction translates an interior sociopolitical situation in his homeland in which the established government
refused to share responsibilities or credit with the
bright upcoming youth. But the novel has a broader
message to convey.

The inability to communicate and the failure to establish an authentic rapport with an interlocutor, that is
the major theme around which the action of Habel centers. The novel offers four major examples of such breakdown by pitting the main protagonist against four figures
in his life: his older brother, two prostitutes, Sabine
and Lily, and the androgynous Dame de la Merci, alias
le Vieux. Each of these flawed relationships is symbolic, beginning initially with spiritual fratricide and
leading to depersonalization, viewed here under three
guises as a prostitution of the self.

As is frequently the case, Dib plays on several registers in this intricately worked novel. To the reader is
left the difficult task of deciphering all possible implications. Furthermore, the events in the hero's life are
not related chronologically but are unfolded as jumbled
medleys. The past exists as a living present in the
hero's mind, right alongside the present he is experi-
encing.

Reorganized sequentially, Habel's downfall begins with
his exile. In his imagination he carries on a false
dialogue with his brother which illustrates that the
process of expatriation is indirectly a sentence of
condemnation to death. (In the name Habel we recognize
the association with the biblical Abel who was annihi-
lated at his brother's hands.) In Paris the nineteen-
year-old Habel wanders the streets, endeavoring to escape
his very essence.

Three encounters mark Habel's delirious ramblings.
First there is the liaison with Sabine. Through repeated
acts of physical possession Habel satisfies his carnal
appetite. These flights from the self, however, bring
only brief release from the consciousness of a painful
existence. On the spiritual plane, Habel finds himself

suffocated by this woman whose pat answers to all of
life's problems seem to emprison his aspirations for freedom. Sabine symbolizes conformity that asphyxiates.
Habel leaves her to return to another partner, Lily, whom
he knew before Sabine.

Lily is the exact opposite of Sabine, quiet, ephemeral,
mysterious, a tempting fantasy that invites but evades.
She represents the inaccessible intangible element of
man's longing. As the outcast child of divorced parents,
she too lives exiled. Unable to cope with her circumstances, Lily is finally committed to an asylum.

An ambiguous third character, "whom we don't know if
it is a man or a woman" (32), remains with Habel the
length of the novel. She/he is la Dame de la Merci,
alias le Vieux ("the Old Man"). Significantly, he is a
writer. The dual nature of this transvestite/prostitute/-
pederast brings to the forefront two main issues: double
culture and the function of the writer. The former is a
judgment upon the failure of cultural integration; the
latter is an attempt to destroy the myth of the writer as
a privileged seer and guardian of eternal Truth. Habel
prostitutes himself to the Old Man, who each day promises
to elucidate the mysteries of existence, but the Word
which Habel's soul craves is not to be heard. The writer
is a travesty and a fraud. Habel steals his manuscript
only to discover that it contains no message. Annette
Bonn-Gualino sees this episode as a stern judgment.
"Writing is only a prostitution of language. . . . The
parody of marriage between Habel and the old writer symbolizes in a terrible way the impossible alliance of two
prostituted cultures, which no longer have any authenticity" (33).

The Old Man commits suicide. Realizing that he has
reached an impasse, Habel decides to stop waiting for
something to happen to him and determines to follow his
brother's advice: "fashion your existence into something
which is like you" (34). Habel, whose name in Arabic
means "crazy," volunteers to work in the asylum in which
the insane Lily is interned. There he will spend his
days keeping vigil over her and with her. Both exiles,
it is in this marginal existence that they find a retreat
where they can hide their incommunicable desolation.
Only in madness, in Lily, who incarnates madness, does
Habel find "a person to justify my life, to excuse it; a
person to accept it and make me accept it. A person to
make of it a thing worth something" (35).

The Stories

Aside from his major prose works, Dib has authored
numerous short stories. Among the more accessible are
those printed in book form, Au Café (At the café,
1955), and Le Talisman (1966). The stories of the
former belong to the author's early realistic vein (except for "L'Héritier enchanté"). Dib's penchant to
probe the secret self and to delve beneath the apparent
are superbly illustrated in two stories of the second
collection, "La Dalle écrite" (The engraved stone) and
"Le Talisman." They are a direct commentary on the task
of deciphering the written code that is the author's sole
tool. They attempt to explain metaphorically the essence
of the writer's dilemma: the communication of meaning
through the sign of the written word. At the same time,
in a broader sense they relate man's inability to "de-
code" the events of his life in order to arrive at an
authentic meaning. The printed word, which is the
writer's vehicle, is a collection of signs that has the
effect of reducing all experiences to a one-dimensional
flat surface, that of the printed page (or the surface of
the stone). Only the mind of the reader is capable of
investing these signs with dynamism. The interpretation
of the signs depends on the reader, for whom they are
destined. But the message they convey will be interpreted differently by each who receives it, because each
recipient is a composite of unique experiences. The
vision of the hero of "Le Talisman" surpasses that of his
counterpart in the first story, however, as he realizes
that apart from the written word, he himself is a "sign
traced on limitless matter . . ." (36).

The short stories of Mohammed Dib are usually passed
over by commentators of his works. That is unfortunate,
for they are truly gems whose very limited length dis-
plays all the more sharply the author's literary talent
and philosophy of life.

Even the so-called children's stories—Baba Fekrane
(1959) and L'Histoire du chat qui boude (The story of
the pouting cat, 1974)—challenge the reader to penetrate
their literal level. Written in the vein of North African oral folklore, their function is didactic. They
follow the pattern of progression through cumulative
addition. Each concludes with the following injunction:
"We walked along the road and found a bag of pearls: the
big ones for me, the little ones for you," which is to

say, a small measure of understanding for him who grasps
only the literal sense of the anecdote, wisdom for him
who penetrates the intertextual level of meaning. Here,
as in his larger works, Dib succeeds in playing on two
registers.

The Poetry

While it is above all for his novels that Dib is known
and acclaimed, he himself maintains that he is primarily
a poet: "I am essentially a poet, and it is from poetry
that I came to the novel, not the reverse" (37). Critics
have been quick to note that "the almost continual presence of a poetic universe underlies, clarifies, or amplifies the fictional universe" (38). Songs and poems
punctuate the early novels. These same verses are
expanded and incorporated into Dib's first collection of
poetry, Ombre gardienne (Guardian shadow, 1960).
Ombre gardienne centers on two major themes: nostal-
gic recollections of the poet's homeland and exile. The
poems that focus on Mère/Algérie are comprised mainly
of short mystical lyrics. They evince the most creative
talent of the poet. Those that are set in France are
comprised for the most part of narrative sonnets and
tercets, and are in a more traditional vein that reveal
the writer's skill more than his artistic genius.
The images that the poet summons forth emerge at the
sensory level, but at the same time bear a profound
spiritual meaning that invites meditation. Against the
bitter-sweet landscapes of his homeland one figure stands
above all, woman, subject of predilection, obsession, and
major symbol of Dib's ars poetica. She is the principal reference point of his universe. Where she is not
seen, the very surroundings and forces of nature suggest
her presence. Contemplating the steppe, the poet notes
that "Everything there palpitates a veil / --Or is it a
woman walking?" (39). Algeria is a woman, a "fraternal
mother," a "fraternal spouse that succors her suffering
children. Woman's beneficient presence permeates everywhere, dissolving into and out of the surroundings.
Dib's penchant for envisaging objects and phenomena as
being in flux, as dissolving from one form of manifesta-
tion and evolving into another, is a characteristic that
intensifies in the later collections of poems.
Whereas the poems consecrated to la Mère/Algérie

invite the reader to let his spirit soar, even when burdened with sadness, those that situate the poet in Europe
constrict and emprison. They spell out graphically
rather than elicit a free play of the imagination. It is
as if the polluted air and the very stones of the cities
and monuments bear down to stifle the poet's evocative
powers, crushing his former élan. His sense of separation is acute: "Now where will you look for asylum? / In
the cinema, in the bar that you see / Full of neon, of
blurred drinkers, of voices?" (40). The poet cries out
in despair but is finally rescued by a guardian angel who
opens a way for him. In his concluding poem in this
collection, "Sur la mort de Nezval," Dib reflects that
"dream and life entangled without harm / Lead man forward
toward goodness" (41). Art and reality intermingle, the
poet implies, conscious of his own role, to lead the poet
to a more profound perception of the world and his place
in it.
    In the poems as in the prose works, life is envisaged
as a spiritual journey in which man must freely cooper-
ate. The underlying elements that convey this theme may
be identified as follows: paradox and contradiction,
multiple levels of meaning, the idea of flux, becoming,
and metamorphosis, and distortion of time, space, and
common relationships. These principles operate across
the whole range of Dib's poetry. Their effect is to defy
the mind's craving to reduce reality to static form and
to summon an ongoing colloquy with the text, indeed with
life itself.
    With his next volume of poems, Formulaires (1970),
Dib embarks on yet another experiment. The collection is
composed of poems in verse and brief anecdotal prose narratives reminiscent of the folktales that are part of
North African oral tradition. Direct references to the
Algerian homeland and the struggle for independence are
noticeably absent, as are punctuation and uppercase letters, while inverted syntax and fragmented phrases are
standard. A work of great density, opaque, disquieting,
it is only thanks to Dib's preceding prose works that the
reader is at all able to penetrate the obscure invention
of the poet's mind and to reconstruct the fragments scattered over the one hundred pages of text. In Formulaires everything conspires to challenge the reader's
powers of comprehension. While the familiar symbols are
ever-present, Dib invests them with multifarious signification in his quest to lend fresh expression to reality as

he apprehends it. His vision and his voice invite us to
marvel at the ordinary while warning us against compla-
cency. Things, concepts, and emotions known universally
are rearranged in a new order that forces the mind from
its lethargy, daring it to contemplate reality in an
unfamiliar form. The poems' titles provide a clue to
Dib's intent: "épeler l'envers" ("spell the inside
out"), "sens inverse" ("opposite meaning"), "nouveau né
sans cesse" ("new-born without ceasing"), "Nous n'enten-
dons pas" ("we don't comprehend").

Parallel to the change of woman's status in his works
of fiction, Dib assigns new significance to her in his
poems. She is no longer the mère or épouse frater-
nelle but an equal partner in the journey of life, one
who will assist man in realizing his full potential as a
human being. In thinly veiled metaphors, Formulaires
sings the agony and the ecstasy of carnal union, passionately and reverently preserving the mystery and sacred
aura that are rightly due it. The poet pays homage to
woman's powers. The act of love is extolled as an echo
of the unity of the cosmos. In it the poet finds renewal. Implied here is not only the invigoration of the
spirit but the renewal of the writer's craft.

Written in a similar vein, Omneros, a new collection
of verses, "poems of love and more literally of the act
of love" (42), appeared in 1975. "The most lucid side of
life, the most perceptible, is certainly the most
obscure. It is no other than the shadow borne by Eros;
it is, and us in it, none other than the plan of Eros
itself in those instants when it hardly seems so" (43),
proposes Dib. The book's title proffers a clue: omni—
all; eros—pleasure-directed life instincts, love
oriented toward self-realization. Love is all, has all
to offer, penetrates all, emanates from all. Through
eros man accedes to brief privileged moments of illumination, all of which are but echoes of the primordial act
of love, creation itself (44). Eros permits finite man
to transcend the common and the ordinary, to tap the
inexhaustible spring from which flows ever fresh inspira-
tions. These the poet would capture, however imperfect-
ly, in his own act of creation, through the evocative
power of the word.

Omneros, notes Charles Bonn, is an orphic voyage of
discovery, comparable to the itinerary of Cours sur la
rive sauvage. It is an act of faith that liberates and
enriches him who has ears to hear. Abstract, obscure,

recondite, the reading of <u>Omneros</u> involves "a perpetual
game of decoding, of transparency and opacity, of shadow
and light, of snow and flame, of water and fire . . ."
(45).
    Dib finds erotic love an inexhaustible source of
poetic inspiration. The act of possession is a "door
opened on an abyss." It is at once paradox and contradiction because just when man seems to have gained his end,
that end escapes him. The subject obsesses the poet
because of the infinite paths of discovery that it opens
to him; when all is said, nothing is yet said. And so
Dib once again takes up the subject in <u>Feu beau beau</u>
(Fire beautiful fire, 1979), the most explicitly sensuous
collection of poems to date. Composed of unpunctuated
prose paragraphs and unrhymed brief sketches, these seemingly spontaneous inventions are litanies of praise to
woman. In their entirety, they are an extended metaphor
linking the intimate knowledge of woman with the mystery
of the cosmos and literary creation itself. Woman invites the poet to an endless exploration. Through her he
tries to "fill up the void and its approaches" (46).
Woman is a link with infinity and eternity. For this
reason Dib finds it fitting that homage be paid her.

Conclusion: Life as Eternal Quest

    In terms of content, form, and manner of expression,
Mohammed Dib clearly ranks among the most fertile of the
North African writers who use the French language. His
oeuvre represents three decades of growth, during which
time he has carved out new paths while steadfastly pursuing the elucidation of eternal truths. Dib's works
have universal appeal because they have as their subject
matters fundamental to all human beings: human dignity,
freedom and responsibility, love, and relationships
between individuals and societies.
    Many of Dib's writings describe Algeria in her darkest
hours, yet underlying the physical pain and suffering and
the metaphysical anguish, there remains a fundamentally
optimistic outlook on life and the future of the human
person in his universe. From the ashes of destruction
brought by colonialism, revolution, and a decaying civilization arises an invitation to rise up, to shed sterile
passivity and wounded pride, and to fully participate in
being, to be in harmony with all of creation. Dib be-

lieves in man and credits him with the ability to bring light to a world invaded by shadow. This is not seen as an easy task; rather it is envisaged as a challenging one that fosters self-growth at the same time that it leads to a strengthening of bonds between human beings. Life, for Dib, is a continual quest, a long forward march, punctuated by trials but also marked by illumination, greater understanding of self and others, the uncovering of hidden beauty and untapped spiritual energies. Even in his early "realist" period, it is the obscure spiritual longings of Dib's figures that resurge, seeking interior liberation, rebirth, and finally resurrection. Life continually offers itself anew, is the message; it is always to be discovered, fresh and inviting. Man is intended to be King of his Kingdom, to assume responsibility, and to rule over it wisely. This is a daily endeavor by which finally he will triumph, even over Death, which, far from being an annihilation, leads man back to the Source of his being.

Chapter Four
Kateb Yacine

Eternal Return

Kateb Yacine (1) can be counted as perhaps the most controversial of the French-language Maghrebian authors. His works, obscure, even hermetic, are alternately praised for their depth and lyricism, or spurned for their incomprehensibility or their lack of relevance. Some recognize the author as a genius who is ahead of his time. The French critic Maurice Nadeau applauds his singularity and finds in him a talent that surpasses that of modern giants like Faulkner and Joyce (2). Claude Roy calls him "an Algerian Rimbaud" (3). But others find his work confusing and difficult to approach. The young in particular, who look forward to the future, find him passé, cut off from the present-day issues that face Algeria. Still others see in him an iconoclast who attacks religious and civil authority. One thing remains undisputed: the originality of this writer's works. In the early fifties, while other novelists of the Maghreb persisted in the realist folkloric-ethnographic vein, Kateb broke away from this trend, producing a remarkable work of fiction that was avant-garde in form as well as in content. Since that time the amount of interest generated by this author's creation has grown. Articles and studies in French, English, and Eastern European languages, by Africans, Europeans, and Americans, abound.

Kateb has published only four major works: two novels, a collection of shorter plays, and one longer work for the stage. A number of other plays in colloquial Arabic remain unpublished. Yet, like Memmi, Kateb himself has clearly stated that he is the author of a single book: "I believe indeed that I am the man of a sole book. In the beginning it was a poem that transformed itself into the novels and plays, but it is always the same work that I will certainly leave after me in the same way that I began it, that is to say, both as a ruin and as a starting point. Exactly like Algeria that is still a ruin and a starting point. You put finishing touches on a book the same way that you do with an object. You feel deep within yourself that the work is not finished. Likewise, Algeria has not finished being born" (4). As with Memmi, Kateb's work is forever in gestation.

Knowledge of the major events in Kateb's life is important for an understanding of his work. As he puts it: "the man is in the child" (5). A review of the events, relationships, and influences that molded him in his youth reveals to what extent this is true.

Biographical Notes

Kateb Yacine was born on 6 August 1929 in Constantine, though his birth is recorded officially at Condé Semendou (today Zirout Youcef), on 26 August. He comes from a well-educated family, some of whose members took an active role in government and the theater (6). It was a close-knit group of relations, with a very keen sense of its common origin. Consanguineous marriages were a tradition, and from an early age Kateb was aware of the fraternal link that bound one generation to another, leading as far back as the mythic ancestor Keblout. These strong family ties engendered a marked sense of the cohesiveness and the tribal rootedness of Kabylian society. But the home situation was not an altogether peaceful one. Father and mother quarreled; at one point he repudiated her, then took her back. Kateb's father, who was a lawyer, was versed in French letters as well as in the Koranic scriptures and Muslim law. His mother, who knew only Arabic, was gifted and composed poetry in addition to writing plays. "She was a theater unto herself" (7), Kateb is fond of recalling. Mother and son enjoyed a warm relationship, and the child took delight in sharing the leggends, tales, and word games that sparked his imagination. The mother nourished the impressionable youngster with superstitions inherited from her ancestors, including reports of what she had seen at the sacred "celebration of the vultures" at Constantine, a festival attended by women who hoped to rid themselves of evil spirits (8). This bit of folklore was later to become a central motif in the works of the mature writer. As an adult, Kateb looked back upon these early years as a period of tranquillity and harmony. In his writings he returns to it as to a haven, an all-protective, nourishing womb.

The father's work required that he travel frequently.
He put his son in a Koranic school at Sedrata, where he
memorized the holy texts without really understanding
their meaning. Had he continued his Koranic studies, the
next step would have been for him to attend the medersa,
the Muslim school of higher education. Unexpectedly,
however, in the child's ninth year, his father decided to
transfer him to a French school, "into the lion's mouth"
(9), as he puts it, undoubtedly motivated by the conviction that he would thus be in a superior position in the
French administered colony: "I don't want you to be like
me, straddling two chairs. . . . French language dominates. You must dominate it, and leave behind what we
inculcated in you during your earliest childhood; once
you have become master of that language, you can then
return to us without danger to your point of departure"
(10). Kateb was an avid student of the French language
and culture, but the new formation estranged him from his
mother, who could not share with him the opening of new
linguistic and cultural horizons. As an adult Kateb
noted with bitterness the traumatic effect of the gallici-
zation process. It was a wedge that gradually pushed
mother and son apart: "Thus did I lose at the same time
both my mother and her language, the only inalienable
treasures—nevertheless, gone" (11). This separation
created a cultural, moral, and psychological conflict
within the youth, as it did with many others of his generation. The double rupture and double exile, interiorized
at this stage of his life, had a profound influence that
would manifest itself later.

When his father was transferred to Lafayette (Bougaa),
Kateb was placed in the French lycée at Sétif. There
he mixed with other students, Jews, Christians, and
Arabs, and was exposed to adult prejudices. On 8 May
1945, the day of the uprising which set off the Algerian
nationalist revolution, the adolescent was among the
excited crowds. In the midst of the confusion during
which hundreds were massacred, he was arrested and thrown
into prison. This was a traumatic experience for a
sixteen-year-old boy, as he himself has admitted; it was
also a period of illumination. It was during his three
months in prison that he discovered two of the most important elements of his life: poetry and revolution. He
became cognizant of the suffering of others and discovered the tragedy of existence as he and others were
subject to it. Cut off from the reassuring milieu of

family and friends, Kateb found in poetry the means to
express his distress. He had been nourished by the
poetry of his mother, by traditional folktales and myths,
by the legends (12) of national heroes such as Abdel
Kader, the nineteenth-century freedom fighter, and by the
great Arab past. He had read the classics of French
literature too, and was influenced by Musset, Baudelaire,
and Rimbaud. But he also discovered Aeschylus and
Sophocles, and would eventually go on to read Marxist
authors, and later Joyce and Faulkner.

Once out of prison, Kateb was to suffer a series of
unfortunate experiences that would quickly catapult him
into an entirely new manner of existence. Kateb's impri-
sonment had a devastating effect on his mother. From an
early age she had suffered from nervous disorders. Now
she thought that her son had been assassinated at Sétif,
and as a result lost her reason and had to be confined to
the psychiatric hospital in Blida. The image of the
femme sauvage ("wild woman") would later find itself
transposed into fiction, alongside that of the protective
and nourishing mother. Kateb did not return to school;
he was expelled as an undesirable. While claiming to no
longer be interested in attending classes, he experienced
this exclusion as a further cause of alienation, and it
marked a turning point in his life. He decided to
travel. His goal was to see the world, but first he
wanted to get to know his own country better. He also
wanted to distract himself from the heartache of losing
the great love of his life, an older cousin, Nedjma, who
was married to another man. He traveled first to nearby
Bône, where he found a French editor on the verge of
bankruptcy who printed his first collection of poetry,
Soliloques (Soliloquies), in 1946. Neither the publisher nor the young poet was able to sell the 400 volumes.
(Not only was the book unsuccessful, it has also completely disappeared. Not even the author kept a copy of it.)
Disappointed, Kateb returned to Constantine with his
unsold books. There he met a certain Si Mohammed Tahar
Ben Lounissi, who became his mentor. (He is the model
for the fictional Si Mokhtar.) Lounissi assumed the task
of selling all 400 copies. At this time Kateb was put in
contact with Gabriel Audisio in Paris, who encouraged him
and advised him on literary matters.

Kateb was caught up in the Algerian independence movement. He became an ardent nationalist militant. In May
1947, at the age of seventeen, he delivered a speech in

Paris to a group of scholars on "Abdel Kader and Algerian
Independence." In 1948 he joined the staff of the Algerian Communist daily, Alger Républicain, for which
Mohammed Dib was also working at the time, as a foreign
correspondent. In this capacity he traveled as far as
Central Asia. In 1948 his poem "Nedjma ou le poème ou
le couteau" (Nedjma or the poem or the knife), was
printed in Mercure de France (13). Other poems appeared in Forge, Soleil, Simoun, and Terrasses
(14).

In 1950 Kateb's father died. Kateb left the newspaper, and in 1951 traveled to France where he tried
various occupations, all in the line of manual labor.
(A number of these odd jobs are assumed by various characters in the novels and plays.) None of these suited
him, however. Already the idea for a novel was ger-
minating, excerpts from which had previously appeared
in periodicals. Kateb began to write furiously, filling page after page. Ideas flowed spontaneously from
him. He brought his manuscript to Jean Cayrol at the
Paris publishing firm of Seuil. The novel, Nedjma,
was refused by the editors as being diffuse and inco-
herent. Kateb reworked it. After much alteration, a
good deal of cutting, and a somewhat arbitrary division
into sections and chapters, a staff editor, who prefaced
the text with a highly debatable preface (15), managed to
get the manuscript accepted. Before its eventual
publication in 1956, Kateb became a nomadic wanderer,
visiting Tunisia, Italy, Germany, Belgium, and Russia.
German romanticism appealed to him, as did the exotic
element of the Slavic countries and the vigor of the
Mediterraneans. Kateb met Bertolt Brecht, who was then
at the height of his fame. He also made the acquaintance
of Jean Marie Serreau, who was interested in Third World
theater, particularly in developing a "new theater" that
would incorporate poetry, politics, and contemporary
history. Kateb began writing for the theater. From his
collaboration with Serreau came Le Cadavre encerclé
(The encircled corpse), staged clandestinely by a student
troupe in Paris in the summer of 1958, and then in
Brussels later that year. This was followed by Les
Ancêtres redoublent de férocité (The ancestors
increase in viciousness), which was not to be produced
until nine years later. In 1959 Seuil published Le
Cercle des représailles, a volume comprised of four
works: Le Cadavre encerclé, a tragedy, La Poudre

d'intelligence (Intelligence powder), a farce, Les
Ancêtres redoublent de féroicité" a tragedy, and "Le
Vautour" (The vulture), a dramatic poem. In 1963 an
augmented form of Le Cadavre encerclé was presented in
Paris, under the title "La Femme sauvage" (The wild
woman). That summer Kateb was awarded the Jean Amrouche
prize conferred by the Congress for Mediterranean Culture. In 1966 Seuil published Le Polygone étoilé
(The starred polygon), a novel composed of an amalgama-
tion of previously unpublished materials, including pages
cut from the original Nedjma and selections that had
appeared in periodicals between 1961 and 1965. This
volume, which could be called Nedjma II, amplifies the
story related in the original.

In 1967 the National Theater of Paris staged Les
Ancêtres redoublent de férocité for its inaugural
performance, and in 1967 the Theater of the Epée-de-Bois
in Paris presented La Poudre d'intelligence. The first
play was translated into literary Arabic and given in
Tunis in 1967 and in Algeria the following year. Kateb
believes that this a deliberate attempt to discredit him
and label him as a writer who catered to a French audience: the people, who speak an Arab dialect, could not
understand the drama.

Meanwhile Kateb continued his peregrinations, going
all the way to Hanoi in 1967. There he found the inspiration for his next play, L'Homme aux sandales de
caoutchouc (The man in rubber sandals), published by
Seuil in 1979, which treats of Ho Chi Minh and the
Vietnamese struggle.

Kateb was aware of the ambiguous position of an Algerian writing in the language of the enemy. He wanted to
write for his own people, and therefore turned to writing
plays in his native colloquial Arabic. In 1971 he created "Mohammed, prends ta valise" (Mohammed, take your
suitcase), in which the central figure, symbol of the
collective whole, serves to illustrate the exploitation
of emigrant workers. In 1974 he wrote "La Guerre de
2000" (The war of 2000), a fresco in thirty-one episodes
that reiterates the same theme over a broader time span.
Deeply concerned for the Arab cause in the Middle East,
in 1977 Kateb produced "La Palestine trahie" (Palestine
betrayed), followed by "Le Roi de l'Ouest" (The king of
the West) in the same year. None of the plays written in
Arabic dialect has been published (16).

Kateb makes his permanent home in France but journeys

to the Maghreb to oversee the production of his plays in
colloquial Arabic.

Kateb calls his work "an autobiography in the plural,"
since in it are recorded his personal experiences and
those of his friends, the crises of his life and of his
country. These have evolved into easily recognized
themes that resound across all of Kateb's oeuvre. Like
other writers of his time, Kateb sought to trace his
roots, to find consolation and stability in a glorious
past, to be reconciled with himself. He felt that his
father and others of his generation who should have
served as guides for the young had, by their association
with France, transgressed their ancestors, leaving the
youth with no valid role models. What was necessary,
therefore, was to revive the past, mythologize it, celebrate it, and make it a sacred and vital part of history.
This Kateb does in a distinct manner, commingling in a
symbiotic relationship elements of fiction, history, and
myth.

For a variety of reasons, it is difficult to analyze
the works of Kateb Yacine. They are rich in symbolism
and are marked by an intentional blending of poetry, theater, and the novel; their structure is complex, at times
seemingly chaotic. Finally, multiple planes of understanding are inherent in each work and chronological
sense of time is absent. "Poetic explosion is at the center of everything" (17), declares the author. From this
premise flow great freedom of expression and the destruction of traditional barriers. Thus Nedjma and Le Polygone étoilé are not novels in the generally accepted
sense, and the plays are of the antitheater variety. The
author's deliberate assault on literary form, a unique
departure in the 1950s, expresses his will to escape
emprisonment and to achieve liberation on both the level
of creative writing and on the sociopolitical plane.

Our approach will necessarily be brief, beginning with
a rapid summary of the works, followed by a review of the
major components that together constitute a poetic whole.
We concentrate our attention on Nedjma (1956), Kateb's
signature piece, because it is a self-contained work in
which may be found the keys to all the others (18).

The Prose Fiction

In Nedjma, as in Le Polygone étoilé, the story

is narrated by the protagonists themselves, but not in
linear fashion. A number of significant events, actual,
remembered, or imagined, unfold in various time frames.
Present situations are interspersed with past history,
legends, and myth (19). The entire narration is polarized around Nedjma (the word means "star" in Arabic), the
central figure of a structure that can be described as a
solar system or a stellar universe. All the other characters are satellites in more or less close proximity to
the attracting sun that keeps them in her orbit.

The novel opens in Algeria in the spring of 1947, and
introduces Mourad, his brother Lakhdar, and their cousins
Rachid and Mustapha. They are employed as laborers for a
Monsieur Ernest, a French colonialist. During the course
of the narration we learn that all of them have at one
time or another been in prison, Mustapha and Lakhdar for
their presence at the 8 May insurrection, Rachid for
evading military service, and Mourad for striking his
colonial employer. These four have one overpowering
obsession: their love for Nedjma, their cousin, a character surrounded with an aura of mystery. One third of the
way into the 256-page novel, Rachid, enfevered with
malaria and in a fit of delirium, relates to Mourad the
details of Nedjma's conception, thereby establishing a
correlation between Nedjma and the forgotten ancestral
past.

Three cousins of the same blood-related Keblout (20)
tribe (Sidi Ahmed, Sid Mokhtar, and Rachid's father), and
a fourth protagonist, the Puritan, abduct a French Jew-
ess. The latter thus defiles the pure blood of the tribe
and instigates rivalry in the heretofore cohesive group.
Si Mokhtar takes as a mistress the Puritan's wife and
from their relationship is born Kamel, allegedly the
legitimate son of the Puritan. Si Mokhtar steals the
Frenchwoman from the Puritan and, together with Rachid's
father, carries her off to a cave (21). The next day
Rachid's father is found dead, shot in the back with his
own rifle. The Frenchwoman gives birth to Nedjma, who in
turn will attract the younger circle of cousins, Mourad
and Lakhdar, the sons of Sidi Ahmed, Rachid, and
Mustapha, the son of a certain Master Gahib. Each cousin
could in fact be Nedjma's brother since their father
slept with the Frenchwoman. When she comes of age,
Nedjma is married to her alleged cousin Kamel, an acceptable practice in Muslim tradition. But in fact Kamel is
Nedjma's brother. Nedjma is doubly alluring, as the
issue of the dispersed and cherished tribe and as the

daughter of the seductive foreigner. Rachid, Mourad, and
Lakhdar consummate incestuous relations with their sister-
cousin. Rachid, who had never learned the name of his
father's murderer, develops ties of friendship with Si
Mokhtar, a man fifty years his senior who acts as his
mentor. Finally the two of them carry Nedjma away to the
site of the tribal ruins at Nadhor and seduce her. Here
follows the famous scene of the ritual bath (22). Nedjma
and Rachid go off to the maquis, leaving Si Mokhtar
asleep in a hut. In a symbolic act of purification, the
naked Nedjma frolics in a copper cauldron, while Rachid,
looking on from behind a fig tree, indulges his passion.
He is disturbed, however, by the discovery that a Negro,
feigning sleep under another fig tree, is spying on the
woman. Worried, Rachid goes to rejoin Si Mokhtar. The
latter has suffered a fatal wound, purportedly inflicted
by the Negro, guardian of Nadhor and protector of the
tribal virgins, who took Si Mokhtar for the amoral spouse
of Nedjma. The Negro removes Nedjma to the sacred confines of the virgins. The scene shifts once again. The
young cousins continue to be haunted by the memory of the
unattainable sister-cousin. The novel concludes in the
same setting in which it began, the work yard of M.
Ernest. Each young man decides to leave his job and go
his own way.

The novel's open-ended conclusion is deliberate:
"The most authentic meaning of Nedjma is to be itself
incomplete, unfinished, uncertain" (23). In this way it
translates the suspense that hung over Algeria during the
1950s.

The intrigue may easily be transposed to a political
plane. The young heroes are entrapped in the prism of
colonialism. Nedjma represents the mythic Algeria, raped
and sullied by succeeding generations of conquerors, whom
they nevertheless dream of as a virgin, "vierge après
chaque viol" ("virgin after each rape") (24). At the
same time, she is the daughter of the foreigner, and as
such possesses the prestige of the superior conquering
force. By her dual nature this sister-cousin repels and
attracts. Jean Déjeux explains the dilemma of the young
men caught in an infernal circle: "The four want at one
and the same time the sister and the foreigner, the daughter of the tribe and the daughter of the 'others,' to be
in the tribe and to be deserters, to be in the circle and
to get out of it" (25).

Kateb's insistence on the tribal origins of the Algeri-

an nation is of the utmost importance (26). At a time
when the revolutionaries were calling for nationhood,
though still uncertain of the foundation on which it was
to be built, Kateb was reminding his people of their genesis, celebrating "the memory of the deceased tribe" (27).
The true reality of Algeria lay in her remote and all
but forgotten past. There was to be found a state of
(hypothetical) primitive purity, free of the centuries-
old accumulation of parasites that threatened to sap its
vitality. In that lost paradise could be identified a
distinct spirit: love of the land, of liberty, and of
independence. It is this that Kateb ardently seeks to
evoke for the present generation: "The history of our
tribe is written nowhere, but not a single thread of it
has been broken for whoever seeks out its origins" (28).
While Kateb inveighs against the French for having
attempted to wipe out the remnants of Algeria's past and
replace it with their Western model, he concludes that
they mark another phase in the country's painful evolution: "The conquest was a necessary evil, a painful
grafting that brought a promise of progress to the nation
split by the ax. Like the Turks, the Romans, and the
Arabs, the French could not help but put down roots,
hostages of the country whose favors they fought for"
(29). The present generation needs to see clearly where
it stands, declares Kateb: "we wanted, before conjuring
up the future, to know all the surviving remnants of the
tribe, to verify our origins in order to establish an
account of failure, or to attempt a reconciliation" (30).
Through the device of the cousins' obsession for the
enigmatic Nedjma, Kateb untangles the mystery of Algeria's clouded origins. He casts a glance backward in
order to link the past with the present at a time when
Algerians were ready to discard all that they had been.
Rachid, alone in his prison cell, recalls Si Mokhtar's
words: "You must think of the destiny of this country
from which we come, which is not a French province, and
which has neither bey nor sultan; you perhaps think of
Algeria always invaded, of its inextricable past, for we
are not yet a nation, not yet, know that: we are only
decimated tribes. It is not a step backwards to honor
our tribe, the only link which remains for us to unite
and find ourselves . . ." (31).

From time to time the scenes of bloody battles give
way to the narrator's recollection of privileged periods
of tranquillity, alternately envisaged as a return to the

womb, where an oceanic calm cradles the promise of renewal, or as a withdrawal to the innocence of childhood
under maternal guardianship. The nurturing reveries of
these periods, brought back by means of the imagination
in search of a utopia, are an aid to healing the mutilated self and restoring wholeness.

   In analyzing the structure of Nedjma, one finds that
the figure of the circle clearly predominates. Beginning
with the tribal circle of old, each generation thereafter, the uncles, and later the cousins, is another cycle
in a closed circular spiral going from birth to death as
one generation after the other picks up the remnants of
its mutilated heritage and passes it on to the next.
Only within the circle, symbolic womb where the values of
the ancestral past are forever preserved, is true liberty
to be found. Though many times violated, it is nevertheless the one sure refuge, the sole link to one's origins.
Despite the seductive attraction of departing for other
horizons, of evading the confines of the circle, true
identity is to be found only within its boundaries. The
circle has a double value, a negative as well as a positive signification. While it is a reassuring sanctuary,
it is also a trap where the threat of decay menaces. Man
is caught. To stay within the circle implies a refusal
of the modern world; to escape it implies loss of
identity.
   We have already spoken of a variety of elements that
distinguish Nedjma as a singular example of uncommon
narrative technique: commingling of genres, absence of
linear time, reverberating symbolism throughout. Aside
from these we may mention some technical devices that
characterize this work as well as Le Polygone étoilé,
that derives from it. First, Kateb uses several perspectives in order to describe a given person or event. The
same people and events are seen by different characters,
each of whom is a simultaneously autonomous voice with
his own specific viewpoint. These figures and happenings, variously picked up and abandoned as the narrative
continues, are related with modifications each time.
Each retelling adds depth and helps to fill in the
contours of past events. Some experiences are related by
characters under the influence of hashish or seized in
the delirium of fever. Their accounts take on an altogether different tone, that of frenzied hallucination.
When the author does intervene, it is only to set a scene

or to coordinate episodes; nowhere does he explain an
action or judge it. Deliberately a system of equivoca-
tions is constructed. The reader perceives the similari-
ties but also the differences in the various accounts.
The alternatives and uncertainties serve to reinforce the
hermeticism of the novel, as they force the reader to
make a continuous effort to sort out what actually hap-
pened and the chronological sequence in which these
things occurred. In some instances lines are blurred,
intentionally, and no definitive conclusion can be made.
This in itself is a commentary on man's inability to deal
conclusively with history.

To further complicate our reading, Kateb intertwines
several narrative levels: pure fiction, history (both
personal and collective), legend, and richly allusive
myth. Thus the reader is simultaneously challenged to
distinguish "reality" from myth at the same time as he
tries to establish their chronology and the details that
attach to each episode. This technique provokes constant
tension in the reader and requires that he perpetually
re-create the whole of the action in a clear, logical
outline. But his efforts are from the start doomed to
frustration, at least to some extent, since alternatives
and ambiguities are built into the literary construct.

The structural and thematic components of Kateb's
works are inextricably bound with a rich and original
poetry that is deliberately disconcerting. This is in
keeping with the writer's goal "to be disturbing in the
bosom of disturbance" (32). Like Rimbaud, with whom he
is often associated (33), Kateb seeks to steal fire and
give it form, to transform reality, to produce a "calcu-
lated derailment of all the senses" (34). Kateb seems to
draw on primordial energies. Words and images spring
forth in an overwhelming torrent; uncommon analogies
erupt, piling one atop the other in profuse succession.
Highly charged multivalent words and word combinations
cascade over an abrupt course and are thrown together
pell-mell, as in a kaleidoscope. These cataclysmic dis-
plays of brilliance, fused and synthesized in anarchy,
render Kateb's phrases obscure and his parables abstruse,
yet not without producing a sensory response in the
reader. A constant, frequently foreboding, tension born
of uncertainty and violence holds everything together.

Kateb dwells on a number of recurrent themes and
images that, like his country, are ever the same yet ever
different. Once the reader becomes familiar with the

author's iconography, he is able to appreciate the varia-
tions, as he would those of a musical composition. Mo-
tifs dear to Kateb that center on such words as <u>virgin</u>,
<u>blood</u>, <u>cave</u>, <u>sun</u>, <u>fire</u>, <u>star</u>, <u>rose</u>, and <u>vulture</u> are
repeatedly reworked throughout the poet's oeuvre, and
while they still retain a certain unsettling ambiguity,
their frequent recurrence is an aid to understanding
their overall significance. The combination of polygonal
words, unwonted imagery, and paradoxical anecdotes
bursting nervously in an atmosphere charged with the
terror of black magic is in keeping with the North African mystique, that inexhaustible source on which Kateb
continuously draws, for therein lie the origins of his
country and his race, their heritage and their identity.

Together with the later works of Mohammed Dib,
<u>Nedjma</u> may be counted as a unique chronicle of colonial
alienation. Its structure, content, and style are revolutionary, reflecting the confusion and degradation of the
country from which it sprang. Kateb himself chose to
extend the meaning of the word revolution, understanding
by it not only an historical occurrence affecting his
country, but an aspect of life itself:

> There are people who fear the word revolution or those
> who do not understand it, or narrow politicians, and
> all that is false. In fact revolution is a natural
> thing. Revolution is inscribed in the stars. Because
> the stars turn the earth turns. Revolution is the
> movement of the world. It is the most natural thing
> that is. Good. As a consequence the revolutionaries
> are not those who want to destroy everything. They
> are the ones who want the world to turn as it must.
> Thus there is nothing extraordinary in being revolu-
> tionary. It is only an attitude. It is simply the
> fact of being in the direction of life. (35)

Seen in this way, the Algerian revolution is but a
speck in the ongoing spinning out of all life. Whether
one accepts the term in the narrow or the broad sense,
Kateb's singular literary achievement is accurately
summed up by Gontard: "the miracle, properly artistic,
comes precisely from the fact that the deepest <u>engage-
ment</u> is communicated by the very form of the work" (36).
This novel is in itself a sign, "a form which contains
its meaning within itself" (37).

Born of the need for renewal, artistic and political,

Nedjma has been compared with the nouveau roman.
However, while the latter is purely the product of experimental technique, Nedjma is deeply rooted in nationalism and translates a situation that is specifically North
African. Nedjma is doubly significant, in its content
and in its form. With respect to the vitality of North
African francophone literature, its greatest import lies
in the impact it had on the concept of writing itself.
In a country where the novel was largely a borrowed form
imitating French models, Nedjma is proof that an original literature could be produced. It is both an example
and a challenge to other artists to celebrate tradition
by forging new paths. The fact that it continues to be
the source of a steady flow of research right up to the
present day is proof of the fertility of a work which
cannot be exhausted.

The Plays

The theater, not the novel, was to become Kateb's
preferred mode of expression, the ideal outlet for his
poetry and his political message, the means by which he
could reach the largest audience and have the greatest
impact. His plays combine Kateb's psychological affinity
with the heroes of ancient Greek drama, his leanings
toward Brechtien didacticism, and his own personal Algerian heritage of myths and legends.

Le Cadavre encerclé (The encircled corpse) was
produced in 1958. The drama opens on Lakhdar, a political demonstrator, symbol of the resistance and the central figure in this tragedy which unfolds in the midst of
the 1945 uprising. Wounded during the fighting, he now
agonizes amid heaps of cadavers. Recalling his country's
glorious past and her subsequent dismemberment, Lakhdar
denounces the treason of her people who sold her out to
the enemy. Through multiple vignettes related on several
planes—fictional, historical, and mythical—the events
that have led up to this moment are recalled. Monologues
employing the stream-of-consciousness technique allow the
characters to give full rein to their imagination and
emotions. As Lakhdar recalls the "sins of the father,"
his memory reaching back to the days of the Numidians, he
assumes a new function, that of the collective unconscious of the people. The return of the country's forgotten sources is the sine qua non for spiritual revivifi-

cation. The enactment of this descent into the past has
a cathartic function: to uncover the mutilated conscience long buried in the confused history of centuries
of invasions in order to bring about a reconciliation
with the individual and the collective identity.

The action is brought back to the present with the
appearance of Marguerite, daughter of a French comman-
dant, who takes the side of the Algerians. She frater-
nizes with Nedjma, Lakhdar's mistress, but the tension of
an implicit rivalry exerts itself. Although Marguerite
is well-meaning, the Algerians do not trust her. No
valid rapport is possible. Unwittingly she is also therefore a victim. Lakhdar's stepfather, who disagrees with
his political ideals, stabs him in the back. Lakhdar is
left alone in the polygonal rifle range where he clings
to a tree. He is caught in the inescapable circle of his
origins and of the endless circle of birth and death. He
dies. But Lakhdar, whose name in Arabic means "fruitful," is a symbol of hope. Atop the tree sits Ali, his
son, sign of regeneration. The action remains deliberately incomplete, to show that Algeria is always in the
process of becoming.

Les Ancêtres redoublent de férocité (The ancestors increase in viciousness), a shorter play, uses
themes, symbolism, and theatrical devices similar to
those of Le Cadavre encerclé, but with one striking
addition: the use of a chorus and choryphaeus borrowed
from classical Greek tragedy. Their alternate incanta-
tions accentuate the mythic roots of the action. The
story is told in flashbacks and may be briefly summarized. Lakhdar, Nedjma's husband, has lost his mind as
a result of the torture he endured while in prison. In
an effort to cure him, Nedjma takes him to the festival
of the vultures, but there he is killed by his stepfather
Tahar. As a result of this, Nedjma goes mad. Apparently
possessed, she comes to be known as la femme sauvage
("the wild woman"), and goes to live at the bottom of a
ravine. A vulture (38) circles overhead and she imagines
it to be Lakhdar. The bird swoops down on her as if to
possess her. Meanwhile, Mustapha and Hassan avenge
Lakhdar's death by killing Tahar, who had become a puppet
in the service of the colonial aggressors. They then go
in search of Nedjma, who has been led away to join the
army of liberation. Hassan and Mustapha, now combatants
in the revolutionary force, carry off Nedjma, but then
engage in fatal rivalry over their prize. Mustapha kills

Hassan and wounds Nedjma. The bird, symbol of destruction, pounces on her, sacrificing her to the war.
Mustapha survives but is blinded by the vulture. The
circle of reprisals is closed. Individual passion must
be renounced in favor of tribal integrity. The ancestors
have been appeased.

La Poudre d'intelligence (Intelligence powder), a
picaresque farce, differs from other Kateb works in its
humor and in its acerbic attack against abuses of power
and justice, religious superstition and trickery (39),
and the gullibility of the people. The principal character, Nuage de Fumée (Cloud of Smoke), is a buffoon who,
thanks to the hypocrisy and foolishness of those who
govern, manages to turn each situation to his advantage.
He is a type character, well known in the Arab–Berber
oral tradition. In fact, many of the anecdotes that
compose the play are drawn from the oral folk heritage.

While the reader of these plays can appreciate their
poetry and message, only the spectator can experience
their artistic dimension to the fullest (40). A variety
of special effects, including concrete music and dramatic
use of lighting and visuals, add vigor to the playwright's militant theater. Clearly Kateb intends that
these additions function as in integral part of the statement that he seeks to make.

During the 1940s, while working as a reporter for
Alger Républicain, Kateb took an interest in the developments in Vietnam. He sketched some rough drafts for a
play but nothing came of them. In 1967 he visited Vietnam and witnessed for himself the struggle of the common
people. The idea for a play began to take shape, and by
1970 L'Homme aux sandales de caoutchouc (The man in
rubber sandals)—the title refers to Ho Chi Minh—was
completed. In 1971 Kateb explained the correlation that
he saw between the Vietnamese peoples' effort to control
their own country and the direction his own country was
taking: "I saw my country as I wanted it to be being
born in Vietnam. Algeria as if projected into the
future. Colonial peoples, if they want to make up for
lost time, must take the path of socialism. . . . What I
saw in Vietnam thus was for me a kind of fountain of
youth, the dawn of a rebirth" (41). In Vietnam Kateb saw
the socialist republic he hoped Algeria would embrace.
As an artist committed to his country's cause, he assumed
the task of presenting the example of Vietnam as a model
for his own people.

That Kateb should have chosen the war in Vietnam as
the subject of his drama is not so difficult to understand once one is aware of the forces that come into
play. The French defeat at Dien Bien Phu had served as a
source of inspiration to the Algerian people, a confirma-
tion that a disadvantaged country could indeed throw off
the colonialists despite the latter's clear economic and
military superiority. Then there were the evident parallels between the two peoples, Algerians and Vietnamese.
Both were a people divided against themselves and manipulated by foreign intervention while thirsting for self-
determination.

L'Homme aux sandales de caoutchouc, an epic military
farce composed of thirteen dramatic sequences, attacks
the hypocrisy and greed of powers who use war to further
their own selfish ends. French, British, Vietnamese,
Vietcong, and Americans are pitted against each other and
against themselves. Other conflicts are also inserted:
guerrilla warfare in South America, exploitation of the
blacks in the United States, and Israeli-Arab conflicts.
Neither is religion spared. The Catholic Church and the
Buddhist faith are shown up as having enfeebled the
people, and their tactics are exposed. A multitude of
abuses are denounced in this play: the unjust nature of
the war, the profiteering that grows along with its esca-
lation, the blasé attitude of the American prisoners of
war who refuse to accept responsibility for having killed
civilians, the crass military who respond that the White
House will send monetary compensation to cover all
losses, including human life. Together with the common
people, Ho Chi Minh, whom Kateb esteems as "the Vietnamese man par excellence," is the victorious hero of
this drama. Statesman, militant, and poet, in him Kateb
recognizes the figure of the ancestor who helps the
people to find the thread of their lost past.

That Kateb should bitterly decry the abuses of colonialist warlords is understandable. That he should select
Vietnam as the model for an ideal state is difficult to
understand. Tyranny and cruelty direct the course of the
new, so-called free Vietnam. Like the majority of his
compatriots, Kateb seems to attach much importance to the
struggle for independence per se, without looking ahead
to the forging of a new nation that prepares to enter
into the twentieth century.

With the performance of his plays in colloquial
Arabic, Kateb came to a heightened awareness of the play-

wright's mission: "my objective has always been to
reach the public of my country. From that point of view,
my itinerary is clear. . . . I am returning to what I
always wanted to do: a political theater in a language
widely accessible to the masses of common people. Hence-
forth I am going to wield two languages: French and
especially colloquial Arabic" (42).

Kateb defines his own role clearly:

> The role of the revolutionary writer is to take into
> account the struggles that set fire to the whole
> world, to transmit a living message, to place this
> public in the heart of a theater that takes part in
> the never-ended combat that opposes the proletariat to
> the bourgeoisie. It is the great confrontation of our
> time. It is logical to promote a theater that stirs up
> class struggle and brings it to its height. The
> theater is the ideal means for a people to enter
> politics on the ground floor. (43)

Kateb Yacine remains the most deeply rooted of leading
contemporary francophone writers of the Maghreb. He goes
beyond individual obsessions to embrace the collective
tragedy of an entire people, tracing its origins in history. Like Proust in search of lost time, he returns to
the foundations. Yet in following the circle of eternal
return, he breaks through the narrow confines of form and
style with a creative tour de force that is wholly
original. The process and the result in themselves mirror the reality of his country that must return to its
sources in order to be born anew. Kateb's poetry both
liberates and elevates him. It is evidence of his refusal to be molded by exterior forces and of his determination to find within the source of renewal. Though he has
to his credit only four books published over a fifteen-
year span, the impact of those four is significant.
Kateb has forged new paths, working out an unparalleled
itinerary and traveling untried routes in order to
complete his circuit which, paradoxically, while returning upon itself never encircles him. He invites his
reader to follow while almost playfully throwing him off
guard at every step of the way. The result is a tempting
adventure, not without rewards for anyone willing to
engage in an exercise of wit and wits.

Chapter Five
Albert Memmi

An Investigation into the Sources of Oppression

Tunisian and Jewish, Albert Memmi occupies a special place among the North African francophone writers. Belonging neither to the world of the colonizer nor, strictly speaking, to that of the colonized, his particular circumstances place him in a unique position to view the ills of colonial rule. His remarkable storytelling ability combined with his masterful handling of form, style, and language have rightly earned for him a position of rank alongside the finest names in Maghrebian literature. His specific situation has inclined him to see true liberation as originating with the individual, hence his preoccupation with the unity and equilibrium of the person. Spurred on by a need to resolve his personal conflicts, Memmi has come to see that universal emancipation of the dominated and oppressed groups within society is dependent on individual freedom born of genuine self-knowledge. The task is envisaged as an ongoing one to be relentlessly pursued because a person's life circumstances are in constant flux. To this end Memmi continues to reexamine, reformulate, and express his views in new and different ways.

A Jewish literature written in French has existed in North Africa since the early part of this century. In fact, as Isaac Yetiv notes (1), it was a whole generation in advance of Muslim literature in French. But the Jewish writers writing in the 1920s and 1930s, of whom Jean Vehel, Victor Danon, and Ryvel are among the best representatives, limited themselves to descriptions of their history, folklore, ancestral customs, religious traditions, and living conditions. Their books do not speak of generation conflicts or of alienation from one's milieu. Without falling into the vein of facile "picturesque" folklore, Memmi's first efforts follow in their tradition as documentary testaments of history. But his works surpass the frontiers opened by them with this important difference: they are a critical self-analysis,

an "auto-dissection," an "introspective plunge into the
darkest recesses of the soul to try to discover there an
elusive identity, always changing, always fleeing, never
fixed" (2).

Memmi's unique contribution to this literature and his
originality stem from his analytical approach, his ability to pitilessly ferret out the precise causes and conditions of all oppression and to state these clearly. His
works remain rooted in the native culture yet at the same
time are of universal interest, for they concern the
humanity of man.

Biographical Notes

Albert Memmi was born in the Jewish ghetto of Tunis on
15 December 1920. As the son of poor Jewish colonized
Tunisians, he suffered a triple alienation, the implications of which are evidenced in his works. As a Tunisian
educated in French schools he endured the intellectual
and cultural estrangement of the évolué caught
between two civilizations; as a Jew he was automatically
ostracized; as the son of a poor artisan (his father was
a harness maker), he was cut off from the bourgeois
milieu of his city of birth. By the time he was twenty
he had come to the following realizations, which he
expresses in his autobiographical first novel, La Statue
de sel:

> I am ill at ease in my native country and don't know
> any other, my culture is borrowed and my mother tongue
> weak, I have no more beliefs, religion, traditions,
> and I am ashamed of what remains of them in me. . . .
> I am Tunisian, but Jewish, that is to say, political-
> ly, socially excluded, speaking the same language of
> the country with a peculiar accent, not in tune emo-
> tionally with what moves the Muslims; Jewish but
> having broken with the Jewish religion and the ghetto,
> ignorant of Jewish cultures and detesting the inauthen-
> tic bourgeoisie. (3)

Memmi's childhood, adolescence, and young manhood are
colorfully described in La Statue de sel. As a youngster he frequented a rabbinical school. At the rather
late age of seven he entered a Jewish Alliance school
where he remained until the age of thirteen. Upon

successful completion of his courses he was awarded a
scholarship that enabled him to attend the French lycée
Carnot in Tunis, where he had the good fortune to have as
his professor of literature the Algerian writer Jean
Amrouche, who also lived the anguish of North African
attraction to Western civilization. Upon completion of
his baccalauréat, Memmi went to the University of
Algiers to study philosophy, but his education was inter-
rupted by World War II. In 1943 he was sent to a forced
work camp from which he later escaped, another experience
that he speaks of in his novel. At the end of the war
Memmi went to Paris, passing the agrégation in philosophy at the Sorbonne. He married a Christian Frenchwoman,
then returned to Tunis to teach philosophy. At this time
he took on a job as director of the literary page of the
first Tunisian daily, L'Action. He took an active part
in the movement for Tunisian nationalism while working as
director of the Center for Child Psychology. When
Tunisia was granted independence in 1956, the return to
sclerotic tradition advanced by the nationalists left him
in an uncomfortable position. He felt there was no place
for him in the new Muslim state run by a narrow-minded
bourgeois government. He therefore returned to Paris,
settling there in 1957. It was at this point in his
career that the young teacher's interest turned to sociology.

As a researcher affiliated with the National Center
for Scientific Research, Memmi gives conferences at
various French institutes of higher studies: the University Center for Jewish Studies, and the Sorbonne, where
he teaches social psychology. Based on his own experience and knowledge, Memmi's great undertaking has been
the study of oppressed groups—the colonized Jew, the
black American, the suffering proletariat, among others—
for the purpose of establishing a sociology of oppression. The influence of Sartre and Camus, whom he knew as
a friend, may be felt in his works. Among the classic
French writers he cites Rousseau and Montaigne as influen-
tial to his development, but certainly his thinking is
not limited by these. Because of the broad scope of his
inquiry into the psychology and behavior of human groups,
and the timelessness of his topic, Memmi's works have
been translated into many languages.

Memmi has written four novels: La Statue de sel
(1953), which won the Carthage prize in 1953 and the
Fenéon prize in 1954, Agar (1955), both published by

the Paris firm of Buchet-Chastel, Le Scorpion (1969),
and Le Désert: ou la vie et les aventures de Jubaïr
Ouali El-Mammi (1977), both published by Gallimard.
Another novel, "Chronique du Royaume–du–Dedans," is in
preparation. From the author's scientific studies have
come the essays: Portrait du colonisé précédé du
portrait du colonisateur (1957), perhaps his best-known
work, first published by Buchet-Chastel, Portrait d'un
Juif (1962), La Libération du Juif (1966), L'Homme
Dominé (1968), and La Dépendance (1979), all published by Gallimard. Apart from the essays there are two
collections of conversations: Entretien (1975), published by the Canadian firm Editions de l'Etincelle, and
La Terre intérieure (1976), published by Gallimard.
The Jewish-Arab conflict in the Middle East led to the
study Juifs et Arabes (1974), printed by Gallimard.
   In addition to these works, Memmi has collaborated
with other authors in carrying out sociological inquiries. Jointly prepared investigations yielded the study
Les Français et le racisme (1965), published by Payot.
   Memmi's interest in North Africa has not diminished as
a result of his residence in France. He is employed by
the Paris publishing firm of Maspero as director of the
series "Domaine Maghrébin," which is devoted to the
study of literary and scientific journals. He is responsible for having written introductions to two important
collections: L'Anthologie des écrivains maghrébins
d'expression française (1964) (4), and L'Anthologie
des écrivains français du Maghreb (1969).
   This prodigious effort had its origins in Memmi's
first student days in Paris. As a youth isolated from
his family and homeland, Memmi felt a need to review his
existence and once and for all to put his early years
behind him. Writing was the tool by which he determined
to accomplish this task, and the result was his first
novel, La Statue de sel. In order to better appreciate
each individual work, one should understand that there is
a structure that unifies the whole of Memmi's work.
   Kateb Yacine, as we have seen, claims to be the author
of a single book. The same can likewise be said of Albert
Memmi. In Kateb's works all action is polarized around
the fictional Nedjma; with Memmi the central figure of
fiction and essay alike is the first-person narrator,
Memmi himself, at different stages in his career, seeking
knowledge and understanding of the self. Each book is a
further step in a lengthy ongoing process of self-

examinations that begins with "me" and proceeds to the
universal. In his excellent study, Isaac Yetiv explains
Memmi's method of investigation, a method that Memmi
himself confirms intermittently by direct reference in
his works: "the author-narrator moves linearly in historic time but by concentric circles in human space; geographic space barely interests him and the rare descriptions, while very successful from a literary point of
view, are only there to cast light on and make clear the
état d'âme of the author and the state of tension
that joins him to men" (5). Certain relationships are
found at each stage of these expanding concentric circles, such as narrator-mother, narrator-father, while
others are found only once, as for example in Memmi's
second novel in which we have the narrator-Marie, and the
narrator-community. In the essays the narrator is projected outward from the center under certain identities:
the colonized, the Jew, man, woman. As the author proceeds from one stage to the next, the narrating "I"
becomes "other," an objectified former self. "All these
manifestations of the 'moi' are so many steps on the road
to self-knowledge and are at the origin of the author's
identity crisis . . ." (6).

The Novels

La Statue de sel (The Pillar of Salt, 1953), Memmi's
first novel, is the poignant tale of one Alexandre
Mordekhai Benillouche of the Tunisian Jewish ghetto.
Unlike the first works of Dib and Mammeri, Memmi's first-
person chronological narrative reads like a diary, for
under the thin veil of the narrator we clearly recognize
the author himself. The reader follows his life from a
blissful early childhood in Tunis, through the milieux of
the artisans, the Jewish school, the synagogue, and the
French lycée, whose influence brings about a gradually
widening rupture with his family, language, tradition,
religion, and his father's goals for him. We see him
lose faith in the all-powerfulness of the father whom he
had so respected. We see him turn away ashamed at the
primitive superstition of the dear mother whom he had
cherished. We observe his disgust at the vanity of the
dirty, ill-clad uneducated rabbis of the temples. In the
French school Alexandre decides upon philosophy as his
field of study. The choice is indicative of his aim at

this stage in his life: to penetrate the most intimate
part of the others, to understand them and thereby, hopefully, to gain entrance into their universe, which he
sees as so utterly different from his. Finally, World
War II, the anti-Semitic laws of the Vichy government,
and the experience of a labor camp open his eyes to the
treason of the West.

Like so many heroes of fiction of this period, the
young man is torn between two cultures, two civilizations. Education, in which he had placed all his trust,
has made him a stranger in his own country. He cannot go
back to his own people because he has forgotten the
native dialect and his people are suspicious of "intellectuals." But the West, with its racial prejudice, will
not accept him either. "I had refused the East and the
West refused me" (7), he comes to understand. He is not
alone in his dilemma: "Millions of men have lost their
fundamental unity, they no longer recognize themselves
and look for themselves in vain" (8). This statement,
uttered at the beginning of the account, as the narrator
looks back, expresses what has become of Memmi and the
course he must pursue. His will be a constant and cruel
process of examination and evaluation. His life advances
in a series of stages, best described by the narrator
himself: "Thus, I passed from crisis to crisis, finding
each time a new equilibrium, more precarious, but always
there remained something for me to destroy. . . . And
each time a part of me collapsed" (9). The hero's quest
is a process and an operation, at which he is at one and
the same time spectator, surgeon, and patient. Periodically he will stop as he proceeds along this existential
journey to ask the questions "who am I?" and "what have I
become?" before embarking on the next phase of a quest
that ends only in death. Finally, the introspective hero-
narrator concludes that there is only one viable option:
to abandon both the native and the learned culture and to
start all over again by building a new identity, without
turning back, lest he become a "statue of salt," as did
Lot's wife in the Bible. (As with other North African
writers, the past for Memmi is equated with petrifica-
tion.) He thus decides to join his friend Henry and go
to South America. His decision to break entirely with
the past is symbolized through the destruction of his
diary, while Henry packs a new notebook on the cover of
which he inscribes the word "Argentina."

Unlike Mammeri's <u>Colline oubliée</u> or Dib's <u>Grande</u>

Maison, which aroused conflicting emotions and even
enraged some readers, La Statue de sel received unani-
mous praise from the critics. It was seen as a reflec-
tive confession, a lucid scanning of a particular case,
and by implication of others similar to it. It was
passionate without inciting anger; it was touching
without being saccharine. The effects of the novel were
not recognized until several years after its publication
in 1953: it raised the question of the sociopolitical
conditionings that encircle man.

Agar (1955), Memmi's second novel, published in
English under the title Strangers, is the logical continuation of the life journey initiated in La Statue de
sel. In it the hero has progressed to the fourth phase
of his existence, his marriage to a French Alsatian
Catholic, whom he had met and loved in Paris while both
were students. Narrated in the first person by an
unnamed hero in whom we recognize a prolongation of
Alexandre Benillouche turned doctor of medicine, the
novel traces the course of the couple's three years
together, beginning with their arrival in Tunis where
they move in with his relatives. From the start things
go badly. Marie at first conceals, then openly admits,
her distaste for everything Tunisian. Alienated by the
language, people, and tradition of her new country, she
tries to block all of these out of her life, but in order
to do so she cuts her husband off from his family and
friends. He, meanwhile, lives a guilt-ridden, divided
existence. (Here we recognize the situation of the young
hero of La Statue de sel transposed to the dimension of
the couple.) The protagonists admit the failure of their
union. Departure is seen as the sole solution. Marie
leaves for France, leaving her husband to ponder the
extent of his alienation. "My misfortune is that I am no
longer like anyone" (10), he laments as the impact of the
situation delivers a telling blow.

Agar was incorrectly interpreted by some critics,
and Memmi found it expedient to explain himself in a
lengthy preface to the 1963 reprinting of his work. The
novel is not an autobiographical account of his own marriage, nor was it intended as a study of a mixed marriage
per se. Memmi expressly states that he did not intend to
imply that communication between two people of different
civilizations, cultures, and nationalities was impossible, nor that such a marriage was destined to failure.
He explains that in emphasizing the negative conditions

that prevent success in a marriage, he wished to describe
the conditions of interior liberation, the end to personal prejudice and close-mindedness that must be present
if political liberation is to reach full flower.

Both foreign and American critics have, with justifica-
tion, faulted Memmi on his approach. The main protagonists are rigid, obviously doomed to failure from the
start. They assume an attitude that is unlikely in young
people who are otherwise liberated. For a man who has
written that his hopes rest with the couple, Memmi's
orientation and the characterizations that he creates in
this novel belie his aspirations.

Fourteen years and four essays later, Memmi once again
turned to fiction to complete the next circuit in the
search for inner peace and enlightenment. This was Le
Scorpion (1969), subtitled The Imaginary Confession.
It is a complicated, bizarre, but original eclectic literary work that combines, or rather juxtaposes, the various
forms of expression practiced by Memmi: fiction, essay,
and chronicle. The action is set in Tunisia during the
tumultuous period of decolonization. The pretext for the
work is simple. Marcel, an opthalmologist, has been
asked to go through the contents of a desk drawer contain-
ing papers belonging to his brother Emile, a writer, who
has disappeared. What he finds is a random collection of
fragments of novels, a personal diary, commentaries,
reflections, and vignettes that reveal to him his
brother's mind and, simultaneously, bring him to uncover
new dimensions in his own life. The confusing assortment
of texts moves Marcel to frustration as he tries to sort
through the muddle. He finds family events recorded,
though not always in the same version in which he remembers living them, and he reads these same events distorted in a fictionalized rendition. All of this goes to
suggest that life is not one dimensional but unfolds on
various planes.

Since Le Scorpion is the sum total of the past,
personal histories related in La Statue de sel and
Agar are reiterated, with further amplifications. As
the reader preoccupies himself with sorting Emile's works
of fiction from fact, he realizes that there is a further
dimension in this novel to be accounted for. As Marcel
pulls his brother's notes out of the drawer one by one,
his own reactions are being recorded by the omniscient
narrator, who intersperses them with Emile's writings.
The complex mosaic is distinguished by the use of four

different typefaces, while, we are told, the notes left
by Emile are written in different colored ink. At first
the reader is disconcerted by the effort to distinguish
the documents, but various clues along the way serve to
reassure him: "Perhaps the best is to advance without
trying first of all to understand. The main story lines
will end up by standing out on their own: if they exist"
(11). The reader is further drawn into the scheme with
Marcel's hypothesis that perhaps there is "neither fiction, nor diary, nor document, but a single complex intention" (12), although, like Marcel, he is vexed at not
being able to find the key to it. Emile's writings
gradually lead Marcel to gain insights into his own
existence, and simultaneously by bits and pieces the
reader comes to grasp the purpose of the whole novel:
"If a writer tried to say all, in a single book, that
book would perhaps be his healing, his reconciliation
with himself and others, with life itself" (13). In
words that echo Memmi's own motivation, Emile reveals
that he had turned to writing as an investigatory device:
"literature is an exploration of limits" (14). It was
for him a means of clarifying: a desperate effort to see
more clearly and a stratagem by which he tried "to re-
achieve his unity" (15). As in previous works, Le Scorpion is Memmi's creative attempt to reexamine his own
life. Emile's obsession with tracing tentative family
roots in ancient times thus becomes clear.

    Marcel surmises that Emile has left Tunis in order to
convalesce, to heal his inner being and find peace. The
doctor concludes that he too must leave this country
shaken by political and social upheaval and ruled by a
new despotic government. The former victims have become
the new tyrants. In a phrase whose double meaning is
unmistakable, Marcel notes "the frequency, variety, and
seriousness of eye disorders in this country" (16).
Neither Emile, with his gift of insight, nor Marcel, with
his ability to restore sight, can ameliorate the forces
at work. In his concluding remarks, as Marcel realizes
how closely he now identifies himself with his brother,
the reader comes to see that the two men are complementary. The divisions of text and characters finally
resolve into a much sought after unity.

    Le Scorpion has aroused the interest of critics on
both sides of the Atlantic. It is related "with the
brio of an oriental story teller" and "with the pirou-
ettes of a master experienced in the secrets of writing

but who mistrusts it" (17), notes Jacqueline Leiner in
the French Review. It certainly departs from the
format of the "standard" novel that has been passed on
for a century. As with the works of Kateb Yacine, the
reader is not allowed to remain a passive bystander, but
must actively participate in the construction of this
novel. Memmi himself writes: "We count on the reader to
offer a complementary imaginative effort. That will be
his contribution to this joint work" (18).

Clever, imaginative, and thought provoking (19) in its
approach to the eternal questions of life, Le Scorpion
has been praised by critics who, nevertheless, do not
seem to agree on its strong and weak points. Emile
Capouya, writing for the Saturday Review, hails Memmi
for "the lively presence of his characters" (20), while
Hugh Kenner in the New York Times criticizes their card-
board nature: "This kind of labyrinth can get so fas-
cinating you almost fail to notice how little the people
come through as people . . . or how shopworn, when you
isolate them, are all those 'ideas.' . . . Albert Memmi
is conducting that very French exercise, an intricate
dialogue with himself, brilliantly disguised as a new way
for a novelist to organize chaos" (21).

Memmi does not really hide this fact from his readers,
but rather scatters throughout the novel revealing clues
about his procedure. In the novel he comments on the personal breakthrough he has made: "Only now do I perceive
that all my published work is only incessant commentary
of a work yet to come; with the insane hope that that commentary might end up itself constituting that work" (22).

Isaac Yetiv sums up Memmi's technique as follows.

This system of mirrors, facing one another and reflecting ad infinitum the evanescent pictures very
often deformed by the different angles of vision of
the protagonists, enables the author to indulge in his
cherished game of contradicting, even antagonizing
himself at will, thus leaving open and unresolved the
great problems of human existence, of love and hate,
of right and wrong, of good and evil. (23)

For Memmi writing is in itself a source of relief;
through it he unloads his metaphysical burden. The
answers to the questions he raises are not of concern to
him here but remain a matter for the reader's speculation.

Le Désert (1977), Memmi's last novel, transposes
the author's eternal quest to a fourteenth-century setting in which the exotic element only veils thinly
Memmi's personal metaphysical history and probings. The
novel relates the life and adventures of one Jubaïr
Ouali El-Mammi, a prince who as a youth was exiled from
the domain that he was to have inherited, the Royaume-du-
Dedans (Kingdom Within). He sets forth on a quest to
regain his throne only to learn, four decades later, that
his kingdom with its population has been destroyed by the
great conqueror Tamerlane. Joubaïr, already a sexagenarian, later surrenders to this leader. The latter, struck
by the old man's unusual personality, invites him to dine
with him and to explain what dangers he must avoid in
order to retain his power. In answer Joubaïr requests
permission to tell his life story, explaining that the
conqueror will perhaps find the answers to his questions
in Joubaïr's adventures. In a manner reminiscent of the
Lettres persanes, what follows are close to two hundred
pages of Oriental tales relating the long and numerous
travels, wars, plots, love affairs, and diverse
happenings in which the hero is caught up. A whole
gallery of characters is sketched. Joubaïr converses
with kings, viziers, esteemed men, and brigands, at times
enjoying high honors, at times humiliated. Each episode
of the lengthy chronicle that Joubaïr is recording
contains a moral that helps him to better understand
other people, civilizations, and life.
        Outside of its value as pure entertainment, two things
are accomplished by the novel: it permits Memmi to trace
his own tribal roots, however mythological they may be,
and it demonstrates the sources of true tranquillity,
that inner equilibrium so highly prized by Memmi. Though
he takes great pains to situate the Royaume-du-Dedans
geographically, even going so far as to include a map in
his book, the kingdom is of course but a thinly veiled
synonym of a state of inner calm that can only be
achieved through an absence of desires: "Haven't I acted
rather as though the sole kingdom to be conquered was
that of the self? Final wisdom or supreme illusion?"
(24).
        Critics have received this novel favorably, praising
it on various counts. Gerard Guillot, writing for the
Figaro Littèraire, describes it as "a vivid chronicle,
thrilling, blinding in its truth, as powerful as a film
with all its images. . . . in the manner of thirteenth-

or fifteenth-century chroniclers. And the verbal richness of the text is so strong that it seems as if one
hears rather than reads the narrative. As if its transmission had only been oral, as if over the centuries it
came down to us generation after generation" (25).

Salim Jay, writing for L'Afrique Littéraire et
Artistique, similarly lauds this book, but goes even
further, noting that it is "full of palpitations, of
scents," by which "the reader is intoxicated and seduced"
(26). True, the reader's imagination is stimulated by
the picturesque, yet though we might agree that "Albert
Memmi has made a success of his enterprise as a virtuoso
of the imaginary" (27), the reader who seeks a more challenging composition might be disappointed, especially
after Le Scorpion, which marked a decisive attempt to
break with traditional narration. The bulk of Le Désert is made up of progression through repetition, a
technique that has been around for centuries and that, in
spite of the elements of local color, palls when one is
looking for an exciting experiment in form. Let it be
noted, however, that Albert Memmi's wish in this instance
is merely to provide "that simple happiness of reading,
too often neglected in our days" (28). To make the
reader go through a game of mental gymnastics is not his
purpose here.

The Essays

It is not principally for his novels that Albert
Memmi's name is known, but for his study on colonialism,
Le Portrait du colonisé suivi du portrait du colonisateur (The Colonizer and the Colonized, 1957), which
has become a classic in its field. This essay was to be
the first in a series of books focusing on oppression.
In the preface written for the second edition, Memmi
explains the genesis of his work.

During the mid-1950s his personal quest for solid
happiness and relief from solitude led him to the conclusion that hope rests with the couple: "the whole world
. . . [is] within the couple" (29). In Agar, however,
he had shown a union doomed to failure. This drove him
to broader considerations:

I felt that to understand the failure of their undertaking, that of a mixed marriage in a colony, I first

had to understand the colonizer and the colonized,
perhaps the entire colonial relationship and situation. All this was leading me far from myself and
from my own problems, but their explanation became
more and more complex; so without knowing where I
would end up, I had to at least try to put an end to
my own anguish. . . . Thus I undertook this inventory
of conditions of colonized people mainly in order to
understand myself and to identify my place in the society of other men. It was my readers—not all of them
Tunisian—who later convinced me that this portrait
was equally theirs. (30)

Thus did Memmi begin his systematic study of a topic
that was to inspire a steady stream of essays: the relationship between the dominator and the dominated. His
approach, however, while analytic, is characteristically
personal. He begins with himself as the point of departure, proceeding thence from the individual to the universal as he carries on a kind of stylized dialogue, a
dialectic of thesis and antithesis. Déjeux has described Memmi's modus operandi as a methodic exposition
that combines "a skillful dosage of objectivity and personal emotion" (31). It is precisely for these personal
and subjective interventions in what otherwise strives to
be objective analysis that Memmi has been criticized.
His answer to his detractors is that one can only proceed
from his own particular case, and this method teaches far
more than general and abstract answers.
Memmi defends the integrity of this method: "Nothing
in the texts is invented or supposed or even hazardously
transposed. Actual experience, co-ordinated and stylized,
lies behind every sentence. If in the end I have con-
sented to a general tone, it is because I know that I
could, at every line, every word, produce innumerable
concrete facts" (32).
Le Portrait du colonisé was published at a critical
moment during the Algerian revolution. When it appeared,
it caused both anger and enthusiasm. Some saw it as an
insolent provocation; others as a flag to which to rally.
French critics applauded its restraint. Jean Paul
Sartre, in his introduction to the text, writes: "this
lucid and sober work may be classed among the 'passionate
geometries,' for its calm objectivity represents tran-
scendence of suffering and anger" (33).
In fact, the book is dispassionate in its analysis,

totally unlike Frantz Fanon's virulent study <u>Les Damnés de la Terre</u> (published in English as <u>The Wretched of the Earth</u>), which made its appearance four years later. Memmi's plan was to write a rational discourse that would "reproduce completely and authentically the portraits of the two protagonists of the colonial drama, and the relationship that unites them" (34). He proceeded like a logician, analyzing the conditions that allow colonialism to take root, and studying its operation over a period of time. Memmi views colonization as a process, a mechanism, and a chain of events destined to lead to an inexorable end. The portrait probes the attitudes assumed by colonizer and colonized, vis-à-vis each other and vis-à-vis themselves, and it debunks commonly held myths, for example, the meritorious concern of the colonizer, consumed by virtuous zeal to protect and instruct the indolent, unpredictable, deficient native; the latter's notorious ingratitude for all these efforts and his irrevocable wretchedness, in which he himself has come to believe. Memmi makes clear that the colonizer is a usurper asserting nonlegitimate privileges, debasing the colonized to exalt himself. While the author's purpose in writing was to understand his own particular situation in society, he acknowledges that his readers later led him to see that the pattern that he deciphered applies to vast multitudes of oppressed people across the globe.

It is all too easy to criticize Memmi's portrayal of colonialism, to haggle over his approach to the topic. We cite but a few of the major comments. Paul Semonin writing for the <u>Nation</u> notes that in certain respects the essay "suffers from an excruciating brevity and a superficial grasp of doctrinal questions involved" (35). It omits entirely the portrait of the colonizer in France, and in this omission "the symmetry of Memmi's analysis is misleading, for it underemphasizes the most essential aspect of colonialism" (36). Jean Déjeux finds the portraits "excessively rigorous, frozen, stereotyped . . ." (37). Isaac Yetiv notes a "deterministic or even fatalistic attitude" (38) of the kind found in the novels.

Despite the author's evident partisanship in a book that strives to be objective in its intention, we must agree that these portraits constitute a document of great value, historical, political, sociological, and even psychological. It cannot be denied that Memmi's predictions have come true. History has vindicated him. Further-

more, the essay's impact cannot be refuted. It unveils
the absolute iniquity of colonization and brings to light
its insidious destructive effects that rot colonizer and
colonized alike. Intellectual circles in black Africa
seized upon the book as an invaluable document in their
struggle for independence. Léopold Senghor, past
president of the Republic of Senegal and himself a poet
of repute, wrote: "Albert Memmi's book will constitute a
document to which the historians of colonization will
have to refer" (39). Alioune Diop, president of the
African Cultural Society, sees it as among "the best
known books on colonial psychology" (40).

Eight years after its writing, the book came out in
its English translation in the United States with a dedi-
cation "to the American Negro, also colonized." While
the book has been used to inveigh against racist white
supremacy, it is hardly adequate to describe the complex
dialectics of racial domination in this country.

Le Portrait du colonisé resulted from Memmi's attempt to understand his position as a colonized person.
In 1956 Tunisia was granted independence. Yet while his
status thus changed, a feeling of uneasiness nevertheless
persisted. Memmi found that in a state whose constitution proclaimed Islam as the official religion, he, as a
Jew, was still a second-class citizen, reduced to marginal participation in the country's affairs. After
moving to Paris in 1957, he elected to carry his earlier
examination one step further to see if the same mechanism
would cast light on his situation as a Jew. He proceeded
to take stock of his life under this particular aspect.
The result was the Portrait d'un Juif (Portrait of a
Jew, 1962). In this substantial four-part study, Memmi
tries to deal with his own personal distress at being
Jewish and what he describes as the constant malaise of
the Jew and the continued threat of others. Setting
aside all taboos, Memmi delves into all the facets of the
Jewish condition. In his preface, the author claims to
be giving his own portrait, which in fact extends to a
general description of other Jews, for as Memmi himself
affirms, Jews share a common destiny since they are among
the oppressed of the earth. Memmi clearly sees himself
as different because of his Jewishness. Not all Jews
agree with his position. Whatever the reader's individual reaction to Memmi's account, and they run to both
extremes, one cannot help but note the courage and lucidi-
ty of this forthright study.

The Portrait d'un Juif is continued in a second
volume, La Libération du Juif (1966), which attempts
to outline the Jew's path to liberation, both the false
and the possible ones. In this three-part essay Memmi
considers a variety of issues under the following head-
ings: self-rejection (name changing, assimilation,
conversion, mixed marriage, self-hatred), self-acceptance
(countermyth, literature, language, art, culture), and
finally, the way out. Memmi believes that the solution
lies in the lay Jewish nation of Israel, separated from
religion, which alone can restore dignity to the Jew.
Le Portrait d'un Juif and La Libération du Juif
are really two parts of a single study. The first part
seeks a definition of the Jew and constitutes, in the
words of Jean-Louis Bory, "a sort of ontology of the
Jew," while the second half explores the role played by
the Jew in the world today, "a dynamic of the Jew" (41).
Jean-François Revel judges the second study superior
to the earlier volume "in that Memmi concentrates on the
present-day experience, and avoids the mixture of bio-
sociological exposé with existential overtones that
somewhat prejudiced the unity of the Portrait" (42).
Stimulating, provocative, and painfully honest, La
Libération du Juif raises burning questions of current
import that concern Jews and non-Jews alike.
The theme of the dominated and oppressed continued to
intrigue Memmi, and he relentlessly pursued it in its
various manifestations. Taking the long view, Yetiv
notes the direction of the author's probing: "In his
introspective, long itinerary to comprehend his 'condition,' he systematically exhausted all possibilities:
his ego, his tribe, the Others; his being a colonized
man, his being a Jew. But the malaise is still there.
Something else must be penetrated, that transcends all
egoistic and ethnic distinctions: the nature of Man"
(43).
Memmi's inquiry attains universal proportions in his
next study, L'Homme dominé (Dominated Man, 1968), a
"sort of panorama of oppression" (44). The book is
inscribed with an epigraph from Ecclesiastes: "I considered all the oppressions that are done under the sun."
In this collection of fourteen essays, Memmi ponders the
specific nature of a variety of oppressions, sketching
the portraits of the black man in America, the French
Canadians, the Jew, the proletariat, woman, and the domes-
tic servant. "These various studies are the first steps

towards a major book on oppression, which I am always
planning, which I might never achieve, but toward which I
advance every day" (45), writes the author in his preface.   Indeed, the subject which he approaches is vast.
The portraits are only partial, as Memmi himself admits.
Whereas in previous books he used his own situation as a
starting point, in L'Homme dominé he departs from that
premise, venturing far beyond those areas that are properly within his domain.   In so doing, his lack of objectivity stands out all the more.   His study of women, for
example, in which he admits to being "on the wrong side
of the fence," is particularly biased and abrasive.
Flirting with his reader from behind the skirts of Simone
de Beauvoir, whom he cites as a feminist symbol but an
unfulfilled woman, he assumes the typical male chauvinist
position, defining woman's nature in terms of her biology
(46).   In so doing, he impugns his own credibility as a
dispassionate observer of impartial judgment.

In 1974, the year following the Yom Kippur war, Memmi
published Juifs et Arabes, classified by his publisher
under the rubric "diverse works."   The book offers a
fresh interpretation of the dispute between two oppressed
peoples.   Identifying himself as "an Arabian Jew and a
Left-wing Zionist," Memmi considers Jewish and Arab movements of national liberation, debunks popular myths, and
raises pertinent questions.   He is critical of contemporary Israel, in particular of the favored position it
accords religion within the state, but sees that Israel
has made better progress than her Arab neighbors with
respect to political democracy.   Like the essays, Juifs
et Arabes is a highly personal statement about delicate
issues.   Understandably, it elicits contrary reactions.

In 1979 Memmi produced yet another essay, La Dépendance, esquisse pour un portrait du dépendant (Dependence, sketch for a portrait of the dependent).   Opening
with the premise that everyone is in some way dependent,
the author goes on to develop the thesis that dependence
involves a tripartite relation: a dependent, a purveyor,
and an object of purveyance.

Conclusion: Writing as Passion for Life

Albert Memmi has earned a truly international reputation as a writer and political commentator.   While
removed physically from his native country, he remains

actively engaged in the concerns of his compatriots who
still make their home in the Maghreb. Like other writers, Memmi has sought liberation from specific constraints that check a human being's full development:
those of family, tradition, religion, and colonialism.
But he has not stopped there. His own inexorable drive
for reconciliation with the alienated self has taught him
that every person has the right to fundamental liberty
and that no group of persons is to be exploited for the
benefit of another. This goal is far from being realized
in our time, yet just by calling attention to the inequi-
ties that persist on every continent, Memmi signals man's
basic need to occupy a position of respect within the
community. Memmi's work is timely and it is rooted in
reality. The author holds no illusions about life, but
while he sees evidence of oppression everywhere, he is
not a dire pessimist, though some might think so.

Isaac Yetiv has observed that Memmi is "in a permanent
state of conflict with himself, trying in vain to sign an
'armistice' with himself, certain that a real peace [is]
not possible" (47). All of the author's writings may be
seen to spring from this fundamental restlessness with
his own situation, a situation at first experienced as
particular but whose universal nature eventually became
apparent to him. This inner state of disquiet, far from
being a yolk of despair, is for Memmi a vital stimula-
tion, a propulsive force that drives him to exercise his
creative powers to the limit. Along the via dolorosa
of existence, writing alone brings comfort, the metaphysical comfort of clarification and enlightenment that
enables him to go on from day to day. Memmi's personal
solution is a relentless probing and persistent willingness to understand one's own condition, to face oneself
honestly, and to value every other person's right to do
the same. It calls for continual evaluation and reevaluation; it calls for fearless investigation and the courage
to persevere even when no solution is in sight. Memmi's
inquiry into man's unhappy condition is a lifelong one
that promises a continued and steady literary output.
"It is not in tracing each one of my different colored
circles that I will approach closer to the center" (48),
notes Emile. Yet Memmi continues to trace these circles
with each succeeding work, for to do so is to live more
completely.

Chapter Six
Driss Chraïbi

In Search of the Authentic Self

One of the most controversial of the North African writers using the French language is the Moroccan novelist Driss Chraïbi. In an interview (1) he admitted to deliberately writing against the grain in order to unsettle the reader and to stir up awareness.

To strip away the mask in order to find the innermost authentic self, to actualize it, to live in harmony with oneself and others, these are the fundamental pursuits of Driss Chraïbi's oeuvre. Progressing from pure revolt to a permanent reevaluation and a desperate need to understand, this author's abundant work continues to generate interest and even debate. Whether treating matters peculiar to North Africa or themes of a more universal nature, the problems that he poses in his fiction remain, demanding fresh answers from a new generation.

Biographical Notes (2)

Driss Chraïbi was born on 15 July 1926 (3) at El Jadida (formerly Mazagan), Morocco. As a youngster he attended a Muslim religious school, then at the age of ten entered a French school. He pursued secondary studies at the Lycée Lyautey in Casablanca, where he was one of two Moroccan students among fifteen hundred French. He began to write in order to prove that he was capable of writing in French. He composed poetry and even won a prize for it. He read a variety of authors—French, British, American (notably Caldwell and Faulkner)—before discovering a wealth of Arab and black African literature. In 1945 Chraïbi left Morocco for Paris to study chemistry, obtaining a diploma in chemical engineering in 1950. He then turned to the study of neuropsychiatry. His background in both these scientific areas is much in evidence in his novels (4). Only two months short of earning a Doctor of Science degree, Chraïbi dropped out of school, under the pretext that science leads men to disavow the spiritual dimension of life. Exchanging formal studies for experiential learning, he traveled throughout Western Europe, a sort of vagabond in search of the meaning of existence, of freedom, and of justice. He held a variety of part-time jobs: chemical engineer, journalist, photographer, laborer, teacher, to name a few. As an existential experiment, he lived in Israel for two years under an assumed Jewish name, later publishing reports of his experience in French and Arab periodicals. In 1947 Chraïbi settled permanently in France. He lives in a suburb of Paris and works for the French National Radio and Television Broadcasting System (l'O.R.T.F.) as a writer and producer. By means of interviews and reports aired by the media, he has tried to promote an understanding between the West and the Arab world. Chraibi is married to a French woman and has five children. In 1970 he was a guest lecturer at the University of Laval in Quebec, Canada, where he spoke on North African literature.

Chraibi's work consists of nine novels and a collection of short stories, all, with the exception of the last novel, published by the Paris firm of Denoël from 1954 to 1981. The last novel was published by Seuil. He has also written screenplays and has adapted works of fiction for French National Television. He contributes articles to periodicals in Morocco and France.

Chraïbi's Fiction

Le Passé simple (The simple past, 1954), Chraibi's first novel and the book for which he is best known, is a volatile work. Composed when he was only in his mid-twenties, it violently denounces in one fell swoop ancestral traditions, Islam, and French colonialism. In the preface to his third novel, L'Ane (1956), he speaks about his first novel: "The hero's name is Driss Ferdi. He is perhaps me. In any case his despair is mine. Despair of faith. This Islam in which he believed, which spoke of equality of reigns, of the gift of God in each individual of creation, of tolerance, of liberty, of love, he saw it, ardent adolescent formed in French schools, reduced to Pharisaism, a social system and propaganda arm. Everything considered he embarked for France: he needed to believe, to love, to respect someone or something" (5).

The novel's hero and narrator, Driss Ferdi, the
nineteen-year-old son of a bourgeois family, seethes with
loathing for the abuses he sees manifested all around
him, in society and in the home. He blames Islam and
focuses his hatred on his father, a rich tea merchant,
who is the crystallization of the hypocritical faith.
The father is a sanctimonious egotist and a despot. He
is depicted as brutal, tyrannical, unscrupulous in business, and given to enforcing the letter of the law while
secretly satisfying his carnal lust. A nerve-racking
tension grips his household, whose members move about
paralyzed by a respectful hatred of their master. The
father's hardness has reduced his wife to the rank of an
object, a receptacle for child bearing. She, in turn,
incarnates ignorance, resignation, and superstition,
rooted more in popular belief than in Islam. Driss
pities her, and hates his father and tradition for having
made of her no more than a "pregnancy chamber" (6).
Father and son are animated by a conflict of mutual
hatred. The elder Ferdi, jealous of his son's learning
and threatened by his revolt against the bond of patriarchal tyranny, blames his rebellion on French schooling,
which he feels poisons the young. He furthermore accuses
his son of having inspired revolt in the mother, leading
ultimately to her act of suicide. Driss temporarily
moves out of his home. When he returns he finds his
father a changed man, still sly and cautious yet ready to
accept his prodigal son as a partner in his business.
Human qualities begin to emerge in him and Driss starts
to comprehend that his father too is a victim of his
formation. This metamorphosis, as the critic Isaac Yetiv
points out, is surprising and not sufficiently prepared
in the novel (7). Driss plays a game of psychological
warfare with his father, threatening the latter's life.
The elder Ferdi, perhaps out of frightened respect for
this offspring whom he can no longer dominate, agrees to
subsidize his sojourn to France. Driss interiorly
rejoices in his apparent victory, affirming that only
when he has triumphed, only when he has obtained a
diploma and a position and when his father offers him his
fortune, only then will he revolt.

Though the author has denied that Le Passé simple
is autobiographical, it certainly expresses the state of
Driss Chraibi's soul during his early years. For
Chraibi this novel is a kind of exorcism, a demystifica-
tion of the past and a means by which he was able to

release pent-up feelings of rage. Chraïbi had, after
all, left Morocco in 1945. The book was finished in
1953. It thus took him eight years to work out his
repressed fury. In Le Passé simple he expresses the
feelings of suffocation imposed by Muslim tradition and
religion: "By the dogma, for the dogma, in the dogma. I
kept quiet, extinguished myself, followed the Straight
and Narrow" (8). His repressed irritation and resentment, for so long carefully controlled and guarded, finally erupted in a violent burst of wrath.

The novel was a succès de scandale. Published at
the height of the French-Moroccan crisis, it had the
effect in Morocco of an exploding terrorist's bomb. It
is a violent revolt against the sclerotic Moroccan way of
thinking and acting, and it is insulting to the most
revered of figures in any household, the father. It
opened a caustic polemic that labeled the book "a tissue
of lies and a bad action" (9), one that assassinated the
hopes of the young generation of Moroccans. It is totally pessimistic and makes the whole of society appear
tainted. Isaac Yetif, setting the work in the context of
the author's evolution as a cultural hybrid, offers
valuable insights into the psychological impetus con-
tributing to and resulting from the novel: "The pseudo-
epic symbolism of the situation, rather maladroit, in a
novel of realist intention, but which passion pushes to
melodrama, escaped Chraïbi's readers. It is in effect
his individual drama that Chraïbi wanted to express and
he gratuitously extrapolated it in the dimensions of the
group. The father is the scapegoat, burdened with all
the evils of the son which are undoubtedly real" (10).
The novel, he further suggests, functions as a psychological device by which the adolescent transfers his guilt to
an expiatory victim, the father.

At first Chraïbi responded vehemently to the accusations made against him, but with the passage of time,
after rethinking his position and after observing that
the foreign press used the work to criticise Morocco, he
did a complete about-face. In a letter of self-criticism
written to the director of the Moroccan nationalist daily
newspaper Démocratie on 28 January 1957, he profoundly
humbled himself and disowned the novel, pleading that he
was not unpatriotic and not a traitor. The prodigal son,
having repented, was accepted back into the flock and was
apprised of his faults. It was not that the abuses that
he signaled were not true, for indeed they were. His

error lay in that he had shouted them to the world. Le
Passé simple had served the cause of the imperialists,
of those who hoped to crush the country by killing her
hope. The book and Chraibi's earlier defense of his
position printed in the newspapers served the antination-
alist cause. Years later Chraibi would come to regret
having repudiated his novel.

In Le Passé simple Chraibi shows himself to be a
talented and gifted writer, though certainly not without
faults. Jean Déjeux aptly describes the manner and
style of the novel as "jerky, abrupt, a style of in-
fighting where one wants by sadomasochism to hurt oneself
and to hurt others, with trenchant sentences, locker room
vocabulary, and very crude images (odors, defecation,
visceral or glandular trickling)" (11). All of this is
deliberate and for a purpose. The chopped sentences and
breathless pace suggest spontaneity and violence. The
narrative spurts and gushes, carried along on a wave of
biting sarcasm and turbulence. The mutilation of French
syntax is in itself a sign of anger and hatred. Dislo-
cating the language of the other constitutes an act of
vengeance against the French acculturation process.
Chraibi seeks to be outrageous and obscene, with scenes
of sadistic eroticism and homosexuality. He tries to
shock by whatever means possible, hence the morbid
delight in offending the visual and olfactory senses, the
repeated allusions to spitting, urinating, breaking wind,
masturbating, and ejaculating sperm. The vocabulary is a
curious mixture of foul language and technical terms
drawn from the lexicon of medicine and physical chemistry, which Isaac Yetiv rightly deems pedantic, "and in
its quest for dramatic effects, almost always useless and
encumbering" (12). Indeed, the frequent use of scho-
lastic expressions and metaphors drawn from biology,
physics, and mathematics betrays Chraibi's difficulty as
a newcomer to the field of literature in handling language. The incongruity of many of his combinations is
all too striking.

With every page Chraibi attempts to jolt the reader,
hammering away at his theme, virtually screaming his
rage. However, it must be pointed out that the extremes
to which the author goes have the effect of making the
whole appear to be a caricature of reality. One of
Chraibi's compatriots, Ahmed Sefrioui, reproached him
for this in an article printed in Démocratie: "I sin-
cerely wondered if Chraibi had known Morocco and the

Moroccans. His book leads one to suppose the opposite"
(13). Certainly some of the situations depicted are
lacking in verisimilitude, as Yetiv points out (14). On
the other hand, the religious practices described by
Chraibi, which do correspond to actual practices, such
as the brutal circumcision, are so ridiculous and outrageous that to the uninitiated they seem unreal (15).

Abdellatif Laâbi says that "Chraibi is probably the
only Maghrebian and Arab author who had the courage to
set a whole people before its cowardice, who displayed
before it its immobility, the motives of its hypocrisy,
of that self-colonization and oppression exerted one on
another . . ." (16). Chraibi's compatriots hated him
supposedly for having so well translated the world of
reality into the world of fiction. Others, more de-
tached, believe that the world depicted in Le Passé
simple is purely a subjective one, a vehicle in which
the author pushes his revolt to the brink of absurdity.
Whichever camp one sides with, this work, by the vigor
with which it names abuses and exposes an unhealthy
milieu, marks an important reference point in the history
of Maghrebian literature in French.

"In France, country of liberty and of fraternity,
above all country of refuge, he [Ferdi] is present at the
slow decrystallization of his own brothers in misery"
(17). This statement, from the preface of L'Ane, sum-
marizes the subject of Chraibi's second novel, Les
Boucs (The goats, 1955). The story relates the experience of one Yalann Waldik (the name in Arabic signifies
"may your father be cursed"), an intellectual who has
gone to France filled with the hope of realizing his
dream of liberty, fraternity, and equality, only to find
that the promises for which he yearns exist solely in
textbooks and in his imagination. (As a precaution,
perhaps, Chraibi took care to make the hero of this
novel and his associates Kabylians from Algeria, not
Moroccans.) Les Boucs traces the gradual disintegration of the hero and of his companions, a group of uneducated laborers stigmatized with the derogatory label
"goats" (a term akin to our American appellation "spic").
Treated as pariahs, this band of men is destined to be
crushed in the vise of French racial prejudice. While in
Le Passé simple Chraibi directs his hatred toward his
own people and culture, in Les Boucs his aim is to
illustrate French intolerance and deceit.

Les Boucs is less a novel than a scathing diatribe

launched against official French hypocrisy. The attack,
however, misses its target. Outside of a few token characters, the French people are noticeably absent from this
novel. The North Africans remain a closed group, a collective singular that does not mingle with others. Les
Boucs, with Waldik as spokesman, purports to translate
the misery of the entire race of victimized "Norafs"
(Nord Africains) condemned to a living death in France.
In fact, however, the hero is such a narcissistic fellow
and so dissimilar from his compatriots that what we hear
is a single voice, as in Le Passé simple, of a being
giving vent to his mutilated and anguished self, a thinly
veiled Chraibi whose lecturing voice emerges indiscreet-
ly in his fiction. All too frequently his is the voice
of the philosophizing essayist.

As a work of fiction, Les Boucs is disappointing.
The reader senses that it is not really a novel at all
but a castigating discourse relentlessly spewing forth
the envenomed état d'âme of its pained author, who
wants to expose the "open wound," the "gaping sore," the
"abscess" that is his very being. Les Boucs is
Chraibi's work of atonement. This word (rachat in
French) recurs periodically in the narration. Waldik is
writing a book, and through him Chraibi explains the
inner propulsion that guides his own composition, the
desire to buy back the honor of his compatriots: "I had
not to redeem myself individually with respect to the
society in which I lived in order to have the right to
its sympathy, but to redeem North Africans. To suffer
for them in my dignity as a man in my human flesh.
That's what I did for five years. Then translate that in
a sort of testimony, not of my senses but of my sufferings" (18).

While in his earlier years Chraibi was unequivocal in
his condemnations, the testimony that he gives in his
preface to L'Ane (The donkey, 1956), his third novel,
illustrates a change of heart: "To choose? I have already chosen but I would so much like not to have to do
it anymore. If I have chosen to live in France . . . I
continue to participate in that world of my childhood and
in that Islam in which I believe more and more" (19).

Indeed, L'Ane retains the full flavor of Chraibi's
North African Muslim heritage. Completed on the eve of
Moroccan independence, the tone of this text is entirely
different from that of the author's preceding works.
Revolt gives way to bitterness, disappointment, and dis-

tress as Chraïbi realizes that nationalist liberation
does not automatically make better human beings of its
citizens, nor does it morally and spiritually transform a
country. L'Ane, an extended metaphor in five parts, is
a plea for men to interrupt the thoughtless, mechanically
performed daily chores that have lulled their brains and
to reflect carefully on the meaning of existence, both on
the individual and the collective level.

To summarize briefly, the hero, Moussa, a simple
country barber, gradually comes to understand that one
must be more than a spectator and a witness to life; one
must fully participate in it. As the country moves into
a new era, "everything has to be reconsidered, everything
has to be remade, values, ideals and morals" (20).
Moussa undergoes a transformation and, as a self-styled
prophet, endeavors to open the eyes of the people.
Chraïbi uses him to express his own hope for a better
world. Moussa makes an appeal to the local blacksmith,
but this proud worker, symbol of the capitalists and the
proletariat, talks only of finding a system "that can
utilize without useless waste this work capital that men
represent, which kills the individual at the profit of
the community . . ." (21). Though deep down he is cognizant of having labored all his life without having fulfilled certain duties toward his fellowman, he drowns out
this inner voice and finishes by kicking Moussa out of
his workshop.

The final chapter of the book is both a lament and an
indictment reiterating ideas expressed earlier. The
people ought to face life but cannot bear looking within
themselves. (This theme runs through all of Chraïbi's
fiction.) The story concludes with an ironic note. Not
wanting to be derided by an uneducated madman, the crowd
burns Moussa to death, then prepares to erect a handsome
mausoleum to keep him always with them.

Both in content and in style, L'Ane contains the
germ of the two Chraïbi works that follow, De tous les
horizons (From all horizons, 1958), a collection of six
short stories, and La Foule (The crowd, 1961), a novel
of humorous satire. Chraïbi's didactic bent remains as
pronounced as ever, though it is far more palatable in
its satiric vein. The author's narrative technique
becomes more refined with each succeeding effort, yet the
individual moralizing voice remains. At this stage in
his development, Chraïbi is preoccupied with the following key ideas: (1) man goes through life without think-

ing, filling his hours with trivia, which amounts to a
deliberate evasion and a form of cowardice by which he
avoids discovering his own being and his purpose in life;
(2) man lives for a future that exists only in his imagination, and thus forever avoids truly actualizing his
being in the only time span in which it is possible to
accomplish anything, the present; (3) man takes the line
of least resistance and allows himself to be exploited;
(4) all peoples of the earth have the same needs and need
each other, but they create false problems that set them
at odds.   These are the idées clés around which the
whole of Chraibi's oeuvre centers.

The stories of De tous les horizons are of the
conte-témoignage ("witness-bearing") genre.   Each
conveys a moral, which is reenforced by philosophical
remarks, attributed to Chraibi's father and collected
by the author, that precede each story and close the
book.

Each story features as its main protagonist one of the
exploited peoples of the earth, Arabs, a black man, and a
Jew, to illustrate that all have the same problems and
want the same things: "liberty, belief, happiness, a
meaning in life, hope" (22).   With this thought the
volume opens.   The stories bear witness to a lamentable
situation in which human beings are victims.   These alienated persons serve as a "living reproach, but also as
the spokesmen of another desirable universe of which they
are the outcast heirs" (23).

These stories are well-written, and their message is a
worthy one.   But Chraibi succumbs to the very temptation
that Dib so ardently sought to avoid: repetition of the
same message through a conventional format—the realistic
depiction of a reality à la Balzac.   For while Chraibi
has gained mastery over his craft as a storyteller, he
has failed to renew the literary form of his expression.
His next work is therefore a welcome change.

In La Foule, revolt, drama, and passion are transposed to the ironic.   The fundamental themes of L'Ane
and De tous les horizons, therein related as solemn parables, are restated in the form of a burlesque, a farce
which is no less a parable.   What is suggested here is
the atmosphere of the music hall where all are invited to
laugh heartily.   Gross exaggeration, for which Chraibi
was faulted in his first two novels, is the principal
device that makes La Foule an amusing though bitter-
sweet comedy.   It is the device à la Ubu Roi through

which men are invited to see the folly of their unthinking existence.

North Africa and her specific concerns are totally
absent from this novel, which is set in France. The moral conveyed here is of universal application. By circumstances unknown to him, the hero, one Octave Mathurin, a
timid, Catholic, sexagenarian, former school teacher, has
been elevated to the position of head of state. Described in the novel as a spinach-eating Popeye who seeks
only to live in unbothered comfort, he is "without an
ideal and without a soul" (24), a sharp criticism directed at the leaders of Western governments. His authority
is supported by the crowd, "that amorphous and floating
mass made of average hearts and brains, indifferent to
events and to all that went beyond the framework of the
daily and material cares of existence" (25). La Foule
attacks corrupt politicians, unproductive figurehead governments, today's manipulative marketing system whose
exploitive tactics can lead the people to consume any and
every product, and the indifference of the mindless mass
of humanity caught up in its petty concerns. Society is
an anonymous "heap of unconsciences" (26) which does not
participate in the making of history but merely contents
itself with reading about events after the fact.

Mathurin's downfall is brought about by two black men
from Africa, who manage to buy off the man responsible
for the marketing and packaging of heads of state, and
everything else in society. (The effects of today's
market-programmed society will be more fully developed in
a later novel, Un Ami viendra vous voir.)

The message conveyed in La Foule is every bit a
serious as that of Chraïbi's preceding works, but
couched in the form of humorous caricature, the lesson
conveys itself the more readily. It is in this vein that
Chraïbi's works have their greatest appeal, and retain a
freshness and universality that make them as valid in
today's world as they were twenty years ago.

Chraïbi's eternal quest for the absolute is pursued
once again in his next novel, Succession ouverte (Heirs
to the Past, 1962). The novel is a continuation of Le
Passé simple, with some noticeable alterations. After
sixteen years of self-exile in France, Driss Ferdi makes
a trip to his native Morocco to attend the funeral of his
father. This is no longer the rebellious youth, but the
confused and somewhat defeated adult, tired of running
after ideas and worn out in his search to find a purpose

for existence. In returning to his roots, Driss wonders
if perhaps there he will find an answer to his unfulfilled self. He has married a French woman, has two
children, and has successfully assimilated himself to his
adopted culture, but he is uneasy. Civilization has not
provided him with the key to a satisfying life. Nor, it
is emphasized, has it done much for the Europeans, for
they are content with mere survival as they go through
life, unthinking beings, "drowned in the torment of their
own existence" (27).

In his homeland Driss sees that the independence of
Morocco has not ameliorated the condition of the ordinary
citizen. Unemployment, poverty, a defeated people that
has lost all but the remnants of human dignity as it
moves through its slums, this is the sight with which he
comes face to face. The status of woman remains un-
changed. She is still a slave of cultural bondage, a
mere object and function. Driss sees that on both sides
of the Mediterranean there is an air of hopelessness
accompanied by the sad awareness that one must nevertheless go on.

The father, now depicted as a beneficent soul who used
his power and money to keep the villagers employed in a
variety of business enterprises of which he was the pro-
prietor, has tape recorded his will, which the family
gathers to hear. Driss's inheritance consists of a hope-
inspiring message: "Dig a well and descend in search of
water. Light isn't at the surface, it's at the bottom,
all the way at the bottom. Everywhere, wherever you are,
even in the desert, you will always find water. It is
sufficient to dig" (28). This is the legacy that Driss
carries back with him to France. This is the open succession. Each person must make his own way; his inheritance
is within him.

Succession ouverte bears witness to the failure of
both Western and Oriental society to satisfy man's
deepest metaphysical needs. As a literary work, this
novel, while well written, is in the same realistic vein
as Chraibi's earlier fiction. It stands as a sort of
progress report on the material, moral, and spiritual
condition of Moroccans in their independent state, while
it emphasizes the need for individual initiative to bring
about effective change. It is a sad lament that nevertheless closes on a note of hope, urging its readers to
pursue life rather than fall into despondency.

In his next novel, Un Ami viendra vous voir (A

friend will come to see you, 1967), Chraïbi departs
entirely from North African themes to dwell on problems
of universal concern: the meaning of existence and the
source of true happiness in a society where the individual's self-concept is forged by exterior forces, in this
case, the media and the marketplace. This is a fundamental consideration, one which the author has examined
in previous works and for which he continues to search
for a satisfying answer. In fact, this is but a transpo-
sition of an earlier problem faced by the colonized North
African who was coerced into living according to the
image that the colonizer imposed. Chraïbi attempts to
show that Western man is no less subject to a similar
kind of pressure, always trying to live up to concepts
presented from exterior sources rather than forging his
own being from within.

Un Ami viendra vous voir is set in France. Its heroine, Ruth Anderet, is presented as the epitome of ideal
modern womanhood: happily married to a wealthy professional, liberated, intelligent, employed in a successful
career, and surrounded with the material goods that make
life easy. Chraïbi deliberately exaggerates her perfec-
tion and her happiness to emphasize that beneath the
veneer of a seemingly quintessential existence there
lurks a growing malaise, which Ruth describes as "the
passion to want to understand, in order to finally be
myself" (29). Ruth volunteers to be the feature subject
of analysis for a weekly television program, "A Friend
Will Come to See You," on which she is to explain to her
audience the source of her happiness. This half of the
book, a veritable tour de force, succeeds brilliantly in
exposing the cheap tricks and the idiocy of commercial
television, an industry which Chraïbi knows from the
inside. Here the author effectively attacks the exploitive marketing techniques directed at contemporary
consumer society and forces the reader to see through the
hoax that is being perpetrated in the name of happiness
and success. Gradually Ruth comes to realize how unhappy
she truly is. She sees that the modern world has
translated her existence in economic terms and values her
only for her purchasing power. Utterly devastated, she
has a breakdown, kills her two-year-old son without knowing why, and is subsequently confined to an asylum.

The second half of the novel, which lacks the incisive-
ness of what preceded, is taken up with the psychiatrist's role in curing Ruth. Dr. Daniels, who is

determined to heal his patient, is being torn between his
professional self and his true being. His dilemma is
similar to Ruth's. Ruth finally perceives the source of
her unhappiness: all her life she was pressured into
trying to live up to the goals that others—parents,
teachers, employers, her husband, media publicity—had
for her: "It was a constraint at every instant, for
years. It was necessary that I respond to that image,
that I be that function" (30). Always she tried to be
"that woman, that those people expected" (31). Thus a
state of anarchy persisted within her as she attempted to
suppress her real self in order to adopt the image that
others deemed appropriate and desirable (like the alienation wrought in the colonized who spent their lives
striving for assimilation). This prefabricated self is
the source of torment because it thwarts the harmonious
entity of body and soul, leading an individual to be
treated in terms of object or function. One must free
oneself to be able to relate authentically to others. In
Ruth's discovery lies the cure for her alienated being
and that of the doctor as well.

We have noted Chraibi's denunciation of the Muslim
code that treats woman as an object and considers her
only in terms of a function. In this novel Chraibi
reveals that Western society, which North African countries try to emulate, does the same to male and female
alike, although on a different plane, programming their
tastes, attitudes, and comportment through sophisticated
means of manipulation. The result is a feeling of alienation. Yet, while Chraibi correctly states the need for
people to be their genuine selves, a concept which he
never makes clear, and to communicate fully with each
other, lamentably he reduces successful communication to
erotic love. It is in the spontaneous sexual encounter
between doctor and patient that both find the solution to
their anguished existence. This is unfortunate for it
merely reenforces the notion that individual transcen-
dence and dialogue between a man and a woman are achieved
through sexual union. The edifice which Charibi wishes
to erect is thus destroyed by the very form in which it
is cast. Writing in Les Nouvelles Littéraires, R.-M.
Albérès applauds the novel for being "clear, direct,
brutal (like Who's Afraid of Virginia Woolf?)," but
finds that "this conclusion smells of rose water and
bitters" (32).

The inferior status of woman in today's world and the

need to restore her to a position of equality in which
she actively participates in the shaping of society is
the subject of Chraïbi's next novel, La Civilisation, ma
mère (Civilization, my mother, 1972). This work traces
the evolution of a bourgeois Moroccan family in Casablanca from 1930 until national independence, but in a
manner totally different from that of Le Passé simple
and Succession ouverte. In this case the central
figure is the mother, the motivating passion is filial
and fraternal love, and the impulse that moves the action
forward is an insatiable thirst for genuine personal
growth. The novel begins in a realistic vein. It
depicts the typical bourgeois Moroccan housewife of the
thirties, ignorant, entirely devoted to her children, her
husband, and her housework, isolated from the outside
world, and totally resigned to her condition. Her husband provides for all her needs and treats her with kind
indifference. She in turn tends to her family's needs,
making her life correspond to what others expect of her.
The action progresses in the form of an ever-broadening
spiral, which crescendos and accelerates in tempo as the
story proceeds. Written in a playful and tender tone, the
first half of the novel focuses on the changes brought
about by the introduction of modern technical inventions
into the home—electricity, radio, telephone—and describes the mother's manner of adjusting her existence to
each of them. Her two sons, students at a French school,
are delighted to aid and abet the course of progress.
They buy Western clothes for their mother, take her on
outings, teach her to read. In sum, they open to her the
outside world and a new concept of herself. They lead
her to see her independent personhood. Self-liberation
does not solve her problem of solitude, however. Liberty,
she discovers, is a condition that permits authentic
action.

The second half of the novel, which is quite improba-
ble, translates with verve and amusement the total transformation of this simple peasant into an educated woman
of the world who makes her voice heard in the political
arena and who crusades for female liberation. She
becomes totally involved in other people and the environment, dumbfounding her husband, whose narrow scope of
concern is confined to his own business affairs. The
mother's awakening and evolution are of course symbolic,
signifying the destiny of the Third World. She represents "the conscience of an unconscious world" (33).

Chraibi correctly affirms that the status of women in a given country is indicative of the state of progress in that country. In what is tantamount to an open indictment of Muslim and Third World countries in general, he rejects societies that keep their women veiled and enclosed and that impede them from carrying on an active role in society.

And the nucleus of the commune is the family. If in the bosom of this family the woman is held prisoner, and what is more, veiled, sequestered as we have seen for centuries, if she has no opening on the outside world, no active role whatsoever, society as a whole feels the effects of it on itself and no longer has anything to bring either to her or to the rest of the world. She becomes incapable of living, exactly as those old family enterprises that crumble on the stock exchange at the merest public offering for sale. (34)

Significantly, the mother of this novel buries religion, which for the Muslim implies not just worship of a deity but a social and political way of life as well, and pushes back her horizon by going in search of the Western world.

La Civilisation is both amusing and didactic. In its Moroccan setting the exaggerated happenings that it depicts are a pleasant fantasy that invites us to laugh, while the truths it conveys bear a strong reminder of the immediate feminist progressive present. Though not unusual in its style, by its content this novel marks a definite victory for the cause of the liberation of woman. In this sense it is truly engagé.

With his next novel, La Mort au Canada (Death in Canada, 1975), Chraibi again passes into the orbit of French writers. He is no longer a "Moroccan francophone author," he is simply "a writer."

In tempo with contemporary "free" society of the seventies, the characters of this work find marriage passé and prefer nonbinding relationships, which nevertheless constrain. Casting off responsibilities and painful memories, it is on the level of the purely sensual that the protagonists attempt to heal their complexes and find the fullness of being. The individual's greatest fear is to be treated as an object and to feel empty, to fail in constructing his own happiness. Chraibi depicts his hero in a furious "pursuit of life" that, however, results in only temporary havens of satisfaction.

From the beginning the reader notes the subtle web that gradually entraps the leading figures in this story, Patrik Pierson, who has abandoned family and career in search of new horizons, and his lover, the gifted psychiatrist Maryvonne. The passion in which both greedily seek full self-realization fails to satisfy.

More than one possible conclusion may be drawn from the example of this couple. At first glance the moral seems to be that perfect relationships between imperfect human beings are an impossibility; it is folly to expect another person to supply one with a sense of personal fulfillment. Additionally, the vacuousness of the protagonists and their failure to pursue life beyond its sensual dimensions may serve as a judgment of contemporary society that has severed itself from the spiritual side of being. But perhaps Chraibi would have us understand more.

In the novel Maryvonne clearly occupies the stronger position in the uneasy relationship, while Patrik tries to live up to the image of the ideal virile male, and in so doing mutilates his personality. Here we have a reversal of the roles generally assigned to the sexes. The woman, traditionally a victim of subjection, assumes the position of dominance in the male/female alliance. This is a phenomenon that has surfaced in the last decade. Chraibi's novels up to now show that whenever one partner takes ascendancy over the other, no genuine sharing is possible; no mutually satisfying accord can be reached. When one person's existence is reduced to a mere striving to live up to the image set forth by someone else, he will be torn in the very center of his being.

Chraibi does make his point, but in a manner that is not without compromise. <u>Mort au Canada</u> is an attempt to probe human needs and human shallowness through a study of the couple. The body, erotic love, freedom to be, to have, and to do, a spontaneous rapport with nature and with others, these form the core of the novel. Chraibi uses these examples to point out their failure to respond to the individual's deepest aspirations. But whereas in the earlier novels the author's intent was clear, in this case the meaning is obscure. Chraibi makes ample use of those elements—banal conversation, melodrama, eroticism—which he holds up to criticism, but in such a way as to play into the hands of the accomplice reading audience that feeds on this very brand of cheap romanticism. The author's purpose may be clear to the

discriminating reader, but a less discerning individual
could easily misconstrue his purpose (35).

Chraïbi's most recent novel, Une enquête au pays
(An inquiry in the country), published by Seuil in 1981,
is set in his native Morocco. The author describes his
peaceful native village that is suddenly thrown into dis-
ruption when two inspectors from the Royal Moroccan
Police come to ferret out opponents to the current
regime. These "pseudo-civilized" intruders, as Chraïbi
calls them, are presented with great brio in a gross
caricature clearly meant to mock the robotlike native
administrators who behave like left-over colonialists.
The author makes full use of plays on words, juggling
French slang, Arab, Berber, and English in side-splitting
dialogues. But all is not presented in such a light
vein. Reflecting on the sufferings of his country's
past, on its unfulfilled hopes, and on what it is to
become, Chraïbi's conclusion is somber. The novel successfully translates the genuine concern of a Moroccan
for his homeland. For it Driss Chraïbi received the
French-Arab Friendship Prize the year of its publication.

Conclusion: Toward Universal Themes

In the words of Driss Chraïbi we observe a revealing
evolution of thought. The young author who was torn
apart by abuses of his native land has grown to understand that the people of the Third World, in elevating
their status through the adoption of Western civilization, run the risk of taking on an equally perplexing set
of problems. In fact, he concludes, all of humankind is
beset by the same problems. All need to identify their
purpose in life, need to reject false values and vacuous
role playing, and must learn to live harmoniously with
themselves and with others.

Chraïbi has come to view life and its problems in
their universal dimensions. Not all critics agree with
this approach. Abdelkébir Khatibi, for example, considers Chraïbi a deserter who has unjustifiably abandoned his native land and its interests:

In a sense, this exile is indefensible on the national
level. If the independence aborted and constituted
principally a substitution of the colonial regime by
the regime of a bourgeoisie and of a feudal system as

Chraibi explicitly states in his novel [Succession ouverte], it is fitting to specify that the fight remains to be led in the very interior of the country. The political unrealism of this very talented novelist is flagrant. In order to understand Chraibi, we must say that his attitude is not based on an objective analysis of the historical and political situation of his country; it is essentially psychological, in this sense that his unrootedness is too great to be able to reconcile itself with his own society. (36)

Such strong judgment seems unduly harsh. To imply that a North African writer must dedicate himself exclusively to problems peculiar to his own milieu, and that because he was a victim of colonization he must forever speak out on this matter, is to limit him to the role of a functionary. Chraibi has turned to universal themes, still seeing in them an expression of his original "revolt against the father," that is, any overbearing force under whatever guise that curtails personal liberty and the growth of the whole person. Periodically he does return to the specific concerns of his homeland. But we must keep in mind that, regardless of the geographic setting, for Chraïbi alienation and authentic liberation of the self are the topics around which his interest centers, topics that he explores through a study of individual cases that imply the whole of society. Some readers try to sympathize with Chraibi's views, to understand him, but they regret the direction he has taken. They see in it a desertion. They see Un ami viendra vous voir and Mort au Canada as an abortion, the suicide of colonial literature. Une enquête au pays will perhaps prompt them to alter their views. As for Chraïbi, he is content to awaken consciences and provoke thought. He sees a mission to be accomplished; he would have all individuals, regardless of ethnic background or national origin, tear away their masks and reflect openly and honestly on life so as to be able to live it more fully.

Chapter Seven
Women of the Maghreb in Life and Fiction

From the male-authored works we have studied thus far, there emerges a composite picture of the North African woman as a subjugated being twice alienated. Since a family's honor rests in a specific way on the protection of its female members from sexual dishonor, every stage of a woman's life is governed by restrictive laws and customs. As we have seen, essentially a woman is a household utensil for childbearing, childrearing, and housekeeping. At the same time, she is a pawn in property and power relations of the families to which she is attached by consanguinity and marriage. Once married, her prestige and the economic stability of her household depend on her capacity to bear many children, especially sons. Her failure to assume this function brings contempt, dishonor, and even divorce, since it is always the woman who is accused of sterility. For the most part the North African woman is illiterate and superstitious, nevertheless she is resourceful and tenacious in the face of great difficulties. Whatever her inner propulsions, her responses are governed by a strict unwritten code of tradition. Her forbearance and conniving spring from her determination to assert the little authority that is hers according to accepted norms and from her fear of repudiation and consequent destitution. Divorced, widowed, or abandoned, an aura of shame and humiliation attaches to her and her future is bleak. If she has no family members to support her, she will be forced to work, occasioning further loss of self-esteem in the eyes of the community. Whatever the circumstances of her existence, she is clearly relegated to a position of inferiority and effaced within society. Few male writers deviate from this portrait. Kateb Yacine sees woman as a demonic force, powerful yet silent. Only Dib and Chraibi, in their later periods, give evidence of seeing in woman's liberation the key to their own authentic personhood. Even here, Dib couches her emancipation in esoteric quasi-

mystical terms, limiting her movements to a dream world
where she circulates under the veil of hermetic poetry.
Chraibi alone comes closest to rooting her liberation in
the reality of the everyday world. The role of woman in
contemporary Muslim North Africa deserves to be probed
more fully so as not to confuse the female's image in fiction with her reality. We shall consider briefly her
situation in its sociological-historical-cultural context
(1).

While the Koran upholds the equality of men and women
in the sight of God, the sharia, the man-made code of
Islamic law based on an interpretation of the Prophet's
teachings, spells out woman's subordinate nature and
inferior status. The notion of "natural" inferiority has
been impressed upon her for centuries so that she has
easily come to accept this male conception of her as
congenital, eternal, and immutable truth. This has hardly encouraged self-transformation. Traditionally formal
education for girls has largely been considered unneces-
sary; what instruction they did receive was, and often
still is, considered a preparation for marriage and childrearing. School attendance in all three former French
territories is only nominally compulsory for children
between the ages of seven and thirteen. In rural areas
girls are withdrawn from school at an early age in order
to be able to engage in agricultural work. In metropolitan centers girls have fared somewhat better (in Tunisia
much more so than in Algeria or Morocco), occupying more
places in the universities, but very few key positions in
government. Educated women who do work are largely
restricted to positions as primary school teachers,
nurses, or secretaries employed by the civil service.
The psychological forces at work here are profound and
far-reaching. Schooling has a modernizing effect on
girls, and helps them to achieve new self-concepts and
aspirations. Male-dominated Muslim society prefers to
keep women from understanding the world, or from realizing their capacities or opportunities. Even today the
majority of girls are withdrawn from school at puberty,
not only to protect their "honor" physically and to avoid
local disapprobation that would condemn them as unfit
wives, but also to guard them from psychological contami-
nation. In order that a husband be better able to manage
his wife, it is best that she not know too much about
life. Certainly she should not be allowed to see that
there are alternatives to the type of existence that

tradition dictates for her. Social pressure makes it
clear to woman that marriage is the only desirable position in life. While preteenage marriages are proscribed,
it is customary to arrange for a girl's marriage at a
very early age. This flows from the parents' fear that
their daughter may be deflowered before marriage, thereby
dishonoring the family and destroying any chance of marry-
ing her off. Every precaution is taken to assure virgini-
ty, which is intrinsically valuable, to be passed on to
its proper owner, the husband. Custom dictates that at
the time the marriage contract is signed the male pay a
certain sum of money. In the case of divorce this money
is to pass to the woman. This device is thus intended to
protect the woman and discourage divorce. However, it
has acquired the taint of money; it puts a price on a
woman and makes of her a "thing" to be bargained for in a
commercial transaction.

In Muslim society women are trained to obey, and in so
     Except for women constrained by circumstances to work
as head of household, the female is seen as a minor in
need of permanent guardianship. At marriage she passes
from the authority of the father or brother to that of
the husband and/or mother-in-law. Later on in life,
should her husband die or abandon her, she would be
subject to an uncle or to her own son if he had reached
his majority. The notion of the "couple," as it is known
in Europe and other Western countries, is rare. The
notion of a mutually fulfilling physical/emotional/
intellectual relationship, of mutual enjoyment and genuine rapport is almost unheard of. Rather, both parties
carry out the roles designated by the marriage contract.
Woman is merely a subordinate in the all-important family
unit in which the extent of her power is clearly limited.
The male holds the position of unquestioned authority
and moderates all disputes. Only when age has desexual-
ized her does the woman take on an independent personality, and at that point she plays an active role in the
selection of mates for her male children, choosing the
daughters-in-law whom she will govern with the same
aggressive nagging that she herself underwent when young.
     In Muslim society women are trained to obey, and in so
doing they perpetuate the male-dominated social structure
that curtails their full realization as mature human
beings. Currently the gradual infiltration of Western
ideas, increasing modernization, high unemployment for
male workers, and the necessity for growing numbers of
women to support themselves make the male all the more

aggressive in defending his prerogatives.

Certainly the most visible sign of woman's effacement in Muslim society is the veil. In the name of preserving family honor, tradition dictates that woman pass unseen. The wearing of the veil is in itself a form of alienation imposed by patriarchy. In the postscript to her latest book, Femmes d'Alger dans leur appartement (1980), the Algerian writer Assia Djebar offers valuable insights into the rationale for this custom. An unspoken symbolism is in fact at play here. Outside of the permitted family circle, a woman's eyes must not meet with those of a male stranger, "for the eye of the one who dominates looks first of all for the other eye, that of the dominated, before taking possession of the body . . ." (2). The eye, liberated and unveiled, suggests that "the other eyes of the body (breasts, genitals, and navel), risk in turn to be stared at. It is the end for men, vulnerable guardians: it is their night, their misfortune, their dishonor" (3). To the male mind, a woman who circulates unveiled is undressed, naked. Her blatant renunciation of a protective covering is a sign of her easy availability. A woman thus exposed signifies to the male that he has been dispossessed. Alienated from his tribe, his land, and his possessions by the colonialist intruder, the male now fears that woman's adoption of Western freedom threatens to destroy something even more intimate, his own position of superiority. A woman's look is seen as one of defiance and "a new menace to [the male's] exclusive privilege to view, to that male prerogative" (4).

In history and in literature we observe that Algerians, Moroccans, and Tunisians have called for sweeping social and political reform, a new concept of man, and especially a restoration of his dignity. But while decolonization removed the yoke that weighed heavily on the colonized male, it did little to alleviate woman's condition. True, the Algerian revolution found woman taking an active part in the struggle against the foreign enemy. These "bearers of fire," as Djebar calls them, walked unescorted in the streets carrying bombs and weapons, yet it was not that woman thus liberated herself; rather she liberated the male so that he might be free to engage in his attack on the enemy. Women were utilized, albeit willingly, as auxiliaries and collaborators. Extenuating circumstances permitted such extraordinary action. While it might be thought that the Algerian woman thus participating actively in such a

serious undertaking would become cognizant of her own
value and of her possible role as an autonomous person in
society, in fact this was not the case. It was implicit-
ly understood that a shortage of manpower and unusual
conditions had made her participation necessary. Furthermore, since national independence, not the transformation
of society, was the Algerian militants' goal, the assump-
tion was that once that was achieved, the country would
return to the norms and way of life of precolonial times
that the foreign presence had disrupted and devalued.
Thus, after independence, women lost rights that they had
enjoyed under colonial rule, for example, in case of
divorce or repudiation. Patriarchy "rewarded" its heroines not with emancipation but with further mythifica-
tion. Women did not demand a greater participation in
the molding of their environment, as one might have
expected. In fact, this failure to claim emancipation
is understandable when one considers that women were
largely illiterate and because of their upbringing as
sheltered dependents were ill-adapted to assume authority
for their own future. They were incapable of imagining
for themselves a way of life different from the traditional one in which they had been raised. Over the years
relatively few women have spoken out (5). Those who
have, such as Fadela M'Rabet in her essays, originally
published separately, Femmes algériennes (1964) and
Les Algériennes (1967), have been criticized for their
"extreme" position. (M'Rabet was exiled.) Still others
find the media unwilling to publish their proposals for
reforms.

The North African woman's view of herself is a subject
of much interest, both to the curious outsider intrigued
by the aura of mystery that surrounds her, and to the
timid Arab female, unaccustomed to placing value on herself outside of the functions assigned to her by tradition. It is engaging to hear from women's voices the
role they wish to assume in society, yet even here there
is cause to wonder if they can extricate themselves from
the effects of centuries of prejudice. As we shall see,
even in literature they are pressured to conform to "acceptable" norms. In 1968 Abdelkébir Khatibi wrote: "we
are still in the prehistory of feminine literature . . .
the representation that woman makes of herself is prisoner of that [representation] made [of her] by man" (6).

North African literature in the French language is
clearly dominated by male writers. Only a dozen female

authors may be cited for making substantial original contributions in the form of novels, collections of short
stories, or volumes of poetry, as opposed to more than
one hundred male authors (7). Among the handful of women
francophone writers who deal with the problem of women's
oppression and liberation, the following may be cited for
the importance of their contributions. We list them
according to their chronological entry into the literary
field: Marguerite Taos Amrouche: three novels—Ja-
cinthe noire (Black jacintha, 1947), Rue des tambou-
rins (Street of tambourines, 1960), L'Amant imaginaire
(The imaginary lover, 1975); translations of folk literature—Le Grain magique (1966); Djamila Debèche: two
novels—Leïla, jeune fille d'Algérie (Leïla, girl of
Algeria, 1947), Aziza (1955); Assia Djebar: four novels—La Soif (Thirst, 1957), Les Impatients (1958),
Les Enfants du nouveau monde (Children of the new
world, 1962), Les Alouettes Naïves (The naive larks,
1947); a play—Rouge l'Aube (Red dawn, 1969); a book of
poems—Poèmes pour l'Algérie heureuse (Poems for happy Algeria, 1969); and a collection of short stories—
Femmes d'Alger dans leur appartement (1980); Zoubida
Bittari: a testimony—O Mes soeurs musulmanes, pleurez
(Oh my Muslim sisters, cry, 1964); Lemsine Aicha: La
Chrysalide, Chroniques algériennes (1976).

Few would dispute the choice of Assia Djebar as the
female writer whose fiction best exemplifies the condition of Muslim women in North Africa. This Algerian
author's works, which span a period of more than two
decades, express from a woman's point of view, the concerns, aspirations, and self-image of women across the
Maghreb. The quality and popularity of Djebar's novels,
as well as the recognition they have received from
critics, lead us to select her as a representative of the
woman's position.

Chapter Eight
Assia Djebar

Women's Voices

Fatima-Zohra Imalayen, better known under the pen name
Assia Djebar, was born on 4 August 1936 at Cherchell on
the Mediterranean, to the west of Algiers (1). Djebar
grew up in a middle-class bourgeois family that was faithful to tradition and to religious and social principles.
Her father, a school teacher, firmly believed in the
intellectual development and formation of his children,
sensing that the country needed its own ruling elite to
direct its future. As an adolescent, Djebar attended a
French lycée at Blida. An avid reader and a star pupil,
the young girl showed great enthusiasm and promise in
literary studies and won a number of prizes. After passing the baccalauréat, she went to Paris where she
earned a license in history and geography. In 1955 she
passed the highly competitive entrance exam of the Ecole
Normale Supérieure, France's elite teacher training
school, but then decided against further studies and
returned to North Africa, where she married. Djebar did
not remain in Algeria during the revolution but took
refuge, first in Morocco where she taught at the University of Rabat, and then in Tunis. After independence she
returned to Algeria, where she taught history. Later she
moved to Paris, supposedly for good. During those years
she was exposed to feminist works and spent some time
investigating them fully. In 1974 she returned to
Algeria to work on a film and teach semiotics at the
University of Algiers.

Djebar has written four novels, published by Juilliard, a play and a book of poems, published by the nation-
alized Algerian firm S.N.E.D., and most recently, a
collection of short stories, published in Paris by Des
femmes. In addition, she periodically writes critical
articles, especially on the subject of bilingualism, for
French and North African newspapers and journals. In
1977 Djebar wrote a film scenario for Algerian television, "Nouba des femmes du Mont Chenoua" (Nouba of the

women of Mount Chenoua), which deals with women's participation in the revolution. A published version with text
and photographs was promised but has not materialized.

La Soif (Thirst, 1957), Djebar's first novel, was
published when she was only twenty years old. Briefly
summarized, it tells the story of Nadia, a snobbish, petu-
lant Algerian adolescent of mixed Arab–French blood, who
tries to steal Ali, the husband of her childhood friend
Jedla, in order to render a former suitor, Hassein,
jealous. Nadia, who narrates the story in the first
person, is a selfish youth of vacillating emotions.
Love, hatred, ennui, jealousy, she experiences all in a
single day. Most of the narration is taken up with
Nadia's self-analysis of her passions and the personal
problems that evolve through the interaction of the four
principal characters around which the entire drama
revolves. La Soif is a novel of extremes, of the
thirst for strong sensations and adventure, of Nadia's
thirst for men and Jedla's thirst for a child. The head-
strong Nadia revels in her freedom and takes perverse
pleasure in her plots to seduce the male of her choice.
Jedla attempts suicide. Later, when she learns that Ali
has had an illicit liaison with a French actress, a union
that resulted in the birth of an illegitimate male child,
jealousy inspires her to make a pact with Nadia to freely
yield her husband to her. This act of infidelity would
give Jedla an excuse to leave her husband. While Ali is
on a trip to Paris to gain custody of his son, Jedla
learns that she is pregnant. Nadia convinces her that
even this pregnancy will not keep Ali faithful to her.
Jedla decides to have an abortion. Only then does Nadia
seem to realize the evil effect of her words. Jedla dies
from the operation and Nadia is left carrying a burden of
guilt.

At the time of the novel's publication in 1957,
critics in France were quick to draw a comparison between
La Soif and Françoise Sagan's Bonjour Tristesse.
The style of the writing and the conception of the heroines are similar. North African critics, however, re-
acted strongly to this book which, published during the
middle of the Algerian revolution, displayed manifest
indifference to the grave political situation. In
Algeria it was seen as an irrelevant and selfish indul-
gence in personal concerns, totally inappropriate for
that time of crisis. Not only is the book lacking in

anticolonialist feeling, equally disconcerting is its
depiction of the Algerian woman. The heroine, as a
Westernized Algerian, is atypical, as Djebar herself
later conceded. She is not, however, autobiographical.
Djebar did not enjoy the freedom she ascribes to her heroine. Rather, the latter is a composite of the author's
adolescent school companions and of the stories that
young girls just embarking on life are wont to tell: "I
have always wanted to avoid giving in my novels an autobiographical character for fear of immodesty and horror of
a certain intellectual striptease in which one often
indulges in the first works. My personal life has nothing in common with my heroines" (2).

In an interview Djebar admitted to not having taken
her first novel seriously: "I didn't really think of
publishing La Soif, which remains for me an exercise in
style" (3). When critics judged it severely because of
its lack of political engagement, Djebar disclaimed her
work. Only after independence, when the expected liberation of women was not effected with the liberation of the
country, was the seriousness of problems raised in the
novel appreciated: the affective relationship between
spouses, infidelity, woman's fear of sterility and of
subsequent repudiation, the subordination of the wife to
the husband. These generally unspoken issues, which come
to bear on the existence of every Muslim woman, are found
in all of Djebar's novels, as is the daring theme of
woman's discovery of her body. Abdelkébir Khatibi
submits that, with respect to the latter, La Soif is
already a kind of revolution.

Today we can see the value of this novel as a social
document. But, perhaps such a quick judgment is superficial. Beneath the surface lies a theme that runs through
all the novels and reaches full flower in Djebar's last
work, Femmes d'Alger. That is, the authentic communication of women with other women and the need for female
bonding. In La Soif Jedla and Nadia recall that as
childhood friends they used to enjoy each other's
company. As adults, what sets them at odds and destroys
their friendship is competition for men. La Soif, like
all of Djebar's fiction, is a novel about women. The
psychology of the male is entirely ignored. The text
implies that the male is the ultimate source of dissen-
sion. He destroys the reverie of the idyllic universe
that women would otherwise enjoy. The dictum that all
Muslim women should marry wreaks havoc within their most

intimate self; it carries a host of psychological burdens
that must be born by the woman. These hover as threats
in her unconscious mind. <u>La Soif</u> describes women's
reactions, including the author's, to that inevitable
event, marriage, that is so fraught with risk. The
language and actions of the characters mask a suppressed
perception: that the male is superfluous, an intruder
and a threat. Djebar repeatedly pictures her heroine as
one who relishes the indolent contentment that comes from
being alone in harmony with nature (especially the sun,
sand, and sea, favorite elements of Mediterranean cultures), or who takes delight in a quiet tête-à-tête
with a close female friend in a self-contained haven of
their own making. It is the male, assuming the role that
patriarchal tradition has assigned to him, who encroaches
upon that tranquil sanctuary and who sets women up as a
threat to one another, causing them to inflict pain on
their own kind. Far from dismissing <u>La Soif</u> as the
superficial and exaggerated piece of an inexperienced
youthful writer, we must recognize between the lines of
the text a cleverly disguised rebellion against that deep-
set system of values that menaces the peace and wholeness
of every Muslim female.

This rebellion persists and is seen more clearly in
Djebar's second novel, <u>Les Impatients</u> (The impatient
ones, 1958), written when the author was twenty-two years'
old. Revolt against tradition and against the family is
the subject of the novel. Perhaps to protect herself
against the criticism of being unpatriotic, Djebar sets
the story in the summer and autumn of 1954, the eve of
the revolution. Dalila, the first-person narrator and
eighteen-year-old heroine, revolts against the suffo-
cating constraints exercised by her stepmother, her brother, and his wife in the name of preserving the family
honor and status in the neighborhood. The pose that the
esteemed bourgeois family is determined to maintain infu-
riates Dalila, who discovers that they have a secret to
hide. Dalila falls in love with and agrees to marry
Salim who, she learns, was formerly the lover of her stepmother Lella, now widowed. When he goes to Paris on business, Dalila, hopelessly in love, follows him. There he
virtually sequesters her and controls her every action.
When he learns that Lella has remarried, he flies back to
Algeria to meet her. Lella's new husband, in a fit of
jealousy, shoots the pair to death. Dalila returns to
Algeria where she learns that she must face up to life.

Set in a Muslim milieu, Les Impatients juxtaposes
the fixed values and attitudes of the more staid generation with the revolt of the young student Dalila, who is
determined to exercise the liberty that she feels should
be hers. Dalila deplores the attitude of her married
sisters and her daughter-in-law for submitting to their
husbands. Yet in the name of love she is frequently
willing to yield her liberty to Salim. Inconstant in her
convictions, she vacillates between a docile surrendering
of her will and a fierce refusal to let others decide her
future for her. She perceives that a woman's idea of
herself is all too frequently based on what others think
of her, yet desperately in search of a definitive image
of herself, she succumbs to this temptation.

While we admire Dalila for her determination to break
away from certain conventions, we do not fully sympathize
with her. She is selfish, stubborn, lacking in compas-
sion, willing to destroy people to get what she wants
though in the end she achieves nothing. She is alienated
from the women around her and isolated in her rage.
Eventually the ferocity of her rebellion is quelled and
she succumbs to the code that society dictates.

Far more interesting and much more developed than La
Soif, Les Impatients offers insights into the mentality of the middle-class Muslim woman. We witness her
fears and her schemes and come to see that despite her
subordination to male authority, she lives an existence
that is distinct from his. The principal action of the
novel is psychological. It is a study in attitudes and
motivations, especially on the part of the young heroine
who analyzes and records every passion, sentiment, and
motive of her daily life. In Dalila we see represented,
though perhaps in exaggerated form, the emerging generation of young Algerian woman. Djebar herself has com-
mented on the importance of this figure: "I wanted to
show how in a calm world, where objectively nothing had
yet changed, there was developing a process that allowed
one to guess future upheaval" (4).

Les Impatients centers on the emancipation of the
individual woman in the domain of the family. Les
Enfants du nouveau monde (Children of the new world,
1962), Djebar's third novel, focuses on women's collective struggle, as exemplified by a variety of individual
women, to emancipate the nation through militant action.
This experience brings with it an awakening through
which, it is intimated, Muslim women will achieve new

status in the future society that is at hand. Unlike the preceding novels in which the heroines are preoccupied with self-realization, the women of this novel are seen to unite and form a bond among themselves. What goes left unspoken, however, is the fact that their efforts support a male cause; in the end they will once again be the losers.

Though Djebar was absent from Algeria during the revolution, she did speak with women in refugee camps in Tunisia and on the border, recording their experiences. These accounts inspired the author in composing her novel.

The action takes place in the spring of 1956 when the middle-class inhabitants of Blida find that their complacent bourgeois existence is being shaken. Some of the men leave for the bush while others stay on to collaborate with the revolutionary underground forces. The women, accustomed to remaining cloistered in their houses and having their actions dictated by tradition or by male authority, are nearly paralyzed when a crisis requires them to act on their own. From the ranks of women unaccustomed to being leaders, Djebar creates a suite of positive female heroines: the passive Cherifa, stereotype of the traditional Muslim woman and one of the major figures in the novel, goes out alone at night to warn her husband; Lila, another major character, is arrested for her alleged conspiracy with the revolutionaries; Anna, wife of a traitor police officer, jeopardizes her security by lying in order to defend the nationalist cause; Salima, a school teacher, is imprisoned and tortured for her beliefs.

Unlike most of the "literature of combat," which vividly and realistically depicts brutal physical suffering, the action of this novel is primarily psychological. In the women's reactions to the happenings of war, we find the feminine expression of engagement, which is no less a testimony than any story of blood and gore. Conquering fear, these women, the "children of the new world," discover what it is to "be."

Written in the third person, Les Enfants du nouveau monde permits the reader to see the war through the eyes of a variety of characters, men as well as women, in a series of distinct accounts. While one critic reproaches the author for "the profusion of characters and the multiplicity of plots that obscure the novel" (5), we must nonetheless insist upon the book's merits. It is a more

mature work than its predecessors, more complete in that
it is not limited to a few major characters but shows the
interactions of a cross section of individuals. This
novel marks a definite progression in terms of technique
and character development and, perhaps more important, in
terms of the hope it offers that women are on the threshold of bettering their situation and earning a new place
for themselves in the society that they are helping to
create,
        Les Alouettes naives (The naive larks, 1967),
Djebar's last published novel, is written in the same
psychological vein as her preceding works, but is more
personal. It explores the problems of the couple,
including their sexual relationship, a delicate subject
in Muslim society. The novel emphasizes man's need to
understand his rapport with woman, a consideration underscored by Djebar's use of a phrase from Aragon as a
chapter heading: "the future of man is woman" (6). It
is concerned with the new man and the new woman who will
emerge once the war is over. There are ties to be broken
and bridges to be built. The male intuits an evolution
and liberation on the part of woman, that being from whom
custom has taken away the power of becoming and who has
been reduced to perpetual infancy. Man has accustomed
himself to thinking that he is the light, when in fact it
is woman who is the beacon. He is uneasy in his realization that she exists independently of him.
        The novel is set in 1962 during the last months of the
revolution, against a background of fire and struggle.
But love, not war, is the subject of the narration, the
love of Nfissa and Rachid. Nfissa's fiancé is killed
while both are fighting in the maquis. After returning
to the city, Nfissa meets and marries Rachid, with whom
she shares a romantic relationship. She awakens physically and psychologically, and the intensity of the couple's
love transports them to a temporary Eden in which they
are removed from time, living at the apogee of conjugal
bliss. Ignoring taboos, Djebar discusses the pleasurable
mingling of their naked bodies and the spiritual delight
that their union brings them, a daring novelty consider-
ing the times and the culture.
        In an interview (7) the author affirmed that Les
Alouettes marked the end of a period and of a style. It
is unfortunate that at a time when it seemed that she
should have been expanding horizons and looking with
greater depth into the problems of woman in Muslim society, Djebar renounced those aspects of her writing that

make her unique and fell in with the scores of uncele-
brated amateurs pouring out a banal "literature of
combat." Her next works, both published in Algeria in
1969, were a four-act play, Rouge l'Aube (Red dawn),
coauthored with her then husband Walid Carn, and a collection of poetry, Poèmes pour l'Algérie heureuse (Poems
for happy Algeria). The play, which is totally unlike
the novels, celebrates the revolution. Like so many
other hymns of praise to the glory of Algeria's heroes,
it is not a compelling work.

The poems too sing the glorious struggle of the
revolution and remind the reader of Algeria's origins.
Déjeux finds them "at times insignificant and often
labored" (8). Perhaps the one aspect worthy of note
is Djebar's expressed nostalgia for her native tongue,
the regret that so much popular literature has been lost
because the poets were often illiterates who did not set
their words down for posterity, and her hope that the
present generation will not forget its mother tongue. In
her preface Djebar embraces the philosophy of bilingualism, convinced that facility in both languages is essential for a true appreciation of the Algerian
mentality.

Mysteriously, after 1969 Djebar produced no further
works. She gave up writing because she felt she could
not reach her female compatriots. Both as a woman and as
a writer she had wanted to give them a voice that had
been denied them. Though she has an impeccable command
of the French language, her feelings toward the use of
that idiom in an Arab society cause her no little discom-
fort. It is the language of the colonizer and the
language of men. It estranges her from other Arab women;
it alienates her from them and even from herself. For-
tunately, rather than renounce all hope of communication,
Djebar concentrated all her energy on this theme. In
1977 she produced a film for Algerian television, "Nouba
des Femmes du Mont Chenoua," in which old women tell of
the struggle of the Algerian people to rid their land of
the colonial oppressor. Unfortunately, while women's
voices are heard, the production marks no progress in the
issue of women's liberation. It dwells on the past and
does not give a hearing to the young, who might have
concerns beyond the transmission of their country's glorious history. Marie-Blanche Tahon, one of Djebar's
severest critics, criticizes the film as being a part of
Algeria's official ideology. Even though it records
women's testimony, that testimony only acts as a support

for "great deeds of an essentially masculine epic . . ."
(9). Djebar, claims Tahon, does no more than adhere to
Islamic tradition that holds that woman's function is to
preserve the nation's heritage. This position is confirmed in Djebar's 1980 work.

The author's refusal to confront women's repression by
the rigid patriarchal society of contemporary North
Africa is indeed to be lamented. Djebar evades the issue
and deflects a direct hit by concentrating on a different
aspect of the struggle: the need for bonding between
women, a phenomenon that is present in all her novels but
that many critics failed to notice. Instead of seeing
other women as potential enemies, they must learn to see
that they share a common complaint. Only from this genuine understanding, whispered among themselves, can there
eventually arise a loud cry for change.

After a decade of silence on the literary scene,
Djebar once again made her voice heard, with Femmes
d'Alger dans leur appartement (1980), a collection of
six short stories composed between 1959 and 1979. The
title of this collection was inspired by Delacroix's cor-
respondingly named 1832 painting, a representation of
which illustrates the cover of the volume. The female
universe is a closed one of "women always in waiting,"
living like prisoners in "that rarefied atmosphere of
close confinement" (10). Like a spy, Delacroix stole
a look into that secret enclosure that as a rule is restricted to the eyes of the family circle. His painting
is in itself a stolen glance. Similarly Djebar, through
the medium of fiction, permits spectators, her readers, a
forbidden glimpse into this milieu. What she finds there
is a muted atmosphere where women speak in whispers. The
harem no longer exists, but its conventions, the law of
silence, the law of invisibility, impose themeslves nevertheless. Woman's voice is stifled, her hearing cut off,
her space limited. The theme of suffocation runs through
the entire volume. The female heroines do not enjoy the
pleasure of open space, as did the earlier rebellious
youths Nadia and Dalila, but are always confined to
closed rooms, walled in. But, suggests the author, if
woman's body and even her language remain prisoners of
the veil and sequestration, her soul is in movement.
There is hope that the young women of contemporary society will cross the threshold and "deliver themselves . . .
completely from the rapport of shadow maintained for
centuries with their own bodies" (11).

The seeming boldness expressed in the book's introduction, however, is not borne out in the narratives that follow. The book looks backward more than it looks forward. Only two of the stories are set in the postcolonial period; the remaining four take place during the revolution or long before it. All manifest the author's continued concern for the condition of women in Muslim society, a condition that lamentably has not been ameliorated, yet they dwell too much on the evocation of misery. Far from awakening consciences, the purpose of these stories hardly seems to go beyond that of the painter's more than a century ago: the communication of an atmosphere, the creation of striking tableaux that touch our sensibilities (the scene in the public bath is a particularly vibrant example).

The opening story, which bears the same title as the volume, is the most timely of the collection. Juxtaposing the modern Muslim woman with her elders, it poignantly illustrates a bonding between women who gradually come to see themselves clearly and to realize that they carry within them their own prisons. Even those who do not wear the ancestral veil remain entrapped by invisible veils. The question is posed: how will the passage for Arab women be made. Djebar's answer is weak: "to talk among ourselves and to look. To look outside, to look beyond the walls and persons!" (12). How timid is this response in contrast to the male hero's vigorous determination to throw off the yoke of the colonialist oppressor. While Djebar urges her heroines to advance with hope, anger, and defiance, she leaves them with no practical program to free themselves from their daily oppression.

Addressing this issue, Marie-Blanche Tahon criticizes Djebar for her too cautious approach and her tenuous position as an intellectual living a life distinct from that of the women of her fiction. Tahon goes on to explain the author's predicament as she perceives it: "she is immediately suspected of wanting to deny the Arab-Islamic values, those of her people, in order to promote Western values, those of the occupier" (13). To depart from established patterns is to be an iconoclast. Djebar learned a humiliating lesson with the publication of her first novel, suggests Tahon, and since that time has taken a guarded approach to the subject of woman's liberation. The solidarity in misfortune that she depicts is only murmured softly. It is far from being an enthusi-

astic cry to create a new order. The women of Femmes
d'Alger who go to the aid of their sisters in distress
are not militants. They mother each other. And as
Djebar herself points out, mothers are asexual beings,
the guardians of cultural identity, the umbilical cord of
the memory. Not insignificantly, the heroine of the
first story, Sarah, a "modern" woman who drives to her
job, is employed as a translator of Arab folk songs,
taped recordings collected from rural illiterates, which
threaten to die out with the older generation. Thus her
professional career falls into the category of acceptable
occupations for women. She assumes the "natural" function of one who preserves the roots of the past.

The most important part of Djebar's newest literary
effort is the twenty-three-page postscript that offers a
diachronic review of woman's position in Algeria since
1830, as well as a review of the psychology that fixes
her position. Djebar brings to the forefront and honestly discusses matters that male sociologists leave untouched; however, her effectiveness in bringing about
any change for the better among her compatriots is slim.
She makes no substantial proposals for reform; her exposé on the conditioning that has held women in bondage is
unlikely to be read by any significant number of literate
female North Africans. In the case of the Arab woman,
progress seems to amount to little more than a rocking
back and forth in place, a straddling of "the past paralyzed in the present and the present mid-wife of the
future" (14). In 1969 the author expressed her confidence in woman as the key to a new future in the Arab
world (15). Her 1980 book is an admission by omission
that her vision was unfounded. Les Alouettes naïves
(1967) issued a bold call for an understanding and a dialogue between the sexes; Femmes d'Alger reiterates no
such hope. It abandons this theme entirely in favor of a
dialogue between women, but this dialogue, which has as
its purpose mutual commiseration in unhappiness, holds
less promise for reform than that conjured up in the
novel.

Conclusion: A Revolution that Failed

Djebar is obviously at her best when she explores the
issue of women's independence and the rapport between
husband and wife. In this lies her original contribution

to North African literature. She lays bare the conflicts
that spring forth from woman's immature soul and catch
her in a struggle between affirming her independent existence or of finding that affirmation only by yielding her
will to the authority of a man. Woman's need for love
and man's recognition of his shortcomings in this area
are topics largely untouched by Muslim writers. For the
most part, love is either transposed to devotion and
adoration (as in Dib's novels where the woman is on a
pedestal, a sort of goddess), or limited to its material
dimensions. The discussion of erotic love (for which
even Dib used a veiled approach) was shocking to Muslim
mentality, and off-limits. Tradition dictated arranged
marriages determined by family status, wealth, and the
need for diplomatic alliances in which the matter of love
was immaterial and beside the fact. Djebar dares to jar
the Arab psyche, though to the Western reader her expression of "sensuality" is bland. Djebar shows woman taking
pleasure in her body. Her preoccupation with this recur-
ring motif is in itself a constrained expression of
revolt against the oppressive dictates of Muslim society
that insists on covering the female body, which it views
as a source of evil, sin, and shame. The body is thus
the locus of the female's alienation. As a result she is
being split in two. Djebar attempts, through various
routes, to show her how she can restore wholeness to her
self. One of the possibilities illustrated is to marry
for love. Thus in Les Alouettes naives she shows her
heroine desirous of loving passionately and pleasurably.
This notion is to be judged as a great step forward in
tradition-bound North Africa. Yet even here Djebar casts
doubts. The women of her creation fall short of authentic self-affirmation. They are lacking in security, able
to confirm their own being only when seeing themselves
reflected in an approving male "refuge" that mirrors
their selves. Déjeux signals the narcissistic nature of
woman's love. Alone she enjoys her body for herself;
with her husband, she exchanges her self to satisfy her
passion. In carnal union it is her own pleasure she
seeks, not an authentic reciprocal exchange. The fact
that this love is egotistical is perhaps to be seen as a
reaction against subservience. The idea of real autonomy
for the woman is not yet a reality. Both in these works
of fiction and in North Africa today, the couple has yet
to exist as an equal partnership.
    In a part of the world where women live a cloistered

existence and still wear the veil and the haïk that make
them invisible to male eyes, Djebar is to be applauded
for having opened a door, for having attempted to cast
light on a subject avoided by the North African male, for
having sought to awaken the conscience of men and women,
for having urged both to examine their relationship and
to consider more openly the needs of each.

Djebar's contributions are unique and praiseworthy.
We can only regret the direction she has taken of late.
Earlier concerns, notably the subject of the couple, are
entirely abandoned. Femmes d'Alger marks a definite
rupture with the earlier novels, and a retreat from the
pressing problems of women's equality and liberation. In
a 1969 interview, Djebar wrote that, while she found it
embarrassing to write about love between male and female,
she thought it was necessary to do so (16). By 1980 she
is entirely mute on the subject and writes that for an
Arab woman "to speak on that terrain becomes . . . a
transgression" (17). Why this abrupt reversal at a time
when we had expected to see the author forge ahead in new
directions we can only surmise. Evelyne Accad in her summary of Djebar suggests that her works reflect

> the exact path of women's liberation in Algeria which
> stopped dead after independence. . . . A reflection
> of her country's line of action, Assia Djebar's novels
> indicate a progression and a regression, because like
> Algeria's revolution, Djebar's was not a total and pro-
> found one. The rebellious rage voiced in the fifties
> and sixties has given way to a moderate whimper. The
> nationalistic spirit so necessary for the revolution-
> aries to oust the French colonizers became counterrevo-
> lutionary after the oppressor had been evicted, in
> that traditional laws were reinstituted which deprived
> women of the rights they had enjoyed under colonial
> rule. (18)

Chapter Nine
Perspectives for the Development of Maghrebian Literature in French

Since the granting of independence to the Maghreb countries, one pressing question has occupied the minds of
North African and French men of letters alike: what of
the future of North African francophone literature?
Already in the early 1960s some predicted that this literature was doomed to an early demise (1).   The evidence
offered in support of this hypothesis was persuasive.
The struggle to throw off the colonialist yoke, which had
given birth to and nourished this literature, had finally
been resolved.   An ongoing effort to Arabize the Maghreb
countries promised to lead to the gradual yet steady
replacement of French by Arabic as the medium of communication, thereby virtually eliminating a French-reading
audience.   The major Maghrebian writers had for the most
part settled in France, thus disassociating themselves
from contemporary problems and issues of their homeland.
Furthermore, it was felt that these writers, imbued with
Gallic culture, were the hybrid products of an elitist
bourgeois class temporarily created by the capitalist
colonial system.   Except for their advocacy of the revolution, they were a minority committed to maintaining their
own status quo; since they did not reflect the popular
concerns the masses but turned to themes of a universal nature, they by their own hand excluded themselves
from the Maghrebian current.   All of these speculations
were true.   Moreover, ever since national independence,
complaints of an ideological void, of stagnation, of
timidity on the part of writers, of a restrictive political climate, of inadequate distribution networks, and of
the lack of authentic literary criticism arose in all the
Maghreb countries.   However, despite this litany of
charges, as late as 1973, a full eleven years after the
declaration of Algerian independence, Jean Déjeux, that

most eminent scholar, wrote optimistically that this
literature was "getting its second breath. It is not a
question of 'drying up,' but of a liberty in action which
refuses all domestication and castration" (2). Déjeux
found the period 1962-72 to be the most productive in
terms of total literary output, as he proves statistical-
ly. And indeed he was correct. In retrospect we may see
the general outpouring of creative works of all genres,
published largely abroad, as a natural response to the
tension to which all the Maghreb countries had been sub-
jected during the protracted crisis in Algeria.

In this chapter we will follow developments affecting
the production of North African francophone literature,
from Algerian independence to the present. We will consider the climate in which it evolved and examine more
closely the major aspects of theme, genre, language, and
audience. We have chosen 1962 as our starting point
because it is largely due to the nationalist struggle in
Algeria that this literature was born, gained momentum,
and drew international attention. Its future development
hinged specifically upon the resolution of the Algerian
dilemma. The greatest number of works produced in the
Maghreb came from the pen of Algerian writers. It is
only natural that it was to be in the country that had
suffered the most from the ravages of colonialism that
the loudest voice was to be heard.

In the autumn of 1963, noted writers dedicated to
their art and to their country founded the Union of
Algerian Writers (l'Union des Ecrivains Algériens, or
the U.E.A. as it is also known) in Algiers, within the
perspective of a broad Federation of Arts and Letters.
Mouloud Mammeri was its president, and Jean Sénac was
chosen as secretary general. The union issued a manifesto that was optimistic and lofty in its ideals. It
called for high standards and bold renewal that would
embrace the aspirations of the young as well as the older
generation; it sought to reenforce ties "with all authentically revolutionary writers of Africa, Asia, and the
entire world" (3).

In fact, however, the Union was not instrumental in
carrying out its self-appointed task; and the hoped-for
harmony between writers of French and those of Arabic was
not achieved. The proclaimed determination to be "brothers among our brothers" was frustrated from the start.
Mutual suspicion and incomprehension created divisions.
Those writing in French were suspect as being of the

"French Party," while writers of Arabic expression were disdained for their "Orientalism," for belonging to the Middle Ages at a time when they were expected to be committed Algerians.

The Union launched a cultural review, Novembre, in 1964, but a year later it ceased to exist. It was decided that a Congress should be held in an effort to bring together the largely dispersed writers. In 1966 fifty-six authors who used either French or Arabic, some well-known, others not, in a formal ceremony attached their signatures to the Union's charter. The U.E.A. created a literary prize to be awarded annually. The union's failure to take a strong stand on the 1967 Israeli-Arab conflict brought criticism on it. That year Jean Sénac resigned as secretary general. While the organization was not officially dismantled, for all practical purposes it ceased to exist. Among the key issues facing writers at this time was the question of freedom of expression. The publication and circulation of all books and periodicals in Algeria was (and still is) controlled by the National Society of Editions and Distribution (Société Nationale d'Editons et de Diffusion, more familiarly known as S.N.E.D.), an official government organ. Writers could thus be manipulated and restricted. Above all they shrank from becoming mere functionaries of a political and social system that sanctions only "official" themes while censoring self-directed criticism. In a 1967 interview Kateb Yacine expressed the problem in these words: "They always commit the same fault, they treat the concept of liberty like a bourgeois concept, as if liberty was good only for the bourgeois. . . . Here there is an important question of principle that all revolutionaries ought to ask themselves. There can be no Union of Writers without total freedom of expression, without which it is always the same thing: the only writers approved by the people are yes men" (4). In search of this freedom, and to escape the suffocation of their less progressive and less broad-minded homelands, many of the Maghreb's finest writers chose to make their home outside of their native land.

In 1968 a National Cultural Colloquium was called in Algiers. It drew members from the Union, as well as artists and prominent figures in radio and television. (But known writers, such as Mohammed Dib, Assia Djebar, and Kateb Yacine were absent, while others, Jean Sénac and Fadela M'Rabet, for example, were not invited.) The

national press attended. The F.L.N. (Front de Libération Nationale), Algeria's single-party government,
proclaimed that the moment had come to organize and
reorganize cultural disciplines along socialist lines.
Representatives of all branches of the arts—writers,
musicians, painters, film makers—were called upon to
participate. All were invited to contribute to help fill
the void of the cultural desert that was left in the wake
of independence. The colloquium produced mixed reactions, which were publicized in the press. Some felt
that good effects would result from the assembly, while
others expressed a desire for concrete results. "Créer
et non pas crier" ("create and not clamor") was a catch
phrase seen in the July 1968 issue of El Djeich (5).
The F.L.N. was to provide the impetus for setting the
machinery in motion, but the results were disappointing.
A period of stagnation followed.

We may summarize the major problems facing North African literature at this time as follows: first, there was
renewal of themes. Such topics as the probing of the
alienated self torn asunder by the colonial experience
and the war for independence, the need for inner reconciliation, the quest for ancestral roots and for a lost
paternity had been reiterated at length, together with
the cry of the young to escape sclerotic tradition.
These themes were valid ones and deserved to be heard,
but profound changes had since been wrought and it was no
longer sufficient to dwell on bygone times. If this
literature were to remain healthy, it must not get mired
in a cult of the past and in celebrating ancestral myths,
but must advance to meet the challenge of changing times.
Without being a slave to official ideology, it needed to
explore current social issues, to venture along new
paths, steering clear of pseudopatriotism and manipulative exploitation. Above all it needed to avoid false
and perfidious exoticism, a prefabricated Orientalism
imposed from without by the foreigner to slake his appetite for the unusual. Furthermore, this literature was
not to be limited to any one class but was to consider
the problems of all levels of society. Among the subjects to be treated was the natives' repossession of
their land after the French exodus, of new responsibilities to be met, of the new citizen to be formed and
integrated into a healthy whole, and of the numerous
tasks that needed to be tended to in order to make this
goal a reality. The highly respected Mostefa Lacheraf

stated that creative works ought to be "a conscience present to a world that is lived in, a current open to all possibilities, to all direct lessons that the movement of society, with its thwarted aspirations, its secular deficiencies, its mortal trials, its active or resigned desperation, its revolts, its anguish imposes on our contemporaries . . ." (6).

In addition to the issue of content, there was that of form or genre. The novel, a European invention, was viewed prejudicially by some as being the adulterous issue of an uneasy relationship between East and West. It was, furthermore, the product of the dominant bourgeois class, created for the consumption and enjoyment of this same class. The theater was the least popular outlet for francophone writers, largely because of the decline of the French-speaking public. Theater being dialogue, it would not hold any interest for those who could not participate by immediate communication. Poetry and the short story were the most popular forms of expression, as they are still today, due in large part to the ease with which they can be circulated in newspapers and journals. New authors may easily make their entrée in this way since no costly production mechanics or high financial risks are involved.

In the 1960s and 1970s it was the essay that grew in importance, undoubtedly because it dealt with the most pertinent questions in an immediate way and bore the mark of authenticity. Among the essayists who have earned a considerable reputation we may cite Abdallah Mazouni, Mostefa Lacheraf, Abdallah Laroui, Albert Memmi, and Fadela M'Rabet. With frankness and audacity, they exposed the ills of society and brought attention to its needs. They probed with a view to awakening consciences, to facing realities, and to proposing solutions, and they approached their task with logic, sensitivity, and genuine concern.

The real decline in the production of francophone literature by North Africans did not make itself felt until the 1970s. Feeble efforts were made to revive the U.E.A. but failed for lack of interest. When a meeting was called in 1972, fewer than three dozen participants were in attendance. This group rejected the original union as being an elitist, closed association. Quarrels ensued and for years interested parties were caught up in an infernal circle of sterile debates, while writers went unpublished or sought foreign editors.

In 1973 the minister of culture laid plans to prepare
the convocation of a General Assembly of Algerian
Authors. Under the sponsorship of the Party and of the
minister of information and culture, this convocation was
finally held in 1974. Writers were interested but had
reservations. They shared common concerns that it was
time to act and not just think about issues, but once
again the same problems surfaced. Kateb Yacine spoke out
in favor of freedom of expression. The relationship with
the S.N.E.D. needed serious reconsideration. There was
debate as to who should be admitted to join the new union
and how to keep it a viable organization. Some sixty
authors signed a preparatory commission, and an executive
bureau, headed by Malek Haddad, was established. Although headed by a francophone writer, in fact it was and
is dominated by Arabic-language writers. The Bureau lent
an official air to the proposals expressed. Still complaints were uttered. There was clearly an imbalance
between writers of the "old guard" and the new, the
average member's age being forty-five. The young felt
excluded. In 1974 one poet wrote: "let's not become
settled into an 'official' literature as one would in a
privileged social cast or a deluxe freemasonry, but
instead, let's open wide the doors of the U.E.A. to young
writers who have a word to say. In view of the insur-
mountable difficulties posed by the publishing industry
in Algeria, the U.E.A. risks being for a long time yet
reserved for those with white hair" (7). Another poet
expressed similar complaints: "the time has come to stop
the wheels of this impersonal machinery that mutilates us
without reason. . . . in our day publication has become
a veritable bureaucratic odyssey" (8). Why, asked some,
does a country that adopts a bold policy of economic
development remain extraordinarily conservative in the
domain of arts and literature. "Conformity, lack of boldness and of imagination characterize the productions of
the soul" (9), laments another young writer.

In the long run, it was the question of language and,
related to it, that of audience, that turned the tide.
The process of Arabization had been ongoing in Tunisia
and Morocco since their independence in 1956. At stake
was not the issue of whether French or Arabic should be
the medium of instruction, but the elimination of illiteracy among the masses through educational reforms. Since
Morocco and Tunisia had been protectorates, not full-

fledged colonies, and since they had been spared the
traumatic experience of war, they did not suffer to the
extent that their neighbor Algeria did. Educated people
from abroad stayed on in Morocco and Tunisia. Gradually
a sufficient number of native teachers were trained, and
the educational system was overhauled. The goal to make
schooling compulsory beyond the elementary level was
achieved, at least in theory. French still retained its
status as the language of commerce and international
diplomacy, and those who had access to advanced instruction at the university level faired best economically and
socially.

The situation in Algeria was entirely otherwise. The
educated French fled the country in fear of their lives
when Algerian independence was imminent, leaving the
country in an educational vacuum. Though the F.L.N. had
long before declared Arabic to be the official language,
the problem was that there was an insufficient number of
trained teachers available to carry out the process of
Arabization or, for that matter, to tackle the overwhelming problem of revamping the entire educational system.
Illiteracy was high and the shortage of instructors made
progress painfully slow. To this day the Arabization
process remains an ongoing effort. In December 1981 the
Higher Council on National Language in a report to the
Central Committee of the F.L.N. called for the conversion
of all sectors of society to the Arabic medium. Thus
even two decades after Algerian independence, this goal
has not been met. However, while French and more recently English compete as prestige languages, we must not
lose sight of the fact that in all of the Maghreb
countries colloquial dialectical Arabic is the most
common mode of expression, both oral and written, among
the masses. French continues to be taught in the
schools, but as one elective among a host of others. The
young people no longer consider French as a source of
alienation. Bilingualism is the useful and desirable
goal. Mastering of the Gallic tongue is, like other
disciplines, a source of enrichment and a door to greater
possibilities. Its acquisition is no longer associated
with the shedding of one's native personality. In more
recent years English has gained in popularity for being a
useful tool in the area of commerce.

The initial burst of creative works in French produced
by Maghrebian writers in the decade after Algerian independence has slowed. The younger generations of writers

in Algeria, Morocco, and Tunisia express themselves in
Arabic. Even one member of the old vanguard, Kateb
Yacine, has seen the necessity of producing creative
works in Arabic in order to reach his people. True, his
compatriots, Mammeri, Dib, Memmi, continue to write in
French. But the question arises: are they not merely
remnants of a generation that is slowly fading? And have
they not lost their right to be classed with Maghrebian
writers in Africa, since they are no longer in direct
contact with their homeland, its people, or its interests, but have turned to themes of a universal nature?

A glance through bibliographies of Maghrebian literature, a perusal of the latest titles appearing in the
windows of bookstores in North Africa, or of the periodicals sold at local newsstands proves that the predictions
of the early 1960s are in fact coming true. The golden
age of North African literature in French has passed.
Some believe that within the decade it may have drawn to
a close. However, it is neither possible nor advisable
to form a definitive conclusion as to its future.
Déjeux prudently warns that there exists no sociology of
this literature and care must be taken not to fall into
facile and abusive generalizations. A methodic multidis-
ciplinary approach is needed (10).

In order to provide a response to the issue of this
literature's future, we are once again forced to consider
the audience to which it is addressed. The bulk of these
works have been published in France. Owing to their controversial nature, some have been outlawed in the Maghreb
countries. Their audience has always been and will
always remain restricted, both in France and across the
Mediterranean. As we have shown, one of the purposes of
this literature has been to arouse and lend encouragement to the peoples of the Maghreb. Ironically, due to
barriers of language and cost, the masses have had no
access to the books whose message was intended for them.
After 1952 most writers strove to avoid the romantic
exoticism on which so many Europeans fed. Today we may
question whether a new variation of this same tendency
has not in fact become a trend. Maghrebian writers seem
to be responding to the morbid craving of European taste
for the unhealthy energy expressed in works of African
writers. Curiously, however, a number of works written
in French are finally reaching the common people, in
Arabic translations printed in inexpensive paperback editions. Perhaps this is one route by which the ordinary

citizen will recapture a part of his rich heritage.

At this time it would be imprudent to make a conclusive judgment as to the future development or demise of francophone literature produced by native writers who make their home in the Maghreb. Certain trends have been noted. It remains for history to bear out the conjectures, both affirmative and negative, that are voiced by concerned critics. Their interest continues and has even picked up momentum, a sure guarantee of the immortality of this literature.

Notes and References

Chapter One

1. The term Maghreb (sometimes spelled Maghrib) is a collective name for Morocco, Algeria, and Tunisia, and sometimes includes Libya. The Arab historian Jamil M. Abun-Nasr explains that this term is preferred to the name "North Africa" which includes Egypt. But "the French have made this last name additionally misleading by using its French equivalent 'Afrique du Nord' to refer to their former possessions on the southern shores of the Mediterranean, thus excluding Egypt and Libya from its connotation" (Jamil M. Abun-Nasr, A History of the Maghrib [Cambridge, 1971], p. 1).

2. Camus was born and raised in Algeria but later expelled for political reasons. He settled in France and has always been considered a French writer. Audisio was born in France but lived most of his adult life in Algeria, a country which he claims was the source of inspiration for all his writings. Jules Roy spent his childhood and adolescence in Algeria, the land of his birth, but lived his adult years in France and abroad, except for brief visits back home.

3. The author's sources for the history of the Maghreb include Abun-Nasr, History of the Maghrib; Charles-Andre Julien, History of North Africa, trans. John Petrie, ed. C. C. Steward (New York, 1960); Abdallah Laroui, The History of the Maghrib: An Interpretative Essay, trans. Ralph Manheim (Princeton, 1977); Algeria: A Country Study, ed. Harold D. Nelson (Washington, D.C., 1978); Morocco: A Country Study, ed. Harold D. Nelson (Washington, D.C., 1978); Tunisia: A Country Study, ed. Harold D. Nelson (Washington, D.C., 1979); Lucette Valensi, On the Eve of Colonialism: North Africa Before the French Conquest, trans. Kenneth J. Perkins (New York, 1977).

4. Abun-Nasr, History of the Maghrib, p. 6.

5. The event has a long prehistory. According to written accounts, during the 1790s the French had made an

agreement to purchase Algerian wheat through a merchant
company in Algiers, but they never paid the bill. When
Hussein Dey demanded tribute from the merchants, they com-
plained that they would be unable to pay unless first
reimbursed by the French. The dey suspected collusion
between the merchants and the French government. At a
meeting with the French Consul in 1827, the dey insulted
the Frenchman, hitting him in the face with his fly
swish. Charles X, the king of France, demanded an apolo-
gy and imposed a naval blockade on the port of Algiers.
The blockade produced no noticeable effect on Hussein Dey
and dragged on for three years. The king's ministers
finally managed to convince him that a successful over-
seas campaign could bolster support at home for his shaky
monarchy. It took the French but three weeks to capture
Algiers, on 5 July 1830. Hussein Dey fled into exile.
Just when the news of the victory reached Paris, Charles
X was deposed and Louis-Philippe was named to preside
over a constitutional monarchy.

6. There are at least two possible explanations for
the origin of the term: one based on the fact that the
French military wore black polished shoes, the other
arising from the patronizing view that the colonialists'
feet were burned black by the intense African sun.

7. Nelson, ed., Tunisia: A Country Study, p. 48.

8. Treaty of Fès, as cited in Morocco: A Country
Study, Nelson, ed., p. 48.

9. Anthologie des écrivains maghrébins d'expression française, ed. Albert Memmi (Paris, 1964), p. 14.

10. Ibid., p. 12: "un enrichissement accidental de
leur palette . . ." and "une terre d'évasion."

11. Louis Bertrand, Les Villes d'or (Paris, 1921):
"Nous n'avons fait que récupérer une province perdue de
la Latinité" (p. 9).

12. Louis Bertrand, "Africa," Revue des Deux Mondes
(1 March 1922):128: "La véritable Afrique, c'est nous,
nous les latins, nous les civilisés."

13. Bertrand, Villes d'or, p. 10: "un magasin de
décors ou une alcove voluptueuse."

14. Robert Randau (1873-1946) had a broad knowledge
of the people, land, Arab tongue, and Muslim texts of his
native Algeria. A man of action, he worked in the official capacity of government administrator, partook in
daring expeditions into the Sahara, wrote poems and
novels, and collaborated on several periodicals. His
jovial tone, his penchant for the outrageous, the vulgar,

and the ribald, and his exuberant and exaggerated style earned for him the title of "African Rabelais."

15. Robert Randeau, De treize poètes algériens (Algiers, 1920).

16. "Il doit y avoir une littérature nord-africaine parce qu'un peuple qui possède sa vie propre doit posséder aussi une langue et une littérature à lui." (Cited by Jean Déjeux in La Littérature maghrébine de langue française [Sherbrooke, 1973], p. 16.)

17. Arthur Pellegrin, La Littérature nord-africaine (Tunis, 1920).

18. Déjeux, Littérature maghrébine, p. 18.

19. Memmi, Anthologie, p. 13: "d'être des écrivains français parmi les autres—ou parmi les meilleurs."

20. Jean Déjeux outlines this early history in his study La Littérature algérienne contemporaine (Paris, 1975), pp. 56-95.

21. Ibid., p. 61: "Toute cette oeuvre est une quête obsessionnelle du paradis perdu, des sources vives de l'enfance, de l'ancêtre, de la pureté prénatale."

22. Jean Amrouche, "L'Eternel Jugurtha," L'Arche, no. 13 (February 1946), pp. 57-70.

23. Déjeux, Littérature algérienne contemporaine, p. 61: "Nul plus que lui n'a eu le goût du beau langage, du drapé, de l'éloquence digne des rhéteurs anciens."

24. An informative history of the principal cultural and literary Algerian periodicals published between 1937-62 has been compiled by Jean Déjeux in his article "La revue algérienne Soleil (1950-1952) fondée par Jean Sénac et les revues culturelles en Algérie de 1937 à 1962," Présence Francophone, no. 19 (Autumn 1979), pp. 5-28.

25. Mouloud Mammeri, Le Sommeil du juste (Paris, 1955), p.75: "Cette guerre a tout brouillé. Nul ne sait plus où est la Voie."

26. Memmi, Anthologie, pp. 14-15: "Pour la première fois, l'Afrique du Nord se voit enfin assumée. Acceptée, revendiquée ou discutée, elle cesse d'être un simple décor ou un accident géographique. Ces nouveaux auteurs sont aux prises avec leur pays comme avec l'essentiel d'eux mêmes. . . . C'est qu'il fallait oser enfin s'en prendre à sa propre vie, à celles de ses concitoyens, aux relations avec le Colonisateur. Il fallait en somme découvrir et affronter son véritable

domaine, son objet spécifique. Et cela ne va pas de soi quand depuis si longtemps on a perdu l'habitude de disposer de son destin."

27. Jean Sénac, Le Soleil sous les armes (Rodez, 1957).

28. Ibid., p. 20: "tout écrivain ayant définitivement opté pour la nation algérienne."

29. Due to the repressive political climate, many works composed during the war years were not submitted for publication until after independence in 1962, hence the large number of creative works on the Algerian conflict appearing after that date.

30. Mohammed Dib, "Les intellectuels algériens et le mouvement national," Alger Républicain, 26 April 1950, p. 5: "Toutes les forces de création mises au service de leurs frères opprimés feront de la culture et des oeuvres qu'ils produiront autant d'armes de combat. Armes qui serviront à conquérir la liberté."

31. "L'écrivain est l'expression des inquiétudes de la société, de ses doutes, de même que de sa lutte contre elle-même, de sa négativité" (cited by Déjeux in Littérature maghrébine, p. 39).

32. Jean Déjeux, Les Tendances depuis 1962 dans la littérature maghrébine de langue française (Algiers, 1973), p. 37.

33. This periodical, which began publication in 1971, is still in existence.

34. Born in Fès in 1942, Laâbi has taken up the cause of other repressed Arab countries, in particular Palestine. For his political activities he has been arrested and has suffered persecution.

35. Abdellatif Laâbi, "Au sujet d'un certain procès littérature maghrébine écrite en français," Souffles, no. 18 (March–April 1970), pp. 62–63.

36. Ibid., p. 62.

37. Abdelkébir Khatibi, "Témoignage," Le Monde, 17 December 1971.

38. Déjeux, Littérature maghrébine, p. 30: "La crise n'est pas une crise de la production, mais une crise de la thématique et de la qualité de l'écriture. . . ."

39. Abdelkébir Khatibi, the Moroccan teacher and writer, warns against giving too much credit to the influence of writers on their country's history: "Balanced between doubt and the affirmation of their role, all those writers—whether they called themselves revolution-

ary or not—knew that history was being made without them; they tended on the other hand to privilege their work and to draw attention to its historic necessity" (Le Roman maghrébin [Paris, 1968], p. 30). And further: "Literature does not change the world; it hardly disturbs it at all . . ." (p. 116).

40. Déjeux, Littérature maghrébine, p. 42: "celle d'un conflit de civilisations."

41. Ibid., p. 43: "sa propre permanence intérieure maghrébine."

Chapter Two

1. "Confronter mon lecteur avec la vérité la plus profonde et quelque-fois la plus désespérée de lui-même" (conversation between Mouloud Mammeri and Abdallah Mazouni, Le Jour [Beirut], 27 May 1966, p. 4).

2. During the last decades of colonization, the French sought to play Berbers against Arabs, favoring the former, especially by providing them with greater educational opportunities. Even today Kabylia resists the imposition of central government power. Each of the hundreds of Kabylian villages maintains its autonomy through the djemaa or village council of elders (as described in Mammeri's novels), which functions informally alongside the official administration. Efforts to preserve ancestral particularities has led to armed insurrection as late as May 1980.

3. Interview, El Moudjahid, 10 December 1967. This Algerian daily newspaper is still in existence.

4. Ibid.: "C'était pour moi une façon de la revivre et de m'en débarrasser."

5. "Les valeurs pour lesquelles il me semblait que l'on pût vivre avaient été élaborées par d'autres hommes pour une société différente de la mienne dans un contexte où aucun des miens ne figurait, sinon accidentellement. Je pensais combler la lacune" (cited by Déjeux in Littérature maghrébine, p. 184).

6. Révolution Africaine, April 1967. This publication is the central organ of the F.L.N.

7. These are summarized in an article by Mohammed-Salah Dembri, "Querelles autour de La Colline oubliée," Revue Algérienne des Lettres et des Sciences Humaines, no. 1 (1969), pp. 166-74.

8. In La Dépêche Quotidienne d'Alger, 24 September 1952; cited by Jean Déjeux in Littérature

maghrébine, p. 185.

9. In L'Effort Algérien, 3 October 1952; cited by Déjeux, ibid.

10. Mohammed Cherif Sahli, "La Colline du reniement," Le Jeune Musulman, no. 12 (2 January 1953); cited by Dembri, "Querelles autour," p. 167.

11. Mostefa Lacheraf, "La Colline oubliée ou les consciences anachroniques," Le Jeune Musulman, no. 13 (February 1953).

12. As cited in Déjeux, Littérature maghrébine, p. 187.

13. So fearful was Mammeri of being used as a political tool that he did not attend the awards presentation.

14. "Je pisse sur les idées" (Mouloud Mammeri, Le Sommeil du juste [Paris, 1955], p. 147).

15. Ibid., p. 253: "il ne sait pas que c'est par accident que nous sommes lui du bon côté de la barre et moi de l'autre. Il ne voit pas combien est fragile entre nous la ligne qui sépare la faute de justicier. S'il cessait un instant d'être bercé par la fausse sécurité du code, . . . il reculerait effrayé de découvrir que la société qu'il défend pourrait ne devoir son pardon qu'à ma mansuétude. . . ."

16. For an excellent detailed analysis see Isaac Yetiv's study, "La technique romanesque du Mouloud Mammeri dans Le Sommeil du juste," in Le Roman contemporain d'expression française (Sherbrooke, 1970), pp. 224-32.

17. "Un monde qui s'accepte condamné en face d'un qui se pense investi par Dieu . . ." (Mouloud Mammeri, La Mort absurde des Aztèques; Le Banquet [Paris, 1973], p. 13).

18. Ibid.: "une vraie expérience de laboratoire."

19. Ibid.: "On subit comme un choc insoutenable cette avancée régulière, implacable de l'événement, le déroulement du mécanisme absurde. Ce n'est pas une guerre, c'est une marche funèbre."

20. Ibid., p. 16: "Car il est clair qu'à mesure que les années passent, des portions de plus en plus vastes d'humanité se fourrent dans les voies royales de la civilisation occidentale technicienne, matérielle, efficace et programmée."

21. Ibid.: "La pensée occidentale est par essence unifiante et réductrice. Elle a inventé le Dieu unique et dévastateur, le Dieu jaloux. Il n'y a de place en elle que pour une seule vérité. Pour elle le crime de

l'autre c'est son altérité: l'autre est toujours in-
tolérable. Il est la fêlure qui menace de briser la
fermeture stupidement ronde de notre être."
    22. Ibid., p. 20: "Le travail même, qui fonde ses
richesse, l'empêche d'en jouir. On lui pèse le loisir
à l'once, on le lui programme et l'engeole dans la paren-
thèse crochue de quinze jours l'an, on le lui vend par
paquets ficelés, pasteurisés, pesés."

Chapter Three

    1. Jean Déjeux, Mohammed Dib, Ecrivain algérien
(Sherbrooke, 1977), p. 7: "Elle se présente comme un
investigation sans cesse plus poussée de la personne
humaine (qu'est-ce que l'être humain, le couple, la
liberté, la destinée?) aussi bien en fonction de ter-
roir algérien (l'homme colonisé d'hier et l'Algérien
d'aujourd'hui en marche vers une exigence plus grande de
libération) que par rapport à l'homme partout où il se
trouve. Cette oeuvre est recherche d'une humanité
réconciliée."
    2. Interview with Claudine Acs, L'Afrique
Littéraire et Artistique, no. 18 (August 1971), p. 12:
"L'essentiel est le fonds d'humanité qui nous est commun, les choses qui nous différencient demeureront toujours secondaires."
    3. Such a house exists. It was used to hospitalize
the wounded during World War I. Dib never lived there,
but his grandmother and an uncle did. See interview by
Acs, in L'Afrique, p. 11.
    4. La Grande Maison (Paris, 1952), p. 115:
"[Omar] n'acceptait pas l'existence telle qu'elle
s'offrait. Il en attendait autre chose que ce men-
songe, cette dissimulation, cette catastrophe qu'il
devinait."
    5. Ibid., p. 184: "sûre d'elle-même de ce qu'elle
portait en elle, inhabile encore mais puissante et
farouche. On les avait toujours aidés à ne pas penser;
à présent surgissait devant eux pleine de menaces
obscure, têtue, leur propre aventure; et tous ces
hommes, toutes ces femmes demeuraient nus devant eux-
mêmes. Ils avaient laissé leur coeur disponible, en
repos. Mais le malheur les touchait de son poing et ils
se réveillaient."
    6. Jean Brune, "Un livre et un pamphlet," La
Dépêche Quotidienne, 7 February 1953, p. 1: "une

oeuvre digne d'entrer dans le prestigieux Olympe de l'Art," and "[l'autre] souffle sur la rancune avec des arguments empruntés à la propagande."

7. Jean Sénac, Terrasses, no. 1 (1953). The article is signed Gérard Comma.

8. Louis Aragon, "Un Roman qui commence," Les Lettres Françaises 8-15 (July 1954).

9. L'Incendie (Paris, 1954), p. 36: "presque tout ce qui fait l'Algérie est en eux."

10. Ibid., p. 154: "Un incendie avait été allumé, et jamais plus il ne s'éteindrait. Il continuerait à ramper à l'aveuglette, secret, souterrain; ses flammes sanglantes n'auraient de cesse qu'elles n'aient jeté sur tout le pays leur sinistre éclat." The phrase is significant. The image evoked will be cast in a different mold in Qui se souvient de la mer.

11. Le Métier à tisser (Paris, 1957), p. 66. "Des gens parvenus au point où ils ne sont rien, où ils sont zéro, des gens comme ça, ne pourraient faire qu'une chose. . . . Réclamer tout."

12. Ibid., p. 67: "Nous sommes descendus trop bas. Nous ne pourrions redevenir des hommes par les voies ordinaires."

13. Qui se souvient de la mer (Paris, 1962), pp. 20-21: "Sans la mer, sans les femmes, nous serions restés définitivement des orphelins."

14. Pierre-Henri Simon, book review in Le Monde, 10 October 1962, p. 11: "Le vertige est trop fort avec Monsieur Dib. Son livre révèle un grand talent, une vigueur d'écrivain parfois admirable; mais il faudrait entrer en transes pour le bien lire."

15. Hassan El Nouty, "Roman et révolution dans Qui se souvient de la mer de Mohammed Dib," Présence Francophone 2 (1971):142-52: "Un texte capital qui répond à un triple dessein: c'est à la fois un commentaire esthétique, un plaidoyer et un manifeste."

16. "Mon souci lors de mes premiers romans était de fondre ma voix dans la voix collective. Cette grande voix aujourd'hui s'est tue. . . . J'ai repris mon attitude d'écrivain qui s'intéresse à des problèmes d'ordre psychologique, romanesque ou de style. . . . Le temps de l'engagement est terminé. J'ai été Africain quand il fallait l'être" (Le Figaro Littéraire, 4 June 1964).

17. Fawzia Mostefa-Kara, "Fantastique, mythes et symboles dans Cours sur la rive sauvage de Mohammed Dib"

(M.A. thesis, Université Paul Valéry, Montpellier, 1971).

18. Ibid., p. 5: "Sous son enveloppe fantastique, Cours sur la rive sauvage est une investigation, une recherche sur le destin de l'homme, sur son immortalité, sur la part de l'amour que l'homme porte à la femme, sur le rôle de la femme béatricienne qui montre le chemin à l'homme. Le fantastique semble être la meilleure voie pour accéder à une vérité profonde, pour explorer l'invisible, l'espace du dedans, l'envers des choses, la seconde moitié obscure de l'homme, 'l'autre côté de l'horizon' pour reprendre l'expression de Marcel Proust."

19. Acs, in L'Afrique, p. 10: "Les Algériens élevés dans un milieu musulman considèrent l'introspection comme un peu malsaine. D'un homme plongé dans des reflexions qui paraissent profanes, le proverbe dit: 'C'est quelqu'un qui mène paître les vaches d'Iblis.'"

20. Ibid.: "la psychanalyse est impensable en Algérie pour l'instant."

21. The very names of the main protagonists are revealing. The name Iven Zohar signifies etymologically "son of light." Radia has two etymologies. In Arabic the term refers to a person well disposed toward others. From the French verb irradier comes the meaning "to radiate." Radia is the luminous one, she who emits light. Her negative counterpart is Hellé, a name chosen for its English etymology, "Hell."

22. Cours sur la rive sauvage (Paris, 1964), p. 44: "une étrangère qui serait constamment à venir. . . ."

23. Maria Antonietta Pendola, in "Cours sur la rive sauvage de Mohammed Dib: l'Autre' et la double culture," Studi e Testi, no. 47 (1975), pp. 148–58, sees in this novel the problem of the North African intellectual torn between two cultures, between the native heritage and the acquired one.

24. Pierre-Henri Simon, book review in Le Monde, 12 August 1964, p. 8: "c'est un fleuve pris très loin de ses sources, et qui paraît riche surtout des affluents de culture qu'il a reçus. . . . c'est plutôt un Africain qui a conquis son droit de cité dans nos lettres."

25. As is frequently the case with Dib, the names are significant. Arfia is a derivative of the Arabic arfia, meaning "fire," and the name Rodwan means "he who accepts the light."

26. See Charles Bonn, "La Danse du roi de Mohammed Dib ou la parodie du vide," Présence Francophone, no. 5

(1972), pp. 67-77.

27. <u>La Danse du roi</u> (Paris, 1968), p. 80: "Y a peut-être une Algérie à tuer. A tuer pour qu'une autre plus propre puisse venir au monde."

28. Kamil in Arabic means "perfect." Kamel Waëd would be the perfect leader of a new nation. Waëd evokes <u>wa'da</u>, the gift or offering, that is to say, the money that has been secretly donated so that the young technocrat could receive an education. The name Hakim means "wiseman"; Hakim would have the people elevate themselves and assume their proper dignity. The term <u>jar</u> in the name Madjar means "neighbor, the near one." Hakim Madjar is near to the peasant.

29. <u>Dieu en Barbarie</u> (Paris, 1970), p. 201: "les Occidentaux sont eux-mêmes déchiquetés et dévorés par leur oeuvre."

30. Dib had anticipated writing another trilogy, but did not follow up with the third phase as expected.

31. <u>Habel</u> (Paris, 1977), from the back cover: "Caïn aujourd'hui ne tuerait pas son frère. Il le pousserait sur les chemins de l'émigration."

32. Ibid.: "dont on ne sait si c'est un homme ou une femme."

33. Annette Bonn-Gualino, review of <u>Habel</u> in <u>L'Annuaire de l'Afrique du Nord</u> 16 (1977):1088: "L'écriture n'est qu'une prostituée du langage. . . . Le marriage parodique d'Habel et du vieil écrivain symbolise d'une façon terrible l'impossible alliance de deux cultures prostituées, qui n'ont plus aucune authenticité."

34. <u>Habel</u>, p. 184: "fais de ton existence quelque chose qui te ressemblera."

35. Ibid., p. 131: "Une personne pour justifier ma vie, pour l'excuser; une personne pour l'accepter et me la faire accepter. Une personne pour en faire une chose valant quelque chose."

36. <u>Le Talisman</u> (Paris, 1966), p. 137: "une graphie tracée sur la matière illimitée. . . ."

37. Interview, <u>Afrique-Action</u>, 13 March 1961, p. 23: "je suis essentiellement poète et c'est de la poésie que je suis venu au roman, non l'inverse."

38. J. Levi-Valensi and J. E. Bencheikh, <u>Diwan Algérien</u> (Alger, 1967), p. 69: "la présence presque continuelle d'un univers poétique sous-tend, éclaire ou amplifie l'univers romanesque."

39. <u>Ombre gardienne</u> (Paris, 1961), p. 22: "Tout

là-bas palpite une voile / Ou est-ce une femme qui marche?"

40. Ibid., p. 43: "Maintenant où vas-tu chercher asile? / Au cinéma, dans ce bar que tu vois / Plein de néon, de buveurs flous, de voix?"

41. Ibid., p. 61: "le rêve et la vie emmelés sans se nuire / Menant les hommes plus avant vers la bonté."

42. Omneros (Paris, 1975), from the back cover: "des poèmes d'amour et plus littéralement de l'acte d'amour."

43. Ibid.: "Le côté le plus clair de la vie, le côté perceptible, est certainement le plus obscur. Il n'est que l'ombre portée d'Eros, il n'est et nous en lui, que le projet d'Eros même dans les instants où il ne le semble guère."

44. See Fawzia Sari-Mostefa Kara, "L'Ishrâq dans l'ouevre de Mohammed Dib," Revue de l'Occident Musulman et de la Méditerranée 22 (1976):109-17. The author proposes a religious interpretation: "the love which the lover feels is the very same by which God loves himself in him, in man, since what God loves in man is His epiphany" (p. 116).

45. Charles Bonn, review of Omneros in L'Annuaire de l'Afrique du Nord 14 (1975):1347: "un jeu perpétuel de déchiffrement de la transparence et de l'opacité, de l'ombre et de la lumière, de la neige et de la flamme, de l'eau et du feu. . . ."

46. Feu beau feu (Paris, 1979), p. 21: "combler le vide et ses abords. . . ."

Chapter Four

1. The author's surname is Kateb but he signs himself Kateb Yacine, after the manner in which school masters called their students.

2. Maurice Nadeau, "Kateb Yacine juge l'Islamisme," France Observateur, 16 August 1956, p. 13.

3. Claude Roy, "Un Rimbaud algérien," Le Nouvel Observateur, 7 September 1966, pp. 31-32.

4. Interview with Lakhdar Amina and Jean Duflot, "Kateb Yacine, les intellectuels, la révolution et le pouvoir," Jeune Afrique, no. 324 (26 March 1967), pp. 26-33: "Je crois bien, en effet, que je suis l'homme d'un seul livre. A l'origine c'était un poème, qui s'est transformé en romans et en pièces de théâtre, mais c'est toujours la même oeuvre que je laisserai

certainement comme je l'ai commencée, c'est-à-dire à
la fois à l'état de ruine et à l'état de chantier,
exactement comme l'Algérie est encore à la fois une
ruine et un chantier. On ne peut pas finir un livre
comme on finit un objet. On sent bien au fond de soi-
même que le travail n'est pas fini. L'Algérie n'a pas
fini de venir au monde."

    5. Ibid., p. 28: "Tout l'homme est dans l'enfant."

    6. One of Kateb's cousins was the first Muslim woman
deputy mayor of Bône. An uncle, Abdelaziz Kateb, who
was equally versed in Arab and French culture, was a high
level functionary in the Muslim Affairs section of the
government. Abdelaziz Kateb's son, Mustapha Kateb, is a
former director of the Algerian National Theater. See
Déjeux, Littérature maghrébine de langue française,
p. 211, n.

    7. Le Polygone étoilé (Paris, 1966), p. 179: "A
elle seule, elle était un théâtre."

    8. For further information on the significance of
the vulture both in Kateb's life experience and in African folklore see Jean Déjeux's "Les Structures de
l'imaginaire dans l'oeuvre de Kateb Yacine," Revue de
l'Occident Musulman et de la Méditerranée 13-14
(1973):286-87.

    9. Polygone, p. 180: "'la gueule du loup.' . . ."

    10. Ibid.: "Je ne veux pas que, comme moi, tu sois
assis entre deux chaises. . . . La langue française
domine. Il te faudra la dominer, et laisser en arrière
tout ce que nous t'avons inculqué dans ta plus tendre
enfance. Mais une fois passé maître dans la langue
française, tu pourras sans danger revenir avec nous à
ton point de départ."

    11. Ibid., p. 182: "Ainsi avais-je perdu tout à la
fois ma mère et son langage, les seuls trésors
inaliénables—et pourtant aliénés!"

    12. Legends and myths abound in Africa, where tribal
social structures have kept alive ancient cults and primitive magic rites. Remnants of ancient pagan traditions
associated with agrarian activities and charged with
sexual overtones have persisted over the centuries. Not
only had Kateb heard these stories from his mother, as an
adult he researched the legends and traditions of his
homeland.

    13. "Nedjma ou le poème ou le couteau," Mercure de
France, no. 1013 (1 January 1948):69-70.

    14. These were literary journals initiated by small

groups of writers, Arab Muslims together with French Algerians desirous of extending fraternal ties. The modest publications were committed to giving a voice to native Algerian writers. Financial difficulties forced the cessation of all of these periodicals.

15. The editors maintain that while European thought follows a linear course, "Arab thought evolves in a circular duration where each detour is a return, confusing the future and the past in an eternity of the instant" (Nedjma [Paris, 1956], p. 6). In support of their view that this phenomenon is inherent in the Arab mentality, the editors state that Arab grammar itself bears the mark of such an orientation. Mohammed Aziz Lahbabi, the noted sociologist, vigorously condemns this claim as totally false. See his "Notes sur la culture arabo-musulmane," Confluent, no. 14 (July 1957), pp. 241-45. Clearly the debate involves an insoluble question, for it is impossible to determine the direction and dimension in which men's thoughts move.

16. For a complete bibliography of Kateb's works, including pieces which have appeared in periodicals and critical studies done on him, see Jean Déjeux, "Kateb Yacine, romancier, poète et dramaturge algérien," Présence Francophone 15 (1977):124-47.

17. "L'explosion poétique est au centre de tout." See interview with Jean Marie Serreau, "Qu'est-ce que le théâtre?" L'Action (Tunisia), 11 August 1958, p. 17.

18. An excellent detailed study of this work has been written by Marc Gontard of the University of Fès, Morocco. See his "Nedjma" de Kateb Yacine: Essai sur la structure formelle du roman (Rabat, 1975). Particularly useful are the three diagrams, one charting the interactions among the characters, the other two illustrating the chronology of events. These orient the reader by permitting him to visualize the chronological unfolding of incidents from the distant past to the present, and the relationships of the protagonists to each other. For a structuralist approach see Francis Gandon's "Le Thème de la 'nuit de l'erreur' dans Nedjma de Kateb Yacine," Présence Francophone, no. 21 (1979), pp. 21-46.

19. Abdelkébir Khatibi makes the following observation: "With Kateb the myth is that mediation which, while underscoring the displacement between history and the activity of the imaginary, constitutes that will to play false on history, to do violence to it, to distort it, to jumble it in a gamelike atmosphere. The myth as

such translates a comportment: beyond a verist history, the myth comes to the aid of history and becomes an historicizing element." See La Roman maghrébin (Paris, 1968), p. 106. Myth has another essential function: it counterbalances the notion of "our ancestors the Gauls" imposed on the gallicized North Africans by the French educational system.

20. "Keblout" in Turkish means "cut cord" (corde tranchée).

21. As with Mohammed Dib, the theme of the return to the cave is to be equated with a finding of forgotten energies hidden during the long night of successive foreign invasions. For Kateb this retreat may be one of religion, sex, or a folkloric ethic. Here man's broken spirit is regenerated. In a footnote, Jean Déjeux cites an article by the psychologist Jacques Berque that demonstrates that the Maghreb can only be understood within the framework of a "return to the cavern in search of the ancestor." See "Structures de l'imaginaire," p. 285, n. 38.

22. The theme of "the bath of the accursed," in which the condemned ones are metamorphosed or turned to stone, is an ancient legend of which many versions exist. Its purpose is to illustrate the divine punishment that befalls partners of incestuous marriages. See Déjeux's "Structures de l'imaginaire," p. 279, n. 22.

23. Gontard, "Nedjma" de Kateb Yacine, p. 110: "Le sens le plus authentique de Nedjma est d'être lui-même incomplet, inachevé, incertain."

24. Polygone, p. 144: "vierge après chaque viol. . . ."

25. Déjeux, Littérature maghrébine de langue française, p. 229: "Les quatre veulent à la fois la soeur et l'étrangère, la fille de la tribu et la fille des 'autres,' être dans la tribu et être déserteurs, être dans le cercle et en sortir."

26. Kateb emphasizes this point in an interview with Jean Prasteau, "La Langue de la révolution, c'est le français," Le Figaro Littéraire, 26 January 1967, p. 13.

27. Nedjma, p. 126: "le souvenir de la tribu défunte."

28. Ibid., p. 146: "Car l'histoire de notre tribu n'est écrite nulle part, mais aucun fil n'est jamais rompu pour qui recherche ses origines."

29. Ibid., p. 102: "Mais la conquête était un mal

nécessaire, une greffe douloureuse apportant une promesse de progrès à l'arbre de la nation entamé par la hache; comme les Turcs, les Romains et les Arabes, les Français ne pouvaient que s'enraciner, otages de la patrie en gestation dont ils se disputaient les faveurs."

30. Ibid., pp. 146-47: "Et puis nous voulions, avant d'envisager l'avenir, connaître toutes les survivances de la tribu, vérifir nos origines pour dresser un bilan de faillite, ou tenter une réconciliation."

31. Ibid., p. 128: "Tu dois songer à la destinée de ce pays d'où nous venons, qui n'est pas une province française, et qui n'a ni bey ni sultan; tu penses peut-être à l'Algérie toujours envahie, à son inextricable passé, car nous ne sommes pas une nation, pas encore, sache-le: nous ne sommes que des tribus décimées. Ce n'est pas revenir en arrière que d'honorer notre tribu, le seul lien qui nous reste pour nous réunir et nous retrouver. . . ."

32. Georges Poulet, "Kateb Yacine et le cercle de la révolution algérienne," La Nouvelle Critique 4 (4 May 1967):14-15: "être perturbateur au sein de la perturbation."

33. Like Kateb, Rimbaud was a wanderer who lived on the margin of society. He believed the poet should be a seer who, through the magic of the senses and hallucinations, would transform his perceptions of the universe and render them in new language. Rimbaud's method of superimposing images, his predilection for enigmatic word associations, and his thirst for the absolute are further reasons for the comparison with Kateb.

34. "Raisonné dérèglement de tous les sens" (Arthur Rimbaud, "Lettre du voyant [15 May 1871]," in Oeuvres complètes d'Arthur Rimbaud [Paris, 1963], p. 270).

35. Interview in Jeune Afrique, p. 33: "Il y a des gens qui ont peur du mot révolution ou des gens qui le comprennent mal, ou des politiciens étroits, et tout ça c'est faux. En fait la révolution, c'est une chose toute naturelle. Elle est inscrite dans les astres, la révolution. Parce que les étoiles tournent, la terre tourne. La révolution c'est le mouvement du monde. C'est la chose la plus naturelle qui soit. Bon. Par conséquent les révolutionnaires ne sont pas du tout ceux qui veulent tout casser. Ce sont ceux qui veulent que le monde tourne comme il doit tourner. Donc il n'y a rien d'extraordinaire à être révolutionnaire. Ce n'est

qu'une attitude. C'est tout simplement le fait d'être
dans le sens de la vie."

36. Gontard, "Nedjma" de Kateb Yacine, p. 110: "le
miracle, proprement artistique, vient justement de ce que
l'engagement le plus profond, se traduise par l'inter-
médiaire de la forme même de l'oeuvre. . . ."

37. Ibid., p. 111: "une forme qui porte en elle-
même sa signification."

38. The vulture, which is considered a noble species
in the Maghreb, the bird par excellence, occupies a very
personal place in Kateb's life. It is specifically part
of Constantine tradition. The scene produced in the play
recalls Kateb's mother's story about the celebration of
the vulture festival, an event that the writer was later
able to witness for himself. See Déjeux's "Structures
de l'imaginaire," p. 286.

39. Some readers and critics wrongly interpret Kateb
as condemning Islam. In fact he only mocks religious
abuses.

40. Critics have drawn different conclusions about
the plays, depending on whether they experienced them as
readers or as spectators. For some interesting compari-
sons see Bernard Aresu, "Les Tragédies de Kateb Yacine,"
Oeuvres et Critiques IV, no. 2 (1980), pp. 29-36.

41. Interview with Jean-Marc Martin du Theil, in Les
Lettres Françaises, 17 November 1971, pp. 16-17: "Mon
pays tel que je voulais qu'il soit, je le voyais sur la
terre vietnamienne. L'Algérie comme projetée dans
l'avenir. Les peuples coloniaux, s'ils veulent combler
leur immense retard historique, doivent emprunter la voie
du socialisme. . . . Ce que j'ai vu au Vietnam a donc
été pour moi un bain de jouvence, l'aube d'une renaissance."

42. Ibid., p. 17: "mon objectif a toujours été
d'atteindre le public de mon pays. De ce point de vue,
mon itinéraire est clair. . . . Je reviens à ce que
j'ai toujours désiré faire: un théâtre politique
dans une langue largement accessible au plus grand
nombre. Je vais manier désormais deux langues: le français et surtout l'arabe populaire."

43. Ibid.: "Le rôle de l'écrivain révolutionnaire
est de rendre compte des luttes qui embrasent le monde
entier. A lui de transmettre un message vivant, de
placer ce public au coeur d'un théâtre qui prenne parti
dans le combat, jamais terminé, qui oppose le prolétari-
at à la bourgeoisie. C'est la grande confrontation de

notre temps. Il est logique de promouvoir un théâtre
qui attise la lutte des classes et la porte à son point
le plus haut. Le théâtre est bien le moyen idéal pour
un peuple d'entrer de plain-pied dans la politique."

Chapter Five

    1. Isaac Yetiv, Le Thème de l'aliénation dans le
roman maghrébin d'expression française (Sherbrooke,
1972), pp. 148-51.
    2. Ibid., p. 153: "une plongée introspective dans
les recoins les plus sombres de son âme pour essayer d'y
découvrir une identité insaisissable, toujours change-
ante, toujours fuyante, jamais fixée."
    3. La Statue de sel (Paris, 1953), p. 282: "Moi
je suis mal à l'aise dans mon pays natal et je n'en con-
nais pas d'autre, ma culture est d'emprunt et ma langue
maternelle infirme, je n'ai plus de croyances, de religion, de traditions et j'ai honte de ce qui en eux
résiste au fond de moi. . . . Je suis Tunisien mais
juif, c'est-à-dire politiquement, socialement exclu,
parlant la langue du pays avec un accent particulier, mal
accordé passionnellement à ce qui émeut les musulmans;
juif mais ayant rompu avec la religion juive et le ghetto, ignorant de la culture juive et détestant la bourgeoisie inauthentique."
    4. The Anthologie des écrivains maghrébins d'ex-
pression française is the first anthology in French to
give an overall view of the Maghrebian literary scene
rather than focusing on a particular theme of the revolution. A second edition of the work appeared in 1965,
only four months after the first. Memmi's introduction
and choice of authors for inclusion in the book aroused a
heated polemic centering on the definition of "Maghrebian." Memmi was accused of unfairly discriminating
between writers of European descent and those of Arab
origin. He labeled as Maghrebian those who had lived
through the colonial period as colonized persons and who
sought to establish separate identity through nationhood.
All others he classified as European. Frustration and
revolt characterize the former; separation describes the
latter, he explains.
    5. Yetiv, Le thème de l'aliénation, p. 157:
"l'auteur-narrateur se déplace linéairement dans le
temps historique mais par cercles concentriques dans

l'espace humain; l'espace géographique ne l'intéresse guère et les rare descriptions, d'ailleurs très réussies du point de vue littéraire, ne sont là que pour éclairer et faire comprendre l'état d'âme de l'auteur et l'état de tension qui le relie aux hommes."

6. Ibid., p. 159: "Tous ces 'moi' successifs sont autant de jalons sur la route de l'auto-connaissance et sont à l'origine de la crise d'identité de l'auteur. . . ."

7. Statue, p. 273: "J'avais refusé l'Orient et l'Occident me refusait."

8. Ibid., p. 39: "Des millions d'hommes ont perdu leur unité fondamentale, ils ne se reconnaissent plus et se cherchent en vain."

9. Ibid., pp. 284-85: "Ainsi, j'ai passé de crise en crise, retrouvant chaque fois un nouvel équilibre, plus précaire, mais toujours il me restait quelque chose à détruire. . . . Et chaque fois s'écroulait une partie de moi."

10. "Mon malheur est que je ne suis plus comme personne" (Agar [Paris, 1955], p. 242). The book was reedited in 1963. Our quotations are from the first edition.

11. "Peut-être le mieux est-il d'avancer sans chercher d'abord à comprendre. Des lignes de force finiront bien par apparaître d'elles-mêmes: si elles existent!" (Le Scorpion [Paris, 1969], p. 16).

12. Ibid., p. 41: "ni fiction, ni Journal, ni document, mais une seule intention complexe."

13. Ibid., p. 62: "Si un écrivain essayait de dire tout, dans un seul livre, ce livre serait-il celui de sa guérison, de sa réconciliation avec lui-même et les autres, avec la vie. . . ."

14. Ibid., p. 227: "la littérature est une exploration de limites. . . ."

15. Ibid., p. 244: "refaire son unité. . . ."

16. Ibid., p. 60: "La fréquence, la variété, la gravité des maladies oculaires en ce pays. . . ."

17. Jacqueline Leiner, French Review 44 (December 1970):417.

18. Scorpion, author's note, p. 295: "Nous comptons sur le lecteur pour un effort complémentaire d'imagination. Ce sera sa part dans cette oeuvre commune."

19. The anecdote of the scorpion is in itself a subject of speculation. It is described as being the

attraction of a carnivallike show. Customers pay to see
it apparently sting itself to death with its own venom
when trapped in a ring of fire. In fact, the beast is
only in a comatose state. After the spectators have
dispersed, the exhibitor returns it to a box where it recovers to be exhibited again.

20. Emile Capouya, "Suicidal Stings of Truth,"
Saturday Review, 26 June 1971, pp. 19-21.

21. Hugh Kenner, "The Contents of a Desk Drawer in
Tunisia," New York Times Book Review, 27 June 1971, p.
7.

22. Scorpion, p. 230: "J'entrevois maintenant
seulement que toute mon oeuvre publiée n'est que l'incessant commentaire d'une oeuvre à venir; avec l'espoir
insensé que se commentaire puisse finir par constituer
lui-même cette oeuvre."

23. Isaac Yetiv, "Albert Memmi: The Syndrome of Self
Exile," International Fiction Review 1 (1973):125-34.

24. "N'ai-je pas agi, plutôt, comme si le seul royaume à conquérir était celui de soi-même? Dernière
sagesse ou suprême illusion" (Le Désert [Paris,
1977], p. 177).

25. Gérard Guillot, "Un écrivain en quête de son
identité," Le Figaro Littéraire, 24-25 September
1977, p. 24: "une chronique vivante colorée, émou-
vante, aveuglante de vérité puissante comme un film par
toutes ses images. . . . à la manière des chroniqueurs
du XIIIe ou du XVe siècle. Et la richesse verbale
du texte est si forte qu'il semble que ce récit on
l'entend plutôt qu'on le lit. Comme si sa transmission
n'avait été qu'orale, comme si à travers les siècles
il nous était parvenu génération après génération."

26. "Pleine de palpitations, de senteurs . . . [le]
lecteur est grisé et séduit" (Salim Jay, L'Afrique Littéraire et Artistique, 46:91-94.

27. Ibid., p. 94: "Albert Memmi a réussi son entre-
prise en virtuose de l'imaginaire."

28. Désert, from the back cover: "ce simple bonheur de lire, trop souvent négligé de nos jours."

29. "Le monde entier . . . était dans le couple"
(Le Portrait du colonisé suivi du portrait du colonisateur [Paris, 1957], p. 15). Our quotations are from the
1966 reprint.

30. Ibid., pp. 15-17: "Et si je voulais comprendre
l'échec de leur aventure, celle d'un couple mixte en
colonie, il me fallait comprendre le Colonisateur et le

Colonisé, et peut-être même toute la relation et la
situation coloniales. Tout cela m'entraînait fort loin
de moi-même et de mes difficultés à vivre; mais l'ex-
plication reculait toujours, et sans savoir encore où
j'allais aboutir, et sans la prétention de cerner une
condition si complexe, il me fallait au moins trouver un
terme à mon angoisse. . . . Bref j'enterpris cet inven-
taire de la condition du Colonisé d'abord pour me comprendre moi-même et identifier ma place au milieu des
autres hommes. Ce furent mes lecteurs, qui étaient loin
d'être tous des Tunisiens, qui m'ont convaincu plus tard
que ce Portrait était également le leur."

31. Déjeux, La Littérature maghrébine de langue
française, p. 322: "un savant dosage d'objectivité et
d'émotion personnelles."

32. Portrait, p. 20: "rien dans ce texte n'est
inventé ou supposé, ou même extrapolé hasardeusement.
Il s'agit toujours d'une expérience, mise en forme et
stylisée, mais toujours sous-jacente derrière chaque
phrase. Et si j'ai consenti finalement à cette allure
générale qu'elle a fini par prendre, c'est précisé-
ment parce que je sais que je pourrais, à toute ligne,
à chaque mot, faire correspondre des faits multiples et
parfaitement concrets."

33. Ibid., p. 32: "Cet ouvrage sobre et clair se
range parmi les 'géométries passionnées,' son objectivité calme, c'est de la souffrance et de la colère
dépassée."

34. Ibid., p. 177: "reproduire, complètement et en
vérité, les portraits des deux protagonistes du drame
colonial, et la relation qui les unit."

35. Paul Semonin, "No Man's Land," Nation, 27 December 1965, pp. 535-37.

36. Ibid.

37. Quoted by Yetiv, "Syndrome," p. 129.

38. Ibid.

39. Portrait, cited in the editor's note, p. 10:
"Le livre d'Albert Memmi constituera comme un document
auquel les historiens de la Colonisation auront à se
référer. . . ."

40. Ibid.: "le meilleur des ouvrages connus sur la
psychologie coloniale."

41. Jean-Louis Bory, "Un itinéraire," La Quinzaine
Littéraire, 15-30 November 1966, p. 24.

42. Jean-François Revel, "La Clé du ghetto," L'Express, 10-16 October 1966: "dans la mesure où Memmi se

place exclusivement dans le vécu actuel, et évite le
mélange d'exposé biologico-sociologique et de notations
existentielles qui nuisait quelque peu à l'unité du
Portrait."
  43. Yetiv, "Syndrome," p. 132.
  44. Madeleine Akselrad, "Albert Memmi et L'Homme
dominé," L'Afrique Littéraire et Artistique, 19
April 1969, pp. 18-21.
  45. "Ces diverses études sont des gammes pour ce
grand livre sur l'oppression, que j'annonce sans cesse,
que je n'achèverai peut-être jamais, mais vers lequel
j'avance tous les jours un peu" (L'Homme dominé
[Paris, 1968], p. 9).
  46. Memmi would have come closer to the truth had he
identified woman with the colonized as he describes them
in the first Portrait: inferiors, economically exploited, excluded from management functions, in need of
"protection," relegated to anonymity, and doomed to exist
only as a function of the needs of the colonizer with no
possible means of escaping from their unhappy state.
  47. Yetiv, "Syndrome," p. 132.
  48. Scorpion, p. 230: "Ce n'est pas en traçant
chacun de mes cercles d'une couleur différente que je me
serai davantage approché du centre."

Chapter Six

  1. Salim Jay, "Un entretien avec Driss Chraibi,"
Afrique Littéraire et Artistique, no. 43 (1977), pp.
26-30.
  2. Most of the biographical information presented
here comes from Jean Déjeux's Littérature maghrébine
de langue française, pp. 278-79.
  3. Since no bureau of records existed at the time
Chraibi himself is uncertain of his date of birth. The
author speaks candidly about this problem in Mirrors:
Autoportraits (Paris, 1973), p. 56.
  4. In both Un Ami viendra vous voir and Mort au
Canada, two of the main protagonists are psychiatrists.
  5. L'Ane (Paris, 1956), p. 13: "Le héros du
Passé simple s'appelle Driss Ferdi. C'est peut-être
moi. En tout cas, son désespoir est le mien. Désespoir d'une foi. Cet Islam en quoi il croyait, qui par-
lait d'égalité des règnes, de la part de Dieu en
chaque individu de la création, de tolérance, de
liberté et d'amour, il le voyait, adolescent ardent

formé dans les écoles françaises, réduit au phari-
saïsme, système social arme de propagande. A tout
prendre, il s'embarquait pour la France: il avait besoin
de croire, d'aimer, de respecter quelqu'un ou quelque
chose."

   6. Le Passé simple (Paris, 1954), p. 124: "Cof-
fre à grossesses."

   7. Yetiv, Le Thème de l'aliénation, p. 98.

   8. Le Passé simple, p. 188: "Par le dogme, pour
le dogme, dans le dogme. Je me tus, m'éteignis, suivis
le Droit Chemin."

   9. "Un tissu de mensonges et une mauvaise action."
See readers' responses to Bernard Simiot: "Espoirs et
tourments de la jeunesse marocaine," in Hommes et
Mondes, March 1965.

   10. Yetiv, Le Thème de l'aliénation, pp. 95-96:
"Le symbolisme pseudo-épique de la situation, assez maladroit, dans un roman d'intention réaliste, mais que la
passion pousse vers le mélodrame, a echappé aux lecteurs de Chraïbi. C'est en effet son drame individuel
qu'a voulu exprimer Chraïbi et il l'a gratuitement extrapolé aux dimensions du groupe. Le père est le bouc
émissaire, chargé de tous les maux du fils qui sont
sans doute réels."

   11. Déjeux, Littéraire maghrébine de langue
française, p. 279: "haché, heurté, un style de corps
à corps, où l'on veut par sadomasochisme se faire mal
et faire mal aux autres, avec des phrases à l'emporte-
pièce, un vocabulaire de corps de garde et des images
très crues (odeurs, déjections, défoulement viscéral
ou glandulaire)."

   12. Yetiv, Le Thème de l'aliénation, p. 101: "et
dans sa recherche d'effets dramatiques, presque toujours
inutile et encombrant."

   13. Ahmed Sefrioui, Démocratie, 25 February 1957:
"Je me demandais alors sincèrement si Chraïbi avait
connu le Maroc et les Marocains. Son livre laissait
supposer le contraire."

   14. See Yetiv, Le Thème de l'aliénation, pp. 91,
95: very unlikely would be the spitting scene in which
all the children march before their father, each spitting
in his face, and the knife scene, in which the father, in
the presence of his dumbfounded family, dares Driss to
stab him before he finishes counting to ten.

   15. See ibid., pp. 110-11: rampant pederasty in the
Koranic schools, extreme physical punishment meted out to

youngsters by Muslim school masters, facile formulas for repudiation of a wife are some striking, true examples.

16. Abdellatif Laâbi, Souffles, no. 5 (1967), pp. 18-21: "Chraibi est vraisemblablement le seul écrivain maghrébin et arabe qui ait eu le courage de mettre tout un peuple devant ses lâchetés, qui lui ait étalé son immobilisme, les ressorts de son hypocrisie, de cette autocolonisation et oppression exercée les uns sur les autres. . . ."

17. L'Ane, p. 13: "En France, pays de liberté et de fraternité, pays de refuge surtout, il assiste à la lente décristallisation humaine de ses propres frères de misère."

18. Les Boucs (Paris, 1955), p. 71: "je devais, non pas me racheter individuellement vis-à-vis de la société dans laquelle je vis pour que j'aie droit à sa sympathie, mais racheter les Nord-Africains. Pour eux souffrir dans ma dignité d'homme et dans ma chair d'homme. Voilà ce que j'ai fait pendant cinq ans. Puis traduire cela en une espèce de témoignage, non pas de mes sens, mais de mes souffrances."

19. L'Ane, p. 14: "Choisir? J'ai déjà choisi mais je voudrais tellement n'avoir plus à le faire. Car si j'ai choisi de vivre en France . . . je continue à participer à ce monde de mon enfance et à cet Islam en lequel je crois de plus en plus."

20. Ibid., p. 82: "tout est à reconsidérer, tout est à refaire, valeurs, idéaux et morales. . . ."

21. Ibid., p. 99: "qui puisse employer sans déchets inutiles ce capital-travail que représentent les hommes, qui tue l'individu au profit de la communauté. . . ."

22. De tous les horizons (Paris, 1958), p. 9: "liberté, croyance, bonheur, sens de notre vie, espérance."

23. Ibid., from the rear cover: "un reproche vivant, mais aussi comme les porte-parole d'un autre univers souhaitable dont ils sont les héritiers réprouvés."

24. La Foule (Paris, 1961), p. 88: "sans idéal—et sans âme."

25. Ibid., p. 19: "cette masse amorphe et flottante, faite de coeurs et de cerveaux moyens, indifférents à l'événement at à tout ce qui dépassait le cadre de souci quotidien et matériel de l'existence."

26. Ibid., pp. 87-88: "amas de déconsciences. . . ."

27. Succession ouverte (Paris, 1962), p. 32: "noyés dans la tourmente de leur propre existence. . . ."

28. Ibid., p. 180: "Creuse un puits et descends à
la recherche de l'eau. La lumière n'est pas à la surface, elle est au fond, tout au fond. Partout, où que
tu sois, et même dans le désert, tu trouveras toujours
de l'eau. Il suffit de creuser."

29. Un Ami viendra vous voir (Paris, 1967), p. 42:
"l'acharnement à vouloir comprendre, pour être enfin
moi-même.

30. Ibid., p. 203: "C'était une contrainte de tous
les instants, pendant des années. Il fallait que je
réponde à cette image, que je sois cette fonction."

31. Ibid.: "cette femme-là, que ces gens-là atten-
daient."

32. "Cette conclusion sent l'eau de rose et la gen-
tiane" (R.-M. Albérès, "En plein délire," Les Nouvelles Littéraires, 16 February 1967, p. 7).

33. La Civilisation, ma mère! (Paris, 1972), p.
174: "la conscience d'un monde inconscient."

34. Ibid., p. 175: "Et le noyau de la commune, c'est
bel et bien la famille. Si au sein de cette famille la
femme est maintenue prisonnière, voilée qui plus est,
séquestrée comme nous l'avons fait depuis des siècles,
si elle n'a aucune ouverture sur le monde extérieur,
aucun rôle actif, la société dans son ensemble s'en
ressent fatalement, se referme sur elle-même et n'a plus
rien à apporter ni à elle-même ni au reste du monde.
Elle devient non viable, exactement comme ces anciennes
entreprises familiales qui s'effritent en Bourse à la
moindre offre publique d'achat."

35. The back cover of the book, obviously composed
with a view to enticing the average adult reader,
promises to conjure up an image of absolute love that
"leaves nothing in the dark, not even the most intimate
scenes."

36. Khatibi, Le Roman maghrébin, p. 27: "Dans un
sens, cet exil est indéfendable sur le plan national.
Si l'indépendance a avorté et a constitué principale-
ment en une substitution du régime colonial par le
régime d'une bourgeoisie et d'une féodalité comme le
constate Chraibi dans son dernier roman, il convient de
préciser que le combat reste à mener à l'intérieur
même du pays. L'irréalisme politique de ce romancier
de grand talent est flagrant. Pour comprendre Chraibi,
il faut dire que son attitude ne se base pas sur une
analyse objective de la situation historique et politique
de son pays; elle est essentiellement psychologique, en

ce sens que son déracinement est trop grand pour pouvoir
se réconcilier avec sa propre société."

Chapter Seven

1. Information has been gathered from a number of
sources, including the U.S. area handbooks cited in chap-
ter 1, the new edition of Fadela M'Rabet's essays, La
Femme algérienne suivi de Les Algériennes (Paris,
1969), Mohammed Aziz Lahbabi's Le Personalisme musulman
(Paris, 1953), Evelyn Accad's Veil of Shame: The Role of
Women in the Modern Fiction of North Africa and the Arab
World (Sherbrooke, 1978), and pertinent chapters of
Women in the Muslim World, ed. Lois Beck and Nikki
Keddie (Cambridge, 1978). Germaine Tillion's Le Harem
et les cousins (Paris, 1966), often cited with reference
to the women's problem, is an important theoretical work.
   For the sake of accuracy, it must be noted that the
consideration accorded women varies from country to country, between metropolitan and rural areas, and between
social classes. While not ignoring these differences, we
have tried to summarize the mentality that best describes
the majority.
   2. Femmes d'Alger dans leur appartement (Paris,
1980), p. 174: "car l'oeil de celui qui domine cherche
d'abord l'autre oeil, celui du dominé, avant de prendre
possession du corps. . . ."
   3. Ibid.: "les autres yeux du corps (seins, sexe,
et nombril), risquent à leur tour d'être exposés, dé-
visagés. C'en est fini pour les hommes, gardiens vulné-
rables: c'est leur nuit, leur malheur, leur déshonneur."
   4. Ibid., p. 175: "une menace nouvelle à leur
exclusivité scopique, à cette prérogative mâle."
   5. We do not mean to imply that the subject has been
entirely passed over, but it has not aroused national
consciousness. Jean Déjeux has compiled a lengthy bibliography of male and female authored documents dealing
with women's issues and the family. See his "Connais-
sance du monde féminin et de la famille en Algérie,"
Revue Algérienne des Sciences Juridiques, Economiques
et Politiques 5, no. 4 (December 1968):1247–1302.
   6. Khatibi, Le Roman maghrébin, pp. 59-60: "nous
sommes encore dans la préhistoire de la littérature
féminine, . . . la représentation que se fait la femme
d'elle-même est prisonnière de celle de la femme faite
par l'homme."

7. Jean Déjeux has outlined and summarized the contributions of female Algerian writers. See his article "Femmes écrivains dans la littérature algérienne de langue française," in the Revue de l'Institut de Belles Lettres Arabes, no. 144 (1979), pp. 307-36.

Chapter Eight

1. Most of the biographical information on Assia Djebar is taken from Déjeux, Littérature maghrébine de langue française, pp. 247-49.

2. "J'ai toujours voulu éviter de donner à mes romans un caractère auto-biographique par peur de l'indécence et par horreur d'un certain striptease intellectuel auquel on se livre souvent avec complaisance dans les premières oeuvres. Ma vie personnelle n'a rien de commun avec mes héroïnes" (cited in ibid., p. 252).

3. "Je ne pensais pas réellement publier La Soif qui reste pour moi un exercise de style" (interview, L'Action, 8 September 1958).

4. "J'ai voulu montrer combien dans ce monde calme où rien objectivement n'avait encore changé se développait un processus qui laissait deviner les bouleversements futurs" (cited in Déjeux, Littérature maghrébine de langue française, p. 252).

5. Mildred Palmer Mortimer, "La Femme algérienne dans les romans d'Assia Djebar," French Review 44, no. 5 (April 1976):759-63.

6. Les Alouettes naïves (Paris, 1967), p. 191: "L'avenir de l'homme est la femme."

7. Cited by Déjeux, Littérature maghrébine de langue française, p. 253.

8. Ibid., p. 266: "parfois insignifiants et souvent laborieux."

9. Marie-Blanche Tahon, review of Femmes d'Alger dans leur appartement, in Ecriture Française dans le Monde, la Tribune des Francophones, no. 5 (1981), p. 114: "les hauts faits d'une épopée essentiellement masculine. . . ."

10. Femmes d'Alger dans leur appartement (Paris, 1980), p. 171: "Femmes en attente toujours [dans] cette atmosphère raréfiée de la claustration."

11. Ibid., p. 9: "se délivrent-elles . . . tout à fait du rapport d'ombre entretenu des siècles durant avec leur propre corps."

12. Ibid., p. 68: "Parler entre nous et regarder.

Regarder dehors, regarder hors des murs et des prisons."

13. Tahon, review, p. 114: "elle est aussitôt soupçonnée de vouloir nier les valeurs arabo-islamiques, celles de son peuple, pour promouvoir les valeurs occidentales, celles de l'occupant."

14. Assia Djebar, "Nous boîtons en croyant danser," Jeune Afrique, no. 351 (1 October 1967), pp. 38-39: "le passé paralysé dans le présent et le présent ac-coucheur d'avenir. . . ."

15. Interview with Monique Hennebelle, "La Femme sera le devenir du monde arabe," L'Afrique Littéraire et Artistique, no. 3 (February 1969), pp. 61-64.

16. Ibid., p. 63.

17. Femmes d'Alger, p. 8: "parler sur ce terrain devient . . . une transgression."

18. Evelyne Accad, Veil of Shame: The Role of Women in the Modern Fiction of North Africa and the Arab World (Sherbrooke, 1978), p. 47.

Chapter Nine

1. As early as 1957 Albert Memmi predicted the dry-ing up of this literature. See Le Portrait du coloni-sé, p. 148: "European language colonized literature seems condemned to die young." See also Khatibi, Le Roman Maghrébin, p. 32; Malek Haddad, Les Zéros tour-nent en ronde (Paris, 1961), p. 37. While trying not to make any definitive judgment, Isaac Yetiv too leans toward a negative view. See his final chapter, "Après 1956 . . . Perspectives d'avenir," in Le Thème de l'aliénation dans le roman maghrébin d'expression fran-çaise, pp. 202-29.

2. "Retrouve un second souffle. Il ne peut donc être question de parler de 'tarissement,' mais d'une liberté en action qui refuse toute domestication et toute castration" (Jean Déjeux, Les Tendances depuis 1962 dans la littérature maghrébine de langue fran-çaise [Algiers, 1973]). This is a conference given at the Centre Culturel Français on February 27, 1973.

3. "Avec tous les écrivains authentiquement révolu-tionnaires d'Afrique, d'Asie, du monde entier, pour que triomphe le socialisme" (from the Manifeste des Ecri-vains Algériens, published in Présence Francophone, no. 4 [1972], p. 207).

4. Kateb Yacine, interview, Jeune Afrique, no. 324 (26 March 1967), p. 30. "On commet toujours la même

faute, on traite le concept de liberté comme un concept
bourgeois, c'est comme si la liberté n'était bonne que
pour les bourgeois. . . . Il y a là une importante question de principe que devraient se poser tous les révolu-
tionnaires. Il ne peut y avoir d'Union des écrivains
sans une totale liberté d'expression, faute de quoi
c'est toujours la même chose: le pouvoir délègue dans
ces unions des écrivains béni-oui-oui."

5. As reported in Déjeux's account, "L'Union des
écrivains algériens," Présence Francophone, no. 10
(1975), p. 173.

6. Mostefa Lacheraf, "Le Roman maghrébin: brève
contribution à un débat," Souffles, nos. 13-14
(1969), p. 3: "une conscience présente à un monde
vécu, un cadre actuel ouvert à toutes les possibili-
tés, à toutes les leçons directes que le mouvement de
la société, avec ses aspirations contrariées, ses
carences séculaires, ses épreuves mortelles, son désespoir actif ou résigné, ses révoltes, ses angoisses,
imposent à nos contemporains. . . ."

7. Arezki Metref, "La Culture: Un bien collectif,"
Echabab, no. 123 (29 January 1974): "Qu'on ne
s'installe pas dans la littérature 'officialisée' comme
dans une caste sociale privilégiée ou un franc-
maçonnerie de luxe, mais qu'on ouvre grandes les portes
de l'U.E.A. aux jeunes écrivains qui ont, eux aussi, un
mot à dire, et pas des moindres ni des châtiés. Vu
les insurmontables difficultés posées par l'édition en
Algérie, l'U.E.A. risque d'être longtemps encore réser-
vée aux têtes chenues."

8. Echabab, no. 126 (20 February 1974): "Il est
temps d'arrêter les rouages de cette machine imperson-
nelle qui nous mutile sans raison. . . . de nos jours
l'édition est devenue une véritable odyssée bureau-
cratique."

9. Abdou B., "Culture, Culture!," El Djeich, no.
129 (February 1974): "Conformisme, manque d'audace et
d'imagination caractérisent les productions de l'esprit."

10. In the third section of his study, La Littérature algérienne de langue française et ses lectures
(Sherbrooke, 1974), Charles Bonn focuses on the reader,
his motivations, and the kinds of books he is known to
read, based on surveys and publication statistics. Algerian novels ranked high, but so too did detective and
love stories in French by foreign authors. Bonn's inquiries are revealing to an extent but are neither sufficiently systematic nor all-encompassing.

Selected Bibliography

PRIMARY SOURCES

1. Chraibi, Driss
a. Novels
Un Ami viendra vous voir. Paris: Denoël, 1967.
L'Ane. Paris: Denoël, 1956.
Les Boucs. Paris: Denoël, 1955.
La Civilisation, ma mère. Paris: Denoël, 1972.
Une Enquête au pays. Paris: Seuil, 1981.
La Foule. Paris: Denoël, 1961.
Mort au Canada. Paris: Denoël, 1975.
Le Passé simple. Paris: Denoël, 1954.
Succession ouverte. Paris: Denoël, 1962. Translated
   by Len Ortzen as Heirs to the Past (Exeter: Heine-
   mann Educational Press, 1972).

b. Short stories
De tous les horizons. Paris: Denoël, 1958.

2. Dib, Mohammed
a. Novels
Cours sur la rive sauvage. Paris: Seuil, 1964.
La Danse du roi. Paris: Seuil, 1968.
Dieu en Barbarie. Paris: Seuil, 1970.
Un Eté africain. Paris: Seuil, 1959.
La Grande Maison. Paris: Seuil, 1952.
Habel. Paris: Seuil, 1977.
L'Incendie. Paris: Seuil, 1954.
Le Maître de chasse. Paris: Seuil, 1973.
Le Métier à tisser. Paris: Seuil, 1957.
Qui se souvient de la mer. Paris: Seuil, 1962.

b. Short stories
Au Café. Paris: Gallimard, 1955.
Le Talisman. Paris: Seuil, 1966.

c. Children's stories
Baba Fekrane. Paris: La Farandole, 1959. Illustrated.

L'Histoire du chat qui boude. Paris: La Farandole,
 1974. Illustrated.

d. Poems
Feu beau feu. Paris: Seuil, 1979.
Formulaires. Paris: Seuil, 1970.
Ombre gardienne. Paris: Gallimard, 1961.
Omneros. Paris: Seuil, 1975. English translation by
 Carol Lettieri and Paul Vangelisti (Fairfax: Red
 Hill, 1978).

e. Theater
Mille hourras pour une gueuse. Paris: Seuil, 1980.

3. Djebar, Assia
a. Novels
Les Alouettes naïves. Paris: Juilliard, 1967.
Les Enfants du nouveau monde. Paris: Juilliard, 1962.
Les Impatients. Paris: Juilliard, 1958.
La Soif. Paris: Juilliard, 1957.

b. Short stories
Femmes d'Alger dans leur appartement. Paris: Des
 femmes, 1980.

c. Theater
Rouge l'Aube. Algiers: S.N.E.D., 1969.

d. Poems
Poèmes pour l'Algérie heureuse. Algiers: S.N.E.D.,
 1969.

4. Kateb, Yacine
a. Novels
Nedjma. Paris: Seuil, 1956. Translated by Richard
 Howard as Nedjma (New York: Braziller, 1961).
Le Polygone étoilé. Paris: Seuil, 1966.

b. Theater
Le Cercle des représailles. Paris: Seuil, 1959.
L'Homme aux sandales de caoutchouc. Paris: Seuil,
 1970.

5. Mammeri, Mouloud
a. Novels
La Colline oubliée. Paris: Plon, 1952.

L'Opium et le Bâton. Paris: Plon, 1965.
Le Sommeil du juste. Paris: Plon, 1955.

b. Theater and essay
La Mort absurde des Aztèques; Le Banquet. Paris:
  Librairie Académique Perrin, 1973.

6. Memmi Albert
a. Novels
Agar. Paris: Buchet-Chastel, 1955. Rev. ed. with pref-
  ace, 1963. Translated by Brian Rhys as Strangers
  (New York: Orion Press, 1960).
Le Désert. Paris: Gallimard, 1977.
Le Scorpion. Paris: Gallimard, 1969. Translated by
  Eleanor Levieux as The Scorpion, 2d ed. (New York:
  O'Hara, 1975).
La Statue de sel. Paris: Buchet-Chastel, 1953; rev.
  ed., Paris: Gallimard, 1966. Translated by Edouard
  Roditi as The Pillar of Salt (New York: O'Hara,
  1975).

b. Essays
La Dépendance. Paris: Gallimard, 1979.
L'Homme dominé. Paris: Gallimard, 1968. Translated
  by various translators as Dominated Man (New York:
  Orion Press, 1968).
Juifs et Arabes. Paris: Gallimard, 1974. Translated
  by Eleanor Levieux as Jews and Arabs (New York:
  O'Hara, 1975).
La Libération du Juif. Paris: Gallimard, 1966.
  Translated by Judith Hyun as Liberation of the Jews
  (New York: Viking Press, 1967).
Portrait du colonisé, précédé du portrait du coloni-
  sateur. Paris: Buchet-Chastel, 1957; rev. ed.,
  Paris: Pauvert, 1966. Translated by Howard Green-
  field as The Colonizer and the Colonized (New York:
  Orion Press, 1965). Several reprintings.
Portrait d'un Juif. Paris: Gallimard, 1962. Also pub-
  lished in the collection "Idées," 1969. Translated
  by Elisabeth Abbott as Portrait of a Jew (New York:
  Orion Press, 1962).

c. Conversations
Entretien. Montreal: Editions de l'Etincelle,
  1975.
La Terre intérieure. Paris: Gallimard, 1976.

SECONDARY SOURCES

1. Bibliography

Déjeux, Jean. Bibliographie méthodique et critique de
   la littérature algérienne de langue française, 1945–
   1977. Algiers: S.N.E.D., 1979. This "inventory of
   the national patrimony" lists and briefly describes
   novels, stories, plays, and essays by authors of
   Algeria, Morocco, and Tunisia. (An appendix includes
   works of Algerian fiction from 1900 to 1945.) It also
   inventories interviews with Maghrebian authors, critical reviews of their works, and articles on the historical background and current cultural problems in the
   Maghreb. An indispensable research tool; the most comprehensive source in the field.

2. Books

Accad, Evelyne. Veil of Shame: The Role of Women in
   the Contemporary Fiction of North Africa and the Arab
   World. Sherbrooke: Editions Naaman, 1978. An excellent presentation of the women's problem in Arab countries. Contrasts the real situation of women in a
   patriarchal society with the representation it is
   given by female and male authors in their fiction.
   Explores in particular the early novels of Assia
   Djebar and Marguerite Taos Amrouche.
Arnaud, Jacqueline; Déjeux, Jean; Khatibi, Abdelkébir;
   and Roth, Arlette. Anthologie des écrivains maghrébins d'expression française. 2d ed. Paris: Présence Africaine, 1965. The first anthology in French
   to give a brief biographical presentation and selected
   excerpts of twenty-one authors. The controversial in-
   troduction by Albert Memmi is of historical interest.
   This work is superseded by Déjeux's later studies.
Arnaud, Jacqueline; Déjeux, Jean; and Roth, Arlette.
   Anthologie des écrivains français du Maghreb.
   Paris: Présence Africaine, 1969. Serves as a contrast to anthology that preceded it under the direction of the same editor.
Beck, Lois, and Keddie, Nikki, eds. Women in the Muslim
   World. Cambridge: Harvard University Press, 1978.
   Excellent source of background material on the social
   position of women in the Maghreb countries. The chap-
   ter on "The Theme of Sexual Oppression in the North
   African Novel" by Evelyne Accad is superseded by her
   book.

Bencheikh, Jamel-Eddine, and Valensi, Jacqueline Levi.
Diwân algérien: La Poésie algérienne d'expression française de 1945 à 1965. Algiers: S.N.E.D.,
1967. A useful overview of major Algerian poets,
including a critical study of representative selections.
Bonn, Charles. La Littérature algérienne de langue
française et ses lectures. Sherbrooke: Editions
Naaman, 1974. Originally a doctoral dissertation
(University of Bordeaux), this intelligent study deals
first with the structures of the creative imagination,
then with the reading public and its demands, in order
to underscore the difficult rapport between these two
aspects of literary production.
Boudjedra, Rachid. La Vie quotidienne en Algérie.
Paris: Hachette, 1971. Describes the customs that are
a part of Arab life. Useful background information.
Daninos, Guy. Les Nouvelles tendances du roman algéri-
en de langue française. Sherbrooke: Editions
Naaman, 1979. Originally a doctoral dissertation
(University of Nancy), this intelligent study focuses
on major themes of Algerian novels in French and illustrates the sociological-historical outcomes in free
Algeria of problems posed in the works of fiction.
Déjeux, Jean. La Littérature algérienne contemporaine. Paris: Presses universitaires de France,
1975. Title is somewhat misleading. A large portion
of this book is given over to a presentation of the
historical evolution of Algerian literature from its
French roots in North Africa in 1830. This all too
brief volume includes a chapter on Algerian literature
in Arabic. Completes the historical overview given in
Déjeux's Littérature maghrébine de langue française.
_____. Littérature maghrébine de langue fran-
çaise. Sherbrooke: Editions Naaman, 1973. The
most comprehensive work available to date on the genesis and currents of Maghrebian literature in French,
with detailed presentations of twelve Maghrebian
writers, followed by brief introductions of other
writers.
_____. Mohammed Dib, écrivain algérien. Sher-
brooke: Editions Naaman, 1977. Excellent overview of
Dib's oeuvre, including an analysis of key themes.
Gontard, Marc. "Nedjma" de Kateb Yacine: Essai sur la
structure formelle du roman. Rabat: Imprimerie de

l'Agdal, 1975. Useful to the reader for organizing the seeming chaos of a difficult novel.

Khatibi, Abdelkébir. Le Roman maghrébin. Paris: Maspero, 1968. Originally a doctoral dissertation (Sorbonne), this "sociological essay," as the author termed it, is a lucid presentation of the social and political conditions that affected the production of the novel in the Maghreb.

Lacheraf, Mostefa. L'Algérie, nation et société. Paris: Maspero, 1965. Several reeditions. In large part a compilation of articles published separately in newspapers and periodicals, this intelligent study deals primarily with sociopolitical and historical concerns. It also treats the issue of culture within the context of Algerian nationalism, a matter that has been the subject of much debate in independent Algeria. Useful for understanding the forces that shape Algerian literature in French.

La Poésie contemporaine de langue française depuis 1945. Paris: Editions Saint-Germain-des-Prés, 1973. Compiled of regional studies by five different contributors, the section on the Maghreb, written by Jean Déjeux, includes critical studies of selected poems. A good introduction that invites further study of individual authors' works.

M'Rabet, Fadéla. La Femme algérienne suivi de Les Algériennes. Paris: Maspero, 1969. Originally published separately in 1964 and 1967 respectively. An indispensable work for the understanding of women's position in Algeria. A frank and forthright explanation of the mindset of the male and the female in Arab Muslim society. Includes case histories and concrete statistics together with psychological insights.

Nelson, Harold D., ed. Algeria: A Country Study. 3d ed. Washington, D.C.: American University, 1979.

_____. Morocco: A Country Study. 4th ed. Washington, D.C.: American University, 1978.

_____. Tunisia: A Country Study. 2d ed. Washington, D.C.: American University, 1979. Each of these three handbooks is especially useful for its concise chapters on the history and social environment of the Maghreb countries from earliest times to the present. These retrospective panoramas provide the necessary information for a clear understanding of North Africa's past. They neither overburden the reader with too many fine details, nor omit essential information.

Yetiv, Isaac. <u>Le Thème de l'aliénation dans le roman</u> <u>maghrébin d'expression française de 1952 à 1956.</u> Sherbrooke: Centre d'Etude des Littératures d'Expression Française, 1972. Originally a Ph.D. dissertation (University of Wisconsin-Madison, 1969), this thematic study is limited in scope but presents an excellent introduction to the beginnings of Maghrebian French language literature.

3. Articles

Déjeux, Jean. "L'Avenir de la langue française en Algérie arabe." <u>L'Ethnie Française</u> 5-6 (1976):199-210. Examines the then current status of French in Algeria and makes some hypotheses as to what bearing Arab language medium will have on the future of francophone literature produced by autochthon writers. Now dated.

     _____. "Femmes écrivains dans la littérature algérienne de langue française." <u>Revue de l'Institut de Belles Lettres Arabes</u> 144 (1979):307-36. A succinct inventory of the major Algerian women writers (of which there are only seven) and a brief presentation of their works and significance.

     _____. "Kateb Yacine, romancier, poète et dramaturge algérien." <u>Présence Francophone</u> 15 (1977):124-47. Provides a useful approach to Kateb Yacine's work and comprehensive bibliography of works by and about him.

     _____. "Les Structures de l'imaginaire dans l'oeuvre de Kateb Yacine." <u>Revue de l'Occident Musulman et de la Méditerranée</u> 13-14 (1973):267-92. Offers penetrating insights into Kateb's works and underlines the rapport between his personal life and his fiction.

Sari-Mostefa Kara, Fawzia. "L'Ishrâq dans l'oeuvre de Mohammed Dib." <u>Revue de l'Occident Musulman et de la Méditerranée</u> 22 (1976):109-17. A sensitive interpretation of Dib's works from a Muslim religious point of view.

Index

DATE DUE
